RURAL PROTEST AND THE MAKING OF DEMOCRACY IN MEXICO, 1968–2000

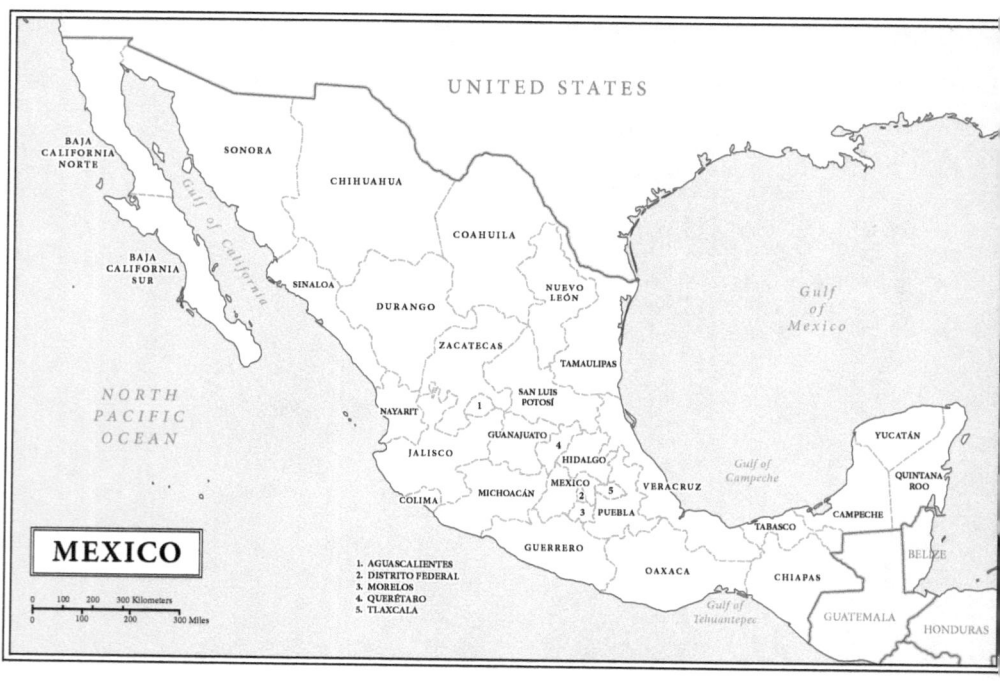

# RURAL PROTEST AND THE MAKING OF DEMOCRACY IN MEXICO, 1968–2000

*Dolores Trevizo*

Portions of chapter 2 originally appeared as Dolores Trevizo, "Between Zapata and Che: A Comparison of Social Movement Success and Failure in Mexico," *Social Science History* 30, no. 2 (Summer 2006): 197–229.
Reprinted by permission of the publisher, Duke University Press.

Portions of chapter 3 originally appeared as Dolores Trevizo, "Dispersed Communist Networks and Grassroots Leadership of Peasant Revolts in Mexico," *Sociological Perspectives* 45, no. 3 (Autumn 2002): 285–315. © 2002 by Pacific Sociological Association.

Portions of chapter 4 originally appeared as Dolores Trevizo, "Interclass Conflict and Political Divisions Among Capitalists: The Remaking of an Agrarian Capitalist Class in Mexico, 1970–75," *Social Science History* 27, no. 1 (Spring 2003): 75–108.
Reprinted by permission of the publisher, Duke University Press.

Library of Congress Cataloging-in-Publication Data

Trevizo, Dolores.
Rural protest and the making of democracy in Mexico, 1968–2000 / Dolores Trevizo.
    p.     cm.
Includes bibliographical references and index.
ISBN 978-0-271-03787-5 (cloth : acid-free paper)
ISBN 978-0-271-03788-2 (pbk. : alk. paper)
1. Mexico—Politics and government—1970–1988.
2. Mexico—Politics and government—1988–2000. 3. Protest movements—Mexico—History—20th century. 4. Social movements—Mexico—History—20th century. 5. Democracy—Mexico—History—20th century.
6. Peasants—Mexico—Political activity—History—20th century.
7. Student movements—Mexico—History—20th century.
8. Mexico—Rural conditions. I. Title.

F1236.T75 2011
972.08′2—dc22
2010046245

Copyright © 2011 The Pennsylvania State University
All rights reserved
Printed in the United States of America
Published by The Pennsylvania State University Press,
University Park, PA 16802-1003

The Pennsylvania State University Press is a member of the
Association of American University Presses.

It is the policy of The Pennsylvania State University Press to use acid-free paper. Publications on uncoated stock satisfy the minimum requirements of American National Standard for Information Sciences—Permanence of Paper for Printed Library Material, ANSI Z39.48–1992.

Frontispiece map and figure 6 were created for the author by Erin Greb.

PARA
*Elisa, Jacob y Warren*

*Contents*

*List of Figures and Tables* ix
*Preface and Acknowledgments* xi
*List of Abbreviations* xiii

Introduction
The Rural Roots of Mexico's Nascent Democracy:
The Role of Peasants and Agrarian Capitalists
in Opposition Politics   *1*

1
Social Movements and Democratization   *29*

2
The "Banner of 1968":
The Student Movement's Democratizing Effects   *57*

3
State Repression and the Dispersal of Radicals into
Mexico's Countryside, 1970–1975   *90*

4
Capitalists on the Road to Political Power in Mexico:
Class Struggle, Neopanismo, and the Birth of Democracy   *126*

5
The Rural Sources of the PRD's Electoral Resiliency   *154*

Conclusion
The Post-1968 Struggle for Democracy
in Rural Mexico   *188*

*Appendixes* 201
*References* 215
*Index* 237

# *Figures and Tables*

## FIGURES

1 Social movements in Mexico by social group, 1964–88   3
2 The formal organizational structure of Mexico's official (PRI-organized) and semi-official (not directly PRI-organized) corporatist system of interest representation   7
3 Movement and countermovement dynamics contributing to Mexico's democratization   20
4 Peasant protests and government responses   102
5 The organizational structure and political orientation of key segments of Mexico's capitalist class   135
6 The 2006 presidential election in Mexico, by the party winning the majority of votes per state   155
7 The ideological orientation of the peasant organizations engaged in 727 cases of peasant protest, 1979–84   160
8 The political issues in 355 cases of peasant protest, 1979–84   169
9 Protest tactic by year in 720 cases of peasant protest, 1979–84   170
10 Demands by tactic and target in 720 cases of peasant protest, 1979–84   210
11 Protest tactic by the role of social control forces in 720 cases of peasant protest, 1979–84   211

## TABLES

1 Chronology of events in the 1968 organized student movement   62
2 Key institutional reforms to Mexico's electoral authority   78
3 Select human rights organizations that emerged as a direct result of Mexico's dirty war   84

4 Mexico's agrarian classes, class segments, and other social strata, 1970   96
5 Characteristics of rural vs. urban population, select census years   99
6 Distribution of thirty-one Mexican states with peasant protest, 1970 to 1975, by whether Communists had organized peasant bases from 1967 to 1975   117
7 Metric coefficients for OLS regression of net differences of all peasant protests on key independent variables, thirty Mexican states, 1970–75   120
8 PAN government officials elected to executive and legislative posts, 1985–2000   149
9 Metric coefficients for OLS regression of net differences of all peasant protests on key independent variables, thirty Mexican states, 1977–83   165
10 Distribution of thirty-one Mexican states showing support for FDN/PRD presidential candidates, 1988 to 2006, by degree of rural protest against government repression from 1977 to 1983   179
11 Distribution of thirty-one Mexican states showing support for PAN presidential candidates, 1988 to 2006, by degree of rural protest against government repression from 1977 to 1983   181
12 Logit coefficients for regression of propensity to support political parties in presidential elections (1988–2006) and PRD governorships, by the number of protests against government repression from 1977 to 1983, in thirty-one Mexican states (excluding Federal District)   183
13 Frequency of peasant demands in 221 protests in Mexico, 1970–75   206

*Preface and Acknowledgments*

My passion for Mexican politics began in my childhood as I heard family members, all born in Chihuahua, debate whether or not the violence of the Revolution of 1910 had been justified. As Chihuahua was the cradle of the Mexican Revolution, my great-grandfathers had seen battle. My maternal great-grandfather, Jesus Duarte, an officer in Francisco Villa's army, never dropped his military "presentation of self." I always wondered about the fear he inspired in other adults, especially the women of the family, who would not dare to disagree with him openly about Pancho Villa's army. The women privately argued that Villa and his men were arbitrary in their use of force, based on the evidence that their aunts had to hide for fear of being raped whenever Villa's army went through their towns or villages. The men in the family, in contrast, held firm that war, by definition, is violence and that the Revolution's goals were historically more important than the local abuses perpetrated by individual and untrained soldiers.

With an equal intensity, the members of my family either supported the ruling party or bemoaned what had happened to the Revolution once it had been institutionalized. My maternal grandfather, Dolores Vazquez, a Bracero who later immigrated permanently to the United States (from the peasant-miner region of Parral, Chihuahua), gave me the intellectual framework with which to understand the discrepancies between revolutionary ideals and revolutionary outcomes. In his typically terse and commonsensical outlook, he explained, "Well, the Revolution was betrayed." His own father, Lucio Vazquez, had been swept away by a swollen river while trying to mobilize poor ranchers to vote.

I was also inspired by my paternal grandmother, María Socorro de Trevizo, with whom I lived in Ciudad Juárez for three months when I was five years old. I'll never forget our daily visits both to church and to fruit markets, as the former yielded song and smells of incense, while the latter smelled of mangoes, earth, and coffee. Those months in Ciudad Juárez fueled my political imagination. As a child from Mid-City, Los Angeles, I had never seen as much bounty as I saw at the government (Partido Revolucionario Institucional, PRI) party my grandmother catered. Nor had I ever witnessed the dehumanizing levels of poverty that I saw in this border town. At the age of five, I was forced to wonder about Native American women who begged on street corners with babies dangling from their nipples, shoeless peasants who exchanged songs for pesos, and street children who sold Chiclets between cars on busy streets. Exposed to what looked to me like inhuman conditions, I learned to think critically about the Mexico that my grandmother loved, the political party she supported, and her nationalist rationale for doing so.

I returned to Mexico many times, including in 1988 during what turned out to be historically pivotal elections. My serious research trips, however, did not take place until the 1990s, first in 1992 and then again two years later. The year 1994 was an exciting and disturbing period in which two politically motivated assassinations (Luis Donaldo Colosio, the PRI's 1994 presidential candidate, and José Francisco Ruiz Massieu, the PRI's secretary-general) and an armed guerrilla movement in the southern state of Chiapas revealed deep and seemingly irreconcilable political differences within the ruling party and the nation. Because I was in Mexico City when José Ruiz Massieu was murdered, I witnessed some of the political drama surrounding the implication of Raul Salinas de Gortari, the brother of the sitting president (Carlos Salinas de Gortari), in that murder, for which he was ultimately convicted. To my surprise, democracy was born without more bloodshed a few years later. The timing of my fieldwork therefore forced me to attempt to analyze a political system that was not only changing rapidly but heading in a direction that seemed uncertain. Given the military repression of armed Zapatistas in Chiapas and even peasants in Guerrero, and given two assassinations of political leaders, I wondered whether the country would move toward even greater authoritarian practices.

The political system was, in other words, a moving target difficult to fully characterize. I am thus eternally grateful to my interview subjects, businessmen and politicians, who were so much wiser than me about my own work. They not only answered my questions but also pointed out the more important issues that my interview guide failed to address. They knew that they had a big story to tell, and they shared it with me even though I initially found it confusing that my interview subjects kept "fast-forwarding" to the 1980s and 1990s when my questions focused on events in 1975. Only after the Partido Acción Nacional's (PAN's) electoral victory in 2000 did I understand the full meaning of the story that businessmen in particular kept trying to share with me. I hope that my chapter on the emergence of the PAN does a good job of representing their experiences. I similarly hope that my observations of leftist political debate and interviews with radicals shed light on the courage of their convictions and their high-risk activism for a better, more just Mexico.

Beyond my research of activists on the left and on the right, my work would not have progressed without the support I received from scholars at Mexico's National Autonomous University (Universidad Nacional Autónoma de México, UNAM). For his mentorship and guidance, I am grateful to Hubert Carton de Grammont. I am also indebted to Blanca Rubio for her incredible generosity. She let me codify her handwritten spreadsheets on peasant protests during the late 1970s and 1980s. I created a digital database of these spreadsheets, which provide the empirical backbone of chapter 5 of this book. Arturo Warman was instrumental in teaching me how to understand the complexities of land expropriations and what to look for specifically when coding. Finally, Matilde Luna and Ricardo Tirado granted me permission to adapt one of their figures from their seminal *El Consejo Coordinador Empresarial: Una radiografía*.

I am also indebted to the University of California's programs and scholars. UCLA's Latin American Studies program funded my first research trip in 1992, and the University of California Institute for Mexico and the United States (UC MEXUS) funded my second trip. I would not, however, have embarked on this research project without the intellectual guidance of my graduate school advisor, Maurice Zeitlin. Over ten years ago, he noted that I had outlined a lifetime of research. I realize now, many years later, that I am still only telling half of the story. The subplot of many of the chapters in this book concerns the armed guerrilla movements of the 1960s and 1970s, the comprehensive analysis for which is yet to be written. I am grateful to Sandy Thatcher for recognizing that the part of the story told here is an important piece in a larger puzzle. Thanks also to Erin Greb for her beautiful maps, to Kathryn Yahner for her attention to details, and to Julie Schoelles for her careful editing.

For their ongoing intellectual and moral support, I thank William Roy, Chris Ehrick, Manali Desai, Alisa Lewin, Dahlia Elazar, and Alec Campbell. For insisting that I had a book-length story to tell, I thank Benita Roth and Karen O'Neil. I am also grateful for the thoughtful and constructive comments on earlier drafts from many anonymous reviewers. Needless to say, the mistakes I have made in this work are completely my own.

Not only was my research first inspired by family members whom I now miss but their storytelling and passionate debates now also influence the lives of my children in Los Angeles, California. For tolerating my endless talk about Mexico, I thank my children, Elisa and Jacob Montag. As they were born while I was either collecting or analyzing data, they have never known anything other than a mother who, as my son once put it, has never left "Mexicoland." For always believing in me, I thank my husband, Warren Montag.

# Abbreviations

| | |
|---|---|
| AC | Antorcha Campesina |
| AMCB | Asociación Mexicana de Casas de Bolsa (formerly Asociación Mexicana de Intermediarios Bursátiles [AMIB]) |
| AMIS | Asociación Mexicana de Instituciones de Seguros |
| CAADES | Confederación de Asociaciones Agrícolas del Estado de Sinaloa |
| CAM | Consejo Agrarista Mexicano |
| CANACINTRA | Cámara Nacional de la Industria de la Transformación |
| CAP | Comandos Armados del Pueblo |
| CCE | Consejo Coordinador Empresarial |
| CCI | Central Campesina Independiente |
| CCI-Danzós | Central Campesina Independiente–Danzós |
| CECVYM | Coalición de Ejidos Colectivos de los Valles del Yaqui y Mayo |
| CEPAL | Comisión Económica para América Latina |
| CFE | Código Federal Electoral |
| CIOAC | Central Independiente de Obreros Agrícolas y Campesinos |
| CMHN | Consejo Mexicano de Hombres de Negocios |
| CNA | Consejo Nacional Agropecuario |
| CNC | Confederación Nacional Campesina |
| CNDH | Comisión Nacional de Derechos Humanos |
| CNG | Confederación Nacional Ganadera |
| CNH | Consejo Nacional de Huelga |
| CNOP | Confederación Nacional de Organizaciones Populares |
| CNPA | Coordinadora Nacional Plan de Ayala |

| | |
|---|---|
| CNPC | Confederación Nacional de Cámaras del Pequeño Comercio |
| CNPI | Consejo Nacional de Pueblos Indígenas |
| CNPP | Confederación Nacional de la Pequeña Propiedad |
| CNPR | Confederación Nacional de Propietarios Rurales |
| COCEI | Coalición de Obreros, Campesinos y Estudiantes del Istmo |
| COECE | Coordinadora de Organismos Empresariales de Comercio Exterior |
| COFIPE | Código Federal de Instituciones y Procedimientos Electorales |
| COMA | Comuneros Organizados de Milpa Alta |
| CONACAR | Consejo Nacional Cardenista |
| CANACO-MEX | Cámara Nacional de Comercio de la Ciudad de México |
| CONAIE | Confederación de Nacionalidades Indígenas del Ecuador |
| CONASUPO | Compaña Nacional de Subsistencias Populares |
| CONCAMIN | Confederación de Cámaras Industriales |
| CONCANACO | Confederación de Cámaras Nacionales de Comercio |
| COPARMEX | Confederación Patronal de la República Mexicana |
| CTM | Confederación de Trabajadores Mexicanos |
| EZLN | Ejército Zapatista de Liberación Nacional |
| FCI | Frente Campesino Independiente de Oaxaca |
| FDN | Frente Democrático Nacional |
| FPPM | Federación de Partidos del Pueblo Mexicano |
| FRAP | Frente Revolucionario Armado del Pueblo |
| FUZ | Frente Urbano Zapatista |
| GATT | General Agreement on Tariffs and Trade |
| IFE | Instituto Federal Electoral |
| IMF | International Monetary Fund |
| INEGI | Instituto Nacional de Estadística y Geografía |

| | |
|---|---|
| INI | Instituto Nacional Indigenista |
| INMECAFÉ | Instituto Mexicano del Café |
| IPN | Instituto Politécnico Nacional |
| ISI | Import substitution industrialization |
| JCM | Juventud Comunista Mexicana |
| LCE | Liga Comunista Espartaco |
| LC23S | Liga Comunista 23 de Septiembre |
| LFOPPE | Ley Federal de Organizaciones Políticas y Procesos Electorales |
| MAP | Movimiento de Acción Popular |
| MAR | Movimiento de Acción Revolucionaria |
| MAS | Movimiento al Socialismo |
| MLN | Movimiento de Liberación Nacional |
| MST | Movimento dos Trabalhadores Rurais Sem Terra |
| NAFTA | North American Free Trade Agreement |
| OCEZ | Organización Campesina Emiliano Zapata |
| OIPUH | Organización Independiente de Pueblos Unidos de las Huastecas |
| OLS | Ordinary least squares |
| PAN | Partido Acción Nacional |
| PARM | Partido Auténtico de la Revolución Mexicana |
| PCM | Partido Comunista Mexicano |
| PEMEX | Petróleos Mexicanos |
| PFP | Partido de Fuerza Popular |
| PIDER | Programa de Inversiones para el Desarrollo Rural Integrado |
| PMS | Partido Mexicano Socialista |
| PMT | Partido Mexicano de los Trabajadores |
| POS | Political opportunity structure |
| PRD | Partido de la Revolución Democrática |

| | |
|---|---|
| PRI | Partido Revolucionario Institucional |
| PROCAMPO | Programa de Apoyos Directos al Campo |
| PRONASOL | Programa Nacional de Solidaridad |
| PRT | Partido Revolucionario de los Trabajadores |
| PST | Partido Socialista de los Trabajadores |
| PSUM | Partido Socialista Unificado de México |
| SAM | Sistema Alimentario Mexicano |
| SARH | Secretaría de Agricultura y Recursos Hidráulicos |
| SITMMSRM | Sindicato Industrial de Trabajadores Mineros, Metalúrgicos y Similares de la República Mexicana |
| SRA | Secretaría de la Reforma Agraria |
| TRIFE | Tribunal Electoral del Poder Judicial de la Federación |
| UCEZ | Unión de Comuneros Emiliano Zapata, Michoacán |
| UGOCM | Unión General de Obreros y Campesinos de México |
| UNAM | Universidad Nacional Autónoma de México |
| UNAN | Unión Agrícola Nacional |
| UNTA | Unión Nacional de Trabajadores Agrícolas |
| UPM | Unión de Pueblos de Morelos |
| URECHH | Unión Regional de Ejidos y Comunidades de la Huasteca Hidalgüense |

## Introduction
### The Rural Roots of Mexico's Nascent Democracy
### The Role of Peasants and Agrarian Capitalists in Opposition Politics

In the last three decades of the twentieth century, urban and rural social movements helped give birth to Mexico's democracy. While democratization was a slow, evolutionary process, the magnitude of change was historically significant. Mexicans transformed their highly fraudulent electoral system into one that most analysts agree is democratic.[1] While numerous studies have focused on these changes, few have systematically explored what rural movements contributed. This empirical neglect is all the more noteworthy given that peasants and other rural poor registered the highest levels of protest as compared to other social groups in the pretransition period (see fig. 1). Their movements, moreover, provoked a countermovement of economically powerful businessmen.

My empirical story begins in 1968, long after a democratically inspired agrarian revolution crystallized into a semi-authoritarian political system. Although the 1910 Revolution broke the postcolonial pattern of autocratic governance and violent political change, by the 1940s Mexico's governing institutions had become authoritarian, if flexibly so, despite the liberal Constitution of 1917. This is evidenced by the fact that the official party, the Partido Revolucionario Institucional (PRI), monopolized power for seventy-one years within a highly centralized "presidentialist" system (Cornelius 1996;

---

1. For an overview of the literature, see Domínguez and McCann (1996), Serrano and Bulmer-Thomas (1996), Domínguez and Lawson (2004), Eisenstadt (2004 and 2007), Middlebrook (2004b), Shirk (2005), and Levy and Bruhn (2006).

Weldon 2004). Yet despite being semi-authoritarian, the PRI ruled hegemonically for many of those years; it operated, that is, primarily through mass support rather than force.

Political support for the PRI state was mobilized by the official party, which organized most groups in civil society into corporatist associations that patronized the masses by providing them with collective and individual benefits (Levy and Székely 1987; Middlebrook 1995; Rubin 1997; Otero 2000; Mitchell 2001; Magaloni 2006). Because these corporatist associations were important vehicles by which the state distributed favors to its clients, the PRI had the capacity to broker compromise between the frequently antagonistic social classes it organized. Such political brokerage explains the organizational incentives for the ideologically "flexible" policy that sustained mass support for the PRI over time. Further, while elections were not serious vehicles for consultation with the masses about policy preferences, they were held regularly (every six years for presidential and senatorial races and every three for congressional ones). As such, the ruling party's candidates mobilized the corporatist associations as electoral machines to renew political support (via the distribution of political favors, or the promise of such distribution) (Cornelius 2004, 48).

The description of Mexico's version of authoritarianism as "soft" derives precisely from the fact that the political system manufactured consent through corporatist organization, ideologically flexible policy, and voter mobilization via patronage. Until the late 1960s, these mechanisms were effective to the extent that the PRI could rule without relying too heavily on political violence. But toward the final third of the twentieth century, the postrevolutionary state saw a rapid loss of hegemony, as evidenced by a rising tide of increasingly organized and disruptive political contention. Middle-class students turned leftists, women, teachers, urban dwellers, informal sector merchants, peasants, workers, and even capitalists forcefully and effectively challenged the state. As seen in fig. 1, however, the largest and most enduring forms of political contention occurred in the countryside.[2] Partly for this reason, I focus primarily (but not exclusively) on the unarmed rural movements that helped democratize Mexico's political arena.

---

2. According to Foweraker and Landman's data from 1964 to 1988, "workers participated in 42 per cent of the total of 560 [social movement] events, peasants in 66 per cent, women in 13 per cent, students in 22 per cent, and the poor in 58 per cent" (1997, 159).

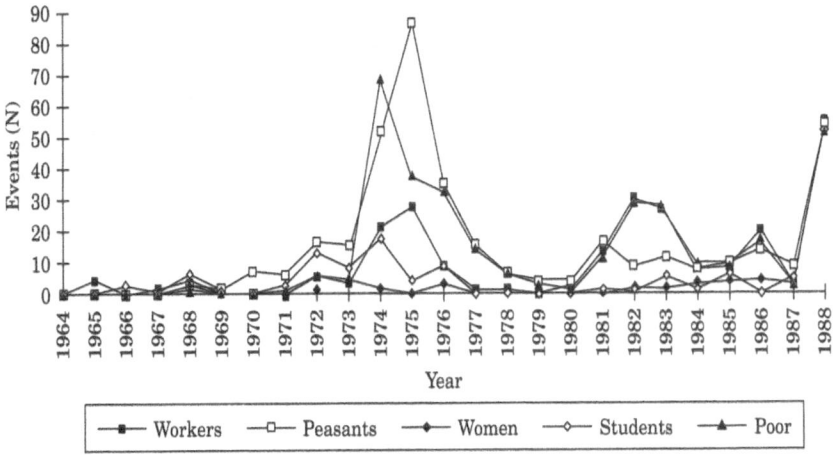

*Fig. 1* Social movements in Mexico by social group, 1964–88
SOURCE: Taken from Foweraker and Landman (1997, 157, fig. 5.6.3). © 1997 by Oxford University Press. Used by permission.

As such, my story sheds light on a paradox of twentieth-century Mexican history: while peasants had historically voted for the PRI, their protest movements in the 1970s through the 1980s contributed to the erosion of the regime's hegemony. Specifically, I explicate how corporatism, a central mechanism for PRI hegemony, alienated the "chosen" children of the regime[3] and how their protest movements for land ultimately provoked a right-wing opposition, or countermovement, led by agrarian capitalists.[4] The leaderships of these nonviolent social movements eventually consolidated support for two opposition political parties, the new left-of-center Party of the Democratic Revolution (Partido de la Revolución Democrática, PRD) and the old right-of-center National Action Party (Partido Acción Nacional, PAN). In other words, I analyze some key movement-countermovement

---

3. Neil Harvey, too, emphasizes the "crisis of corporatist representation" that occurred when peasant groups in Chiapas, and even in Michoacán, Oaxaca, and Guerrero, organized independently of the government's peasant association. They did so because the National Peasants' Confederation (CNC) proved itself to be arbitrary, politically corrupt, repressive, and irrelevant in their pursuit of land (N. Harvey 1990).

4. Agrarian capitalists produce for markets (domestic and/or export), employ wage labor on a significant and permanent basis (as opposed to seasonally), and reinvest profits in the agrarian means of production—labor, machinery, productive inputs, and possibly the land to further accumulate capital (see table 4).

dynamics that helped give ideological expression to the social bases of support for the opposition political parties that successfully pressed for electoral democracy.

The following section describes the key institutions that made the state's relation to civil society nondemocratic. It also outlines why the state institutions set up to discipline politics and control social groups sowed the seeds of political discontent, and how political protest ultimately contributed to a more pluralistic political system. A discussion of how my research contributes to the empirical literature on Mexico's democratization follows. As the broader theoretical implications about the relationship between social movements and institutional political change will be drawn out in chapter 1, I conclude this introduction by defining theoretical concepts, offering a book plan, and discussing the limitations of the data.

## The Semi-authoritarian State of the Revolution

Mexico's twentieth-century state was born indebted to the rural masses. In 1910, tens of thousands of peasants, landless peons, villagers, sharecroppers, dispossessed *serranos* (mountain dwellers), and workers mobilized and successfully overthrew Porfirio Díaz's dictatorship (1876–1911). After the collapse of the ancien régime, the agrarian masses continued to risk their lives in what proved to be one of the bloodiest revolutions of the twentieth century.[5] Their revolutionary potential did not escape the middle-class liberals who, in writing a new constitution, sought bourgeois reforms of the state.[6] Consequently, these liberals were forced to compromise by modernizing the state while also attempting to demobilize the rural masses with political concessions to their social justice claims. The Constitution, for example, incorporated contradictory economic principles, recognizing such competing types of property as private and social property. While private property is owned by an

---

[5]. One out of every eight people died between 1910 and 1917, and hundreds of thousands of the estimated 1–2 million deaths were those of innocent civilians.

[6]. The liberals who wrote the Constitution of 1917 modeled the new state after the United States' federal republican system of government, comprising a bicameral Congress (with a Senate and Chamber of Deputies as equal partners), an executive, and a judiciary. Mexico's Constitution, however, has a strict no-reelection clause that applies to both the executive and legislative branches. Presidential elections are held every six years, and congressional elections are held every three years.

individual or partnership of individuals[7] with rights to sell, rent, mortgage, or bequeath it, social property was inalienable for most of the twentieth century. Because it was possessed, as opposed to owned, social property in the form of either *ejidos* or *comunidades* could not be sold, rented, or mortgaged until the 1990s.[8]

The Constitution, moreover, contains various rules for eminent domain and clearly stipulates that land and water belong to the nation. Until the 1990s, it had powerful legal codes by which to redistribute land to those who could prove that they needed it, so long as land was available for redistribution. Exceeding the legal caps of rural property made the land vulnerable to expropriation, and this was one of several ways that it became "available" for redistribution.[9] In theory, land caps were supposed to prevent the reemergence of the *latifundio* (a massive concentration of land), the grossly unequal pattern of landholding that provoked rural dwellers into revolutionary action in the first place. To prevent large landholding, constitutional law sought to create a class of small rural proprietors called *pequeños propietarios*.[10] Like those who possessed ejidos, small rural proprietors were called *campesinos* (peasants)[11] because they directly cultivated the soil.

The nationalist state further defined citizenship rights as collective social rights (Tamayo Flores-Alatorre 1999; Wada 2006). Citizens were promised public education, a national health program, food subsidies, urban infrastructure, and labor protections. Regardless of whether Mexico's welfare state lived up to its social justice claims and distributive promises, many people believed

7. Mercantile societies were juridically barred from owning rustic lands.

8. The property is communal in that it is theoretically owned by the village. However, most ejidos were subdivided among the usufruct beneficiaries and exploited individually.

9. During Luis Echeverría's presidency, land was defined as being "available" for expropriation for redistribution purposes if it was located within seven kilometers of an "eligible" land reform village (which had petitioned for the surplus land) and exceeded the legal caps. Significantly, *ejidatarios* were also subject to expropriation if they failed to cultivate their plots for two or more consecutive years. Echeverría, for example, stripped more than 160,000 ejidatarios and *comuneros* (indigenous communal farmers) of their usufruct rights for failing to work their parcels (*Excelsior*, 8/31/75). This land was redistributed.

10. While the legal definition of "small" agrarian property changed several times in the course of the twentieth century, the size at which to cap a rustic estate was always partly determined by a combination of land use and land quality.

11. In the strictest sense of the term, a peasant cultivates a parcel primarily through family labor and specifically for his family's subsistence. In Mexico, however, even agricultural workers and landless rural dwellers are called campesinos because they work the land or because they continue to hope that they can possess or, better still, own a parcel. Informally, indigenous people are also called campesinos.

that they had constitutionally backed rights to an education, affordable food, and land (Williams 2001, 70; Wada 2006, 98).[12] And though it is arguably the case that Native Americans were economically and politically forgotten by the Revolution, government officials sought to assimilate them into the nation. Official nationalist discourse generally emphasized some form of indigenism, whether the whitewashing variety that overstated *mestizaje* (racial mixing) or the more multicultural kind that formally granted Indians some legal privileges.[13]

But while the Constitution of 1917 and subsequent laws codified important democratic and social justice principles, the political institutions that ultimately replaced the Porfiriato were decidedly undemocratic. The consensus among most scholars is that Mexico's postrevolutionary political system was semi-authoritarian, at best (see Middlebrook 1995; Loaeza 1993; Levy and Székely 1987).[14] To begin with, the postrevolutionary state was a presidentialist system that concentrated power in the executive. For most of the twentieth century, presidents commanded the entire federal state apparatus, controlling the judiciary, national legislature, and military (Middlebrook 2004b, 24). During their nonrenewable six-year terms, they also presided over the ruling party. In this role, they exercised metaconstitutional powers, including the right to select their successors via a secretive process called the *dedazo* (meaning to "handpick" by pointing with one's finger) (see Garrido 1989).[15] As head of both the ruling party and the nation, presidents helped select the PRI's state-level gubernatorial and mayoral candidates, who, in turn, were elected by the populace. Local legislatures and courts also tended to follow the presidential line (Cornelius 1996, 26; Gómez Tagle 2004, 84). According

---

12. Heather Williams astutely observes that "in the United States, claims to subsistence may be seen as equally or less legitimate than counterclaims that such redistribution violates taxpayers' liberties. In Mexico, revolutionary nationalism is still a hegemonic public ideology and generally precludes any outright denial by officials that protestors' claims are legitimate" (2001, 71).

13. For example, indigenous communities were supposed to be given a legal preference in the government's land reform policies. Further, although most land was distributed as ejidos, many of the comunidades that did exist functioned with a degree of political and economic autonomy from local and national authorities (Esteva 1983, 162).

14. Protracted violence, the continued revolutionary potential of the masses, and even rogue generals help explain why Mexico's modern state was semi-authoritarian despite its democratic potential. In a nutshell, government officials were pressed to maintain political stability but frequently did so in ways that stymied democracy (Levy and Bruhn 2006).

15. Other metaconstitutional powers exercised by Mexican presidents included the power to alter the Constitution and arbitrate all electoral disputes. For a review of all such discretionary powers, including "anticonstitutional" powers, see Garrido (1989).

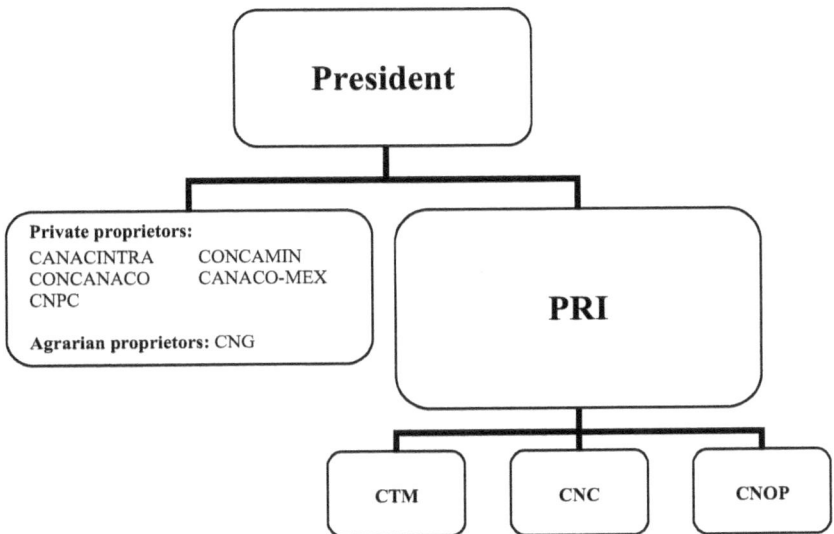

*Fig. 2* The formal organizational structure of Mexico's official (PRI-organized) and semi-official (not directly PRI-organized) corporatist system of interest representation

*The PRI's official corporatist associations*
CNC: National Peasants' Confederation
CTM: Confederation of Mexican Workers
CNOP: National Confederation of Popular Organizations

*Semi-official corporatist associations (excluded from the PRI)*
CANACINTRA: Cámara Nacional de la Industria de la Transformación (National Chamber of Manufacturing Industries; small- and medium-sized manufacturers)
CONCAMIN: Confederación de Cámaras Industriales (Confederation of Industrial Chambers)
CONCANACO: Confederación de Cámaras Nacionales de Comercio (Confederation of Chambers of Commerce)
CANACO-MEX: Cámara Nacional de Comercio de la Ciudad de México (National Chamber of Commerce of Mexico City)
CNPC: Confederación Nacional de Cámaras del Pequeño Comercio (National Confederation of Chambers of Small Commerce)
CNG: Confederación Nacional Ganadera (National Confederation of Cattlemen; as 94 percent of the CNG's members were cattle ranchers during the 1970s, I translated *ganadera* to "cattlemen." The remaining 6 percent raised pigs, poultry, bees, or sheep.)

to Wayne Cornelius, Judith Gentleman, and Peter Smith, presidential power "commanded supreme authority . . . [as presidents] had the final word on all major policy questions" (1989, 8). Worse still, many presidents made arbitrary decisions without congressional consultation and sometimes even extinguished Mexican lives by fiat.

This presidentialist system was structurally reinforced by a corporatist system of interest representation.[16] Corporatist organizations are compulsory, state-chartered, interest-representing monopolies.[17] In addition to the National Peasants' Confederation (CNC) and the Confederation of Mexican Workers (CTM) shown in fig. 2, the PRI organized teachers, women, professionals, government bureaucrats, and small merchants in the National Confederation of Popular Organizations (CNOP). While numerous other organizations were formally affiliated with the PRI,[18] peasants and workers were the most important official "clients" of a "patron" state. Their primary function was to exchange votes and other legitimacy signs for material favors (Mitchell 2001; see also Williams 2001).[19] Rural patronage, for example, could range from production inputs all the way to settling land disputes in a village's favor.[20] For this reason, the government's peasant confederation, the CNC, was one of the largest organized bases of support for the ruling party through

16. In the 1930s, President Lázaro Cárdenas defeated political conservatives by encouraging militant workers and peasants to form unions (Hansen 1971). He then incorporated their unions into the ruling party structure in 1938, per fig. 2.

17. According to Schmitter's classic definition, corporatism is "a system of interest representation in which the constituent units are organized into a limited number of singular, compulsory, noncompetitive, hierarchically ordered and functionally differentiated categories, recognized or licensed (if not created) by the state and granted a deliberate representational monopoly within their respective categories in exchange for observing certain controls on their election of leaders and articulation of demands and supports" (1974, 93).

18. For example, the Confederación Nacional de la Pequeña Propiedad (National Confederation of Small Proprietors, CNPP) was formally affiliated with the PRI despite the fact that it represented private agrarian proprietors, many of them capitalists. Its name derived from the fact that it was unconstitutional to be anything other than a "small" agrarian proprietor. The CNPP changed its name to the Confederación Nacional de Propietarios Rurales (CNPR) during the transition period.

19. In the urban centers, for example, the government could demand wage increases from employers or declare that a strike was legal.

20. As the PRI went into crisis, its last two governments of the twentieth century resorted to distributing financial aid directly to millions of poor families. According to Otero, this "neocorporatist" strategy, exemplified in the Programa Nacional de Solidaridad (PRONASOL) and Programa de Apoyos Directos al Campo (PROCAMPO), was "more direct, paternalistic, and client-efficient in electoral terms" (Otero 2000, 198; see also Olvera 2004, 417). According to Wayne Cornelius (2004), the PRI's vote buying through patronage and manipulation of social welfare programs proved electorally inefficient by 2000.

the 1980s. Organizing two million peasants and nearly one million more would-be peasants, the CNC's mobilization of the peasant vote[21] made the rural areas Mexico's primary "electoral fraud belt" (R. Bartra 2002, 115–18).[22]

While most businessmen were technically excluded from the PRI, from the 1930s on, they too were required by law to join noncompetitive trade associations (see examples under "private proprietors" in fig. 2).[23] These trade associations were also compulsory representational monopolies recognized by the state despite their formal exclusion from the ruling party. In addition, government officials used political office as a selective incentive for those corporatist and quasi-corporatist leaders who played by the official rules of the game. Opportunities for political office extended from public sector jobs to the PRI's congressional candidacies, as well as to appointments to ministries or parastate organizations (Tirado 1982, 150–51; Cornelius 2004).

With the power of economic and political patronage, the postrevolutionary state had the capacity to impose tripartite negotiations among the government, capitalists, workers, or peasants. This meant that government officials could compel union leaders and business representatives to negotiate wage rates and labor conditions. The outcome was widespread corruption, given that political advancement depended on being responsive to the PRI and the president rather than on finding solutions to the problems faced by workers or peasants.[24]

It is difficult to overstate the leverage that government officials had over most social groups and classes, including economically powerful businessmen. As demonstrated by other authoritarian political systems, rather than functioning as vehicles for authentic interest representation, corporatist organizations are "devices for social control."[25] Social groups and classes in

---

21. While the official unions and the CNC were generally effective in distributing patronage and garnering votes, sometimes local political bosses called *caciques* were better at the village level, especially in indigenous communities (Rubin 1997; on rural caciques, see Villarreal 2002).

22. Roger Bartra specifies that the rural areas registered high rates of electoral support for the official party partly because the state failed to provide any significant electoral oversight there.

23. As with those associations organized directly by the PRI, Mexico's president influenced the election of business leaders, went to some national-level business meetings, and otherwise interfered with the articulation of business interests (Tirado 1982, 83). Business-related licenses and permits, limitations on wage increases, the declaring of strikes illegal, favorable audits and inspections, and the possibility of avoiding taxes on specific kinds of capital gains were among the PRI favors on which businessmen relied. Further, the Ministry of Agrarian Reform was responsible for investigating violations of land tenancy laws, expropriating large private proprietors for any such violations, and granting private landowners official guarantees against expropriation (called *certificados de inafectabilidad*).

24. On the CNC, see N. Harvey (1990, 184) and Levy and Bruhn (2006, 75).

25. On Portugal, Spain, and Greece, see Drake (1996, 43).

Mexico indeed felt like "supplicants at the feet of the state" (Drake 1996, 43). As the following chapters demonstrate, antagonistic classes independently concluded that the government's corporatist associations failed to represent their interests by forcing them to accept political compromise.

Boldly put, the Mexican state had colonized civil society by trying to secure social peace through corporatist cooperation. In doing so, officials neglected to build democratic institutions and processes. Without politically independent organizations, civil society was weak. Consequently, social groups had little space or capacity to discern, articulate, and assert their interests effectively. Not only did the corporatist organizations fail to genuinely represent social groups vis-à-vis government officials, but they further sacrificed political rights by undermining the democratic potential of regularized elections. Because corporatist associations organized and mobilized PRI voters, presidential elections were reduced to mere performances in which the dominant party worked to ratify its candidate, the lame-duck president's handpicked successor.

Further, until 1996, the dominant party controlled the very institutions that decided either the legal registration (*registro*) of real political parties or the legitimacy of contested electoral results (see table 2). Electoral laws also ensured that the ruling party had greater financial resources than its competitors, as well as the greatest share of congressional seats. The PRI even received more favorable media attention than the opposition because the privately owned media were financially dependent on the government.[26] Journalists who dared to criticize the government were intimidated.

Electoral law, public spending, and a financially dependent media created a "hegemonic party system" in which the PRI had a monopoly on political power, even though some (not all) parties were legally allowed to compete in elections (Crespo 2004, 59; Gómez Tagle 2004, 82).[27] In reality, the PAN was

---

26. While privately owned, Televisa depended on the government's broadcasting concessions, licenses, and tax exemptions. Further, about half of the print media's advertising revenue derived from government ads, and many newspaper reporters were on the government's direct payroll (Lawson 2004). According to Lawson, "The vast majority of Mexican journalists also accepted regular cash payments from the government agencies they covered," and the income from such government payments was "more than the average reporter's salary" (2004, 379–80).

27. Both far-left and extreme right-wing parties were excluded from the electoral arena. The excluded left-wing parties were the Mexican Communist Party (PCM) and the more moderate Federation of Parties of the Mexican People (Federación de Partidos del Pueblo Mexicano, FPPM). The extreme right-wing party that was banned from electoral participation in 1949 was the Popular Force Party (PFP) (Gómez Tagle 2004, 84).

the regime's only real opposition, and until the early 1980s, it was a weak one at that. From its origins in 1939 until the early 1980s, the PAN was ambivalent about legitimating an unfair and fraudulent electoral system, even by participating in elections (Crespo 2004; Shirk 2005). In 1976, for example, it opted out of the presidential election, leaving the official party's candidate, José López Portillo, to campaign unopposed. Concerned about the threat to democratic appearances if the PAN withdrew from the electoral arena altogether, the regime sponsored satellite parties to offer token competition.[28]

Thus, although held regularly, presidential elections were not used as a serious means for consulting with citizens about policy options. Rather, the electoral system was such that political power at the presidential level did not alternate for seventy-one years (and for six decades at the gubernatorial level). Its democratic façade made it possible for Peruvian novelist Mario Vargas Llosa to call it a "perfect dictatorship."

While not a true dictatorship, Mexico was clearly semi-authoritarian, even if it ruled hegemonically for most of the years that the PRI held power. In the absence of a financially and politically independent media, an organized civil society, and truly competitive elections, Mexicans lacked the capacity to independently formulate and communicate public opinion. This resulted in an almost unidirectional system of communication running from state to civil society (see Lawson 2004, 385; Olvera 2004, 410). The weakness of civil society[29] was aggravated by the exclusion of some groups from organized political action. As we shall see in chapter 4, while capitalists had direct access to the president with respect to most economic issues, they tacitly agreed to refrain from organized political activity. Further, the 1917 Constitution made it illegal for religious institutions, such as the once powerful Catholic Church, to participate in politics (or own property).[30]

---

28. Over time, however, these nominal parties began publicly treating the ruling party's presidential candidates as their own nominees (Crespo 2004, 65).

29. Mexico was not unlike other Latin American states that, in their efforts to foster economic development, concentrated power between 1930 and 1980. The development of state capacity in Latin America is evident in the exponential growth of ministries, agencies, and other bureaucracies. The dramatic increase of such state structures is widely seen as having weakened Latin America's civil societies. However, as I argue in this introduction, the weakness of Mexico's civil society was also bound up with the state's corporatist control of social groups that emerged for political reasons.

30. The clergy were also denied individual voting rights. As Levy and Bruhn put it, the radical separation of church and state was intended to protect the state from the financial and social power of the Catholic Church (and not the other way around) (2006, 56).

But while presidentialism, corporatism, noncompetitive elections, and the PRI's monopoly on power weakened civil society, they did not completely disable the political opposition. On the contrary, the exclusion of genuinely alternative political voices from public debate forced political minorities to function outside of the institutionalized political arena (N. Harvey 1990). As we shall see, the difficulty that social groups faced in articulating their interests independently of the state politicized economic issues or radicalized moderate political ones (N. Harvey 1990, 196; Olvera 2004, 413). More broadly, much policy that sought to mollify peasants or workers came at the expense of capitalists, and vice versa.

As a consequence, basic interclass struggles about land or wages became complicated political contestations about Kafkaesque policies, the corrupt or inefficient implementation of policy, or state institutions. Further, social movements were radicalized by virtue of the fact that they were forced to confront corporatism, presidentialism, or both. In other words, movements arose not just at the margins of the political system but frequently in strong opposition to it. According to Foweraker and Landman, this process was not unique to Mexico. Rather, struggles over material resources turned into movements for civil and political citizenship rights precisely where authoritarian political systems in Latin America (and Spain) proved intransigent (1997, 30).

To manage political unrest, presidents resorted to *pan y palo* tactics (the Spanish equivalent of the carrot and the stick); these consisted of efforts at both co-optation and selective repression.[31] Until the 1968 massacre of students (described in chapter 2), the state tended to eschew generalized violence (except when applied to armed guerrilla movements). Low-intensity selective repression worked through the 1950s but turned into a dirty war as political discontent and protest generalized after 1968. Presidents and other state agents came to approve of torture, long-term disappearances, and extrajudicial executions of armed guerrillas and even unarmed radicals after 1968.

While the armed movements received the brunt of human rights abuses, increasing state repression formed the general political context faced by nonguerrilla activists. As Luisa Paré argues, "In many ways the state used the guerrilla movement as an excuse to attack organizations involved in legal, democratic struggles which challenged interests protected by the ruling party" (1990, 83). Nonguerrilla activists understood that they could be jailed or even

---

31. For a discussion on political co-optation, see Hellman (1994) and Zermeño (1989).

disappear for their political activity. In other words, from 1968 onward, the Mexican government sacrificed its "soft" version of authoritarianism to the extent that it increasingly relied on repression, including dirty war tactics, in the name of political stability.

As repression further radicalized and multiplied political dissidents, it is fair to conclude that neither the economic/political power of corporatist patronage nor the ultimate power of state violence would contain political discontent. The thesis to be demonstrated, however, is that some of the rural social movements that responded to the failures of corporatism, presidentialism, and dirty war tactics helped democratize both civil society and the state.

## The Emergence of Political Pluralism

This book tells the story of how some of the unarmed rural movements undermined the PRI's hegemony among one of its most important clients, the peasantry. I also explain why agrarian capitalists led other segments of the capitalist class in a powerful countermovement. The leaderships of these movements and countermovements then mobilized their social bases, forming the opposition political parties that weakened the PRI by shaming it in postelectoral mass rallies protesting electoral fraud (see Williams 2001, 73).

On July 2, 2000, the right-wing opposition PAN defeated the once invincible PRI. When it did, it peacefully removed from power a party that had ruled Mexico longer than a single party had ruled any other nation in the twentieth century. In 2006, the country underwent a highly competitive, yet remarkably peaceful, presidential election in which the winning PAN candidate prevailed over the losing PRD candidate by less than 1 percent of the vote. That there was no major outbreak of political violence during mass demonstrations and a monthlong sit-in at the Zócalo after a partial vote recount suggests that Mexico's newly democratized electoral processes are robust and have legitimacy among two-thirds of the electorate.[32]

Beyond the presidency, opposition candidates have increasingly won power in municipalities and governorships. This is evidence of rising pluralism at the local level; such pluralism has both increased local political autonomy

---

32. The potential for political violence was palpable, given that roughly one-third of the electorate believed that the PAN had engaged in electoral fraud. The 2006 presidential election further revealed deep regional (north-south), social (rich-poor), and even ideological (left-right) divisions.

and eroded presidential power (Rodríguez 1997; Hernández Rodríguez 2003; see also Weldon 2004; Grindle 2007). According to Hernández Rodríguez, pluralism in Mexico goes beyond political alternation and increasing electoral competition between parties. Pluralism, he argues, "also made it possible for basic institutions, such as the federal and state congresses and the governorships, to enhance their constitutional powers, after the political homogeneity resulting from the PRI's national dominance had disappeared. Pluralism put an end to the compulsory discipline under the executive and enabled both the legislative branch and the governorships to become efficient political counterweights to balance the executive and revitalize federalism. This process changed many traditional political practices before alternation finally reached the presidency of the republic in July 2000" (2003, 123; see also Weldon 2004).

To be clear, my claim that Mexico has evolved robust democratic electoral processes does not suggest a complete or unilinear development; nor does it suggest that procedural democracy is a panacea for all of Mexico's social problems. In terms of the latter, democratic electoral processes can, *by themselves,* do little to reduce the poverty, crime, and deadly drug trade–related violence that have brought the nation to the brink of chaos.[33] These problems can only be remedied by policies that lead to the kind of economic development that closes the gulf between the rich and poor, as well as generate the necessary state resources to adequately fund local judicial and law enforcement authorities and public prosecutors (see Magaloni and Zepeda 2004).

In addition, regimes democratize unevenly, and this seems to be especially true at the local level, where much depends on the outcome of local struggles (see N. Harvey 1998). Thus, even when there are fair and competitive procedures for the alternation of national political power, there may still remain authoritarian relations between patrons and clients, particularly in impoverished rural and urban areas (J. Fox 1990 and 1994a; Hellman 1994; Shefner 2001; Avritzer 2002; Middlebrook 2004b; Holzner 2006).[34] Further,

---

33. On "democracy without equity," see Weyland (1996) on Brazil.

34. Jonathan Fox points out, for example, that Mexico has evidenced "a gradual and uneven transition from clientelism to citizenship that involves the coexistence under the same formal regime of three different de facto political systems: entrenched redoubts of authoritarianism, broad swaths of modernized semiclientelism, and enclaves of pluralist tolerance that exhibit elements of citizenship" (1994a, 183). Similarly, Holzner notes that patron-client cliques have not disappeared in urban squatter communities despite democratization. He argues that patrons manipulate poor communities by policing their behavior and by controlling information (2006, 82).

as Seymour Martin Lipset notes, since newly democratizing countries are "inherently low in legitimacy," they can *potentially* revert back to some version of authoritarianism even at the national level (1994, 8).[35] President Felipe Calderón's current war against the drug cartels may be an example if the militarization of policing functions erodes some of the newfound strength of civil society.

Despite strong countercurrents, one can still argue that Mexico's development of democratic electoral processes is both significant and robust, even if far from perfect. The PRD's Andrés Manuel López Obrador ran a highly competitive campaign in the 2006 presidential election despite the PAN's and PRI's efforts to undermine his candidacy. Further, unlike the electoral farce of 1988,[36] the charges of fraud in the 2006 election resulted in a serious investigation in which recently independent electoral institutions annulled 237,736 votes after a partial vote recount.[37] Mexico, in short, is more democratic today than it has ever been and *begins* to meet many of the theoretical criteria of democracy described below (see Domínguez and McCann 1996; Serrano and Bulmer-Thomas 1996; Domínguez and Lawson 2004; Eisenstadt 2004; Shirk 2005; Levy and Bruhn 2006).

According to McAdam, Tarrow, and Tilly (2001), democracy involves a consultative, constitutionally bound relationship between states and people in civil society. In their view, a society is democratic if the government has the capacity to enact policy per the "protected consultation" of electorates in civil society (see also Dahl 1971).[38] Lipset contends that democracy not only requires a strong, vibrant, and politically autonomous civil society capable of influencing state policy, but must also have "social requisites." Specifically,

---

35. As José Antonio Crespo (2004) argues, federal electoral law also had regressive moments as the PRI regime struggled to preserve its party's electoral dominance.

36. The left-of-center opposition candidate, Cuauhtémoc Cárdenas, is widely believed to have been cheated out of the presidency in the 1988 elections. Mexicans suspected electoral fraud because the minister of the Interior stated on national television that a computer crash prevented the government from showing more of the vote tally. The PRI's candidate, Carlos Salinas de Gortari, was declared the winner even though Cárdenas had been in the lead before the computer crash.

37. Mexico's Federal Electoral Tribunal (TRIFE), a panel of seven judges responsible for arbitrating electoral disputes, recounted 9 percent of the precincts (or a total of 11,839 precincts); this was well short of the PRD's demand for a vote-by-vote recount.

38. Protected consultation involves the following four components: (1) broad citizenship (wherein a large percentage of the population is afforded all rights of citizenship); (2) equal and autonomous citizenship (wherein the people have equal access to governmental agents and state resources); (3) binding consultation (via referendum on policy choices and competitive elections); and (4) protection of citizens from arbitrary action by government officials, as well as autonomy from the state.

democracy requires capitalism, a large middle class, a growing and increasingly egalitarian economy,[39] and even a supportive political culture. Democratic political cultures are those that, at a minimum, value tolerance (including tolerance of political and religious differences), practice pluralism, and have nonauthoritarian religious beliefs and traditions.[40] Lipset emphasizes that citizens, as much as political elites, must accept such principles as "freedom of speech, media, assembly, religion, of the rights of opposition parties, of the rule of law, of human rights, and the like" (1994, 3).

Combining these two working definitions of democracy makes it possible to analyze changing political dynamics. The point of this book is not, however, to engage in the theoretical debate surrounding the question "What is democracy?" (see Touraine 1997). Rather, I will concentrate on some heretofore ignored actors that help account for the democratic transformation of Mexican civil society as well as its electoral arena. Specifically, I intend to show that political protest by rural actors contributed to that transformation. The working definitions of democracy outlined above simply focus the analysis on some of the changes in the way that the Mexican state relates to social groups in civil society.

## Rural Sources Contributing to Mexico's Democratization

As chapter 1 makes clear, the literature on Mexico's democratization tends to concentrate on the 1980s, a period of serious economic and regime crises and, toward the end, greater electoral competition. Much of this scholarship emphasizes that economic globalization led to the eventual emergence of political liberalism. Specifically, the globalization literature argues that the international pressures that resulted from having to refinance the debt in 1982 led to economic neoliberalism, which, in turn, led to political decentralization and eventually electoral pluralism.

While the international pressure to liberalize the economy is indeed important, I will show that civil society blossomed well before the mid-1980s.

---

39. The point of an increasingly egalitarian economy is also noted, but not stressed, by Tilly (2005). Alejandro Moreno (2001) shows that socioeconomic status (income, occupation, and education) is positively correlated with individual-level support for democracy among people in Latin America.

40. An example of authoritarian religious beliefs would be pre–Vatican II Catholic dogma.

This goes a long way toward explaining some of the historically significant PRI reforms of the political arena. Electoral reforms were initiated in 1977, for example, and these paved the way for real electoral competition. It follows that Mexico's political liberalization began well before the adoption of neoliberal economic reforms in the mid-1980s and 1990s.

I argue, moreover, that organized and disruptive political protest not only antedated the emergence of neoliberalism and its economic shocks but also contributed to economic liberalization. This is to say that in addition to the well-documented pressure that the United States and the International Monetary Fund (IMF) placed on Mexico to liberalize its economy, there were *internal* political dynamics pressing for the state's withdrawal from direct production and from the subsidization of specific industries and sectors, and for economic deregulation and free trade (see also Gates 2009). Chapter 4 documents, for example, that Mexican businessmen pressed for both political and economic liberalization in reaction to internal class struggles. While their demands did not play the dominant role in Mexico's economic reversal, the part that they did play has been overlooked by the scholarship.

Further, persistent internal political pressure could well explain why Mexico was one of the first Latin American countries to adopt neoliberal economic reforms. As Leslie Gates emphasizes, the long-term viability of neoliberalism in Mexico suggests that the internal political forces favoring economic liberalization have been crucial. Indeed, the very way in which promarket state bureaucrats (called "technocrats") reorganized the state was responsive to the political mobilization among Mexican business leaders (Gates 2009, 68–69).

Yet scholars who stress processes internal to Mexico have either focused on electoral reforms (Avritzer 2002; Eisenstadt 2004; Lawson and Klesner 2004; Shirk 2005) or on how political campaigns since 1988 have influenced voter preferences (Domínguez and McCann 1996; Domínguez and Lawson 2004). Thus, Lawson likewise notes that "over the last decade, research on Mexican politics has focused on 1) institutional reform, especially in the electoral sphere, and 2) mass behavior, especially voting" (2007, 45). While important, Mexico's democratization story neither begins nor ends in the electoral arena. Electoral reforms, new courts, and changing campaigns are indeed significant, but the impetus for the change of these institutions and processes requires explanation.

My research explores the origins of such change by looking outside of the institutionalized political arena controlled by political elites. As social movements are the central subjects of civil society (Foweraker 1989), I examine how some politically disruptive rural movements and countermovements were catalysts for legal-institutional change as well as for the making of party constituencies and ideologies. According to Foweraker (1989), change in civil society not only precedes a democratic transition, but the prior transformation of civil society is itself important to the viability and consolidation of democracy (see also Avritzer 2002). As such, I examine some movement-countermovement dynamics in civil society in the final third of the twentieth century. I pause at key moments of conflict so as to understand the changing political conditions in civil society that made Mexico's democratization possible.

While I focus on how some movements eventually supported opposition political parties, I neither trace the origins nor explore the development of the PAN (Shirk 2005) or the PRD (Bruhn 1997). Intraparty struggles over strategy are important, but such analyses tend to gloss over the bigger social-political context. These accounts also neglect to illuminate how and why social actors adopt the political positions necessary for party militancy and/or constituency in the first place. Even research that surveys political attitudes on the individual level finds it hard to unpack when or why people adopt their political views.[41]

My analysis explains the origins of some of the political allegiances on the left and on the right that were clearly brought to the fore during the 2006 presidential election.[42] I argue that a shift to the right resulted from the fact that key sectors of the business community were led by an agribusiness leader, Manuel Clouthier. Clouthier and his fellow businessmen revitalized the PAN as part of a general strategy to influence political power directly. By strategically framing the issues, they not only led a movement of key sectors of the capitalist class but also built a mass base of support among the middle class for the PAN. The businessmen's political mobilizations, in turn, were counterpunches to peasant protest and mounting interclass struggles led

---

41. Roderic Ai Camp notes, for example, that "we do not have a means of determining when this ideological shift began, but it became clear in the late 1990s that [many] Mexicans began to conceive of themselves as being on the right of the political spectrum" (2004, 28).

42. In the 2000 presidential election, 57 percent of those (randomly) surveyed considered themselves to be on the right of the ideological spectrum, and about 20 percent identified themselves as being on the left of that spectrum (Camp 2004, 28–29). Six years later, according to *Reforma*'s 2006 national exit poll, fully 34 percent of voters said that they were right of center while 20 percent continued to identify themselves as ideologically left of center. About 18 percent reported that they were squarely in the center, and 28 percent marked "no placement" in 2006 (Moreno 2007, 17).

by leftists during the 1970s. For its part, the left's involvement in earlier rural social movements had an enduring political legacy that helps account for some rural voters' long-term loyal support of left presidential candidates. This legacy also helps explain why some local electorates proved decisive in electing left (PRD) governors in some states. In other words, over the course of two decades, movement and countermovement dynamics in the countryside polarized activists and, as a consequence, the political ideologies that they developed. These struggles eventually led to the revitalization/formation of two opposition parties that successfully pressed for democratization (Bruhn 1997; Shirk 2005).

My research contributes to this historiography insofar as I identify the role of actors outside of state elites—specifically students, peasants, and businessmen—in changing state-society dynamics over time. This is not, however, an argument about "the" most important determinant. Since the literature on the transition to democracy focuses on the 1980s, the prior transformation of civil society is the least understood part of the process. Specifically, this book traces when, how, and why some politically significant rural forces shook off the shackles of corporatism to become politically contentious and how their disruptive mobilizations mattered over time. Understanding the contribution of these earlier movements illuminates some of the transformations within civil society that made structural change and the ultimate transition to democracy possible.

Fig. 3 illustrates my general argument about how the student, and subsequent rural movements, helped catalyze democratic change. At a theoretical level, this story about the relationship between social movements and institutional political change is consistent with recent work on the democratizing impact of social movements in Latin America and Spain (Foweraker 1989 and 1990; Munck 1990; Schneider 1995; Foweraker and Landman 1997; Paige 1997; Avrtizer 2002). As the theoretical implications of my research are discussed in the next chapter, the section that follows defines key theoretical concepts.

## Theoretical Concepts

According to the classic definitions in the literature, social movements are networks of people and organizations engaged in ongoing and challenging

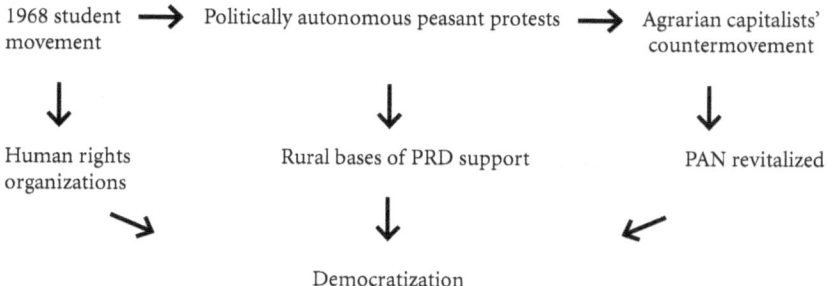

Fig. 3 Movement and countermovement dynamics contributing to Mexico's democratization

noninstitutionalized political practices so as to change society according to their ideologies (Tilly 1978; Tarrow 1994; McAdam, Tarrow, and Tilly 2001).[43] A countermovement is essentially an opposing movement comprising its own networks and organizations that have opposing political ideologies and, consequently, goals. While a movement in its own right, the term "countermovement" signals that people mobilize reactively to make "contrary claims . . . to those of the original movement" (Meyer and Staggenborg 1996, 1631).

Although the boundaries between them are always permeable, social movements are distinguished from political parties not only in that the latter seek to govern but also in that social movements operate primarily, though not exclusively, through disruptive political contention. Whereas political parties tend to play by the institutionalized rules of the game and compete peacefully in elections, social movements rely more heavily on politically disruptive tactics than on such normal politics as voting, lobbying, or petitioning. Nonviolent politically disruptive tactics run the gamut from symbolic acts, such as demonstrations and rallies, to tactics that directly challenge established social relations, including land occupations, blockades, and sit-ins (Schock 2005, 39–40; see also Sharp 2005).

As Goldstone (2003) points out, rather than perceiving social movements and political parties as constituting a simple binary, it is more accurate to

---

43. The theoretical debates about "popular" versus "social" movements, and "new" versus "old" social movements, are beyond the scope of this analysis. My emphasis throughout is that social movements engage in politically disruptive tactics such as demonstrations, rallies, land invasions, blockades, occupation of government offices, etc. As Hellman (1994) points out, many of the protest tactics in Mexico's countryside during the 1970s and 1980s were similar to those of the 1940s through the 1960s.

describe them as being located along a continuum in which the latter have the most access to and influence over policy and power and the former have the least access to these things. Goldstone (2003) emphasizes that social movement organizations and political parties can slide up or down that continuum. When they are viewed from the perspective of a continuum, rather than as a simple dichotomy, it becomes clearer that political parties will sometimes mobilize disruptively in the streets and social movement organizations will sometimes operate peacefully in electoral parties.[44]

Another example of the large gray area between the extremes is that some organizations may call themselves political "parties" even though they neither compete in the electoral arena nor engage in normatively acceptable forms of communicating policy preferences. In this analysis, for example, I treat the Mexican Communist Party (PCM) as a social movement organization on the grounds that for much of its history it was not allowed to compete in elections. When this was so, the PCM adopted an antiparliamentarian stance and engaged in politically disruptive protests both in the urban centers (among teachers, electricians, and railroad, steel, and telephone workers) and in the countryside. It called itself a "party" to signal that it had a rigorous political ideology and because it expected a certain amount of Leninist discipline among its cadre. But for most of the twentieth century, it could not compete in elections and, as I will show, both its cadre and its grassroots networks engaged in politically disruptive contention.

## The Book Plan

Because I argue that Mexico's democratization was the outcome of rural movement and countermovement dynamics unleashed by a massacre of students in 1968, I present a path-dependent analysis of "reactive sequences" of causally linked events.[45] The chapters are arranged chronologically to offer what Mahoney (2000) refers to as "scene-by-scene" descriptions of the causal paths for subsequent events. The historical narrative is punctuated by occasional quantitative techniques used to make and assess causal claims.

---

44. For the Brazilian example, see Dagnino (1998).
45. Following Mahoney's (2000) distinction between "self-reinforcing sequences" and "reactive sequences," my method employs the second type of path-dependent analysis.

Chapter 1 argues that one theoretical implication of my research is that social movements are politically consequential in the short through the long term and in unexpected ways, even in repressive contexts. As in democracies, movement characteristics interact with the political opportunity structure and cultural context to shape movement outcomes. However, in repressive contexts, leadership and politically independent organizations seem especially helpful to movement success by offering key cultural, social, and material resources, such as political ideology, social networks, information, hiding locations, and effective movement frames. In combining the framing literature and social movement outcomes literature, I illuminate not only the role of leadership within civil society but also movement-countermovement dynamics. These micro- and meso-level phenomena have historically been neglected by the focus on single-movement emergence. Finally, my emphasis on how social movements on the left and on the right democratized Mexico complements, rather than refutes, the globalization thesis. I demonstrate how domestic social movements prior to the 1980s gave shape and culturally specific depth to democratizing processes within Mexico.

Chapter 2 examines the 1968 student movement that emerged in Mexico City. This urban detour is necessary because most scholars agree that 1968 was a historical catalyst, not only because of the legitimacy crisis of the state but also because so many of the social movements that constituted a cycle of protest lasting from the 1970s to the end of the 1980s were led by ex-student radicals (Monsiváis 1987; Foweraker 1990, 9; Pérez Arce 1990; Bennett 1992). This book argues that they also participated in nonguerrilla rural protest by working with communist militants (of all political tendencies) and especially with members and former members of the PCM and its youth wing. In the context of increasing state repression, former students and other leftists mobilized in clandestine or loose networks and helped organize a flurry of nonviolent peasant protests from the 1970s through the 1980s.[46] In addition

---

46. In the countryside, a second wave of peasant protest peaked in the mid-1980s and then began to decline. As compared to the flurry of protest activity in the 1970s, by the early 1990s, the countryside was relatively quiescent, save for two spectacular movements. The armed Zapatista uprising in Chiapas (1994–) and the concurrent unarmed movement of rural debtors (the El Barzón movement) made international headlines. While both movements have been written about extensively, as an armed movement, the Zapatista uprising is outside of my theoretical interests. That said, José Antonio Crespo (2004) offers an analysis of how the Ejército Zapatista de Liberación Nacional (EZLN) unwittingly contributed to electoral democratization. Although the El Barzón movement is one of the most important struggles among small- and medium-sized rural producers since the mid-1990s, it is not exclusively a peasant movement.

to consolidating a left activist identity among youth, 1968 also spawned human rights organizations composed of ex-students and their families. I conclude that both the radicalization of youth and the mobilization of human rights organizations led to important legal reforms that contributed to the democratization of the political arena.

Chapter 3 documents how and why ex-student radicals and peasants mobilized despite the state's intensification and extension of a dirty war. I argue that they were motivated by their deep ideological commitment to a definition of social justice and to their leftist activist identities, although they risked jail sentences, indefinite disappearances, and even death. The chapter further examines what this peasant/left collaboration contributed to Mexico's democratization.

Chapter 4 shows that agribusinessmen responded to peasant protests for land in defensive countermovements that helped transform their entire class as well as Mexico's subsequent economic and political development. To defend themselves in the course of class conflict, businessmen created politically autonomous peak associations that functioned like radical social movement organizations. Their doing so created the organizational infrastructure through which to develop and disseminate neoliberalism—the ideology promoting the rights of private property, deregulation, "free" markets, and capitalism. Though once an "alternative" ideology, neoliberalism became policy in part because of the businessmen's mobilizations.[47] By the 1980s, businessmen had not only helped push a neoliberal agenda onto the nation but also succeeded in mobilizing middle-class people for the PAN by strategically reframing their grievances. In so doing, radical businessmen turned the PAN into a competitive political party capable of defeating the once invincible PRI.

Chapter 5 focuses squarely on the rural sources of electoral support for the left-of-center party, the PRD. I argue that some rural voters have been loyal to the PRD in presidential races since 1988 because of the history of left-led movements in the countryside. This history created pockets of rural supporters who, along with the left in general, have helped prop up the PRD, leading it to gubernatorial victories in some states. The PRD's electoral resiliency since 1988 has contributed to democratization in part by making Mexico's political system more pluralistic. The PRD has blocked the road to

---

47. Not all businessmen benefit from neoliberalism and free trade. Levy and Bruhn point out that businessmen organized by the Cámara Nacional de la Industria de la Transformación (CANACINTRA) oppose neoliberal policy (2006, 86).

a two-party system, and viable three-way electoral competition has ensured that policy options do not regress toward the center. In offering Mexicans genuine political alternatives to neoliberalism and economic shock therapy, the PRD has played a leading role in turning elections into increasingly ideological races between the left and the right. Indeed, the PRD's definition of social democracy as social justice turned the 2006 presidential election into a referendum on neoliberalism. As such, the critical voice offered by the PRD both engaged citizens in a public conversation about Mexico's future and helped activate civil society. As C. Wright Mills noted, such critical publics are central to democracy (1956, 323; see also Avritzer 2002; Olvera 2004).

Chapter 6 concludes that the struggles on which I focus were not just class conflicts over economic interests. Although peasants and agribusinessmen first opposed each other because of material interests, they also had in common their increasing alienation from the PRI state. Peasants and businessmen would eventually find it more effective to mobilize for their resources by focusing on organizational autonomy from the state. By their very existence, the voluntary (as opposed to compulsory) associations that they created contributed to the democratization of civil society to the extent that they undermined corporatism and confronted presidentialism. In breaking free from the state's control, peasants and businessmen created organizations through which to articulate their policy preferences and defended their political autonomy from the state. In increasing their bargaining capacity with state officials, they also expanded the very boundaries of civil society (see N. Harvey 1990). Over time, both peasants and agribusinessmen would incorporate democracy as a goal and either directly or indirectly play an important role in strengthening or consolidating the opposition parties that ultimately defeated the PRI.

The evolution of economic struggles into political ones is, according to Foweraker, a common feature in democratizing stories. He argues specifically that grassroots mobilizations rarely start out focusing on democracy. Ordinary people frequently engage in interclass conflict, the contingent outcomes of which may (or may not) move civil society in the direction of democracy (Foweraker 1989). Mexico's story departs from other democratizing stories, not so much in the evolution of interclass conflicts into political struggles but in the fact that the cycle of protest began with a moderate, but violently repressed, prodemocracy student movement. As I will show, youth who had survived the repression of 1968 were behind many peasant struggles for land.

Thus, while students did not get what they demanded in 1968, they contributed to democratization through their continued involvement in left protest activities despite increasing state repression.

To conclude, my contribution is in offering an explanation of the rural sources of left vs. right movement-countermovement dynamics that significantly contributed to electorally competitive political parties in Mexico. I show that while the PAN and left opposition parties have long independent histories, they were ultimately transformed by post-1968 political crises, including movements in the countryside. This analysis suggests a relationship among social movements, political ideologies, parties, and institutional change.

## Data Limitations

As the reader will undoubtedly want a more nuanced analysis of the people engaged in high-risk protests, I explain here what this book will not address. The existing data do not permit giving the percentage of protestors who were women or Native Americans, because the newspaper stories on which the data sets were built reported "campesino" unrest by state (not always the *municipio,* or county). Rarely did those brief stories provide details as to whom the campesinos comprised (see appendix B). What we can say for certain is that extralocal peasant leaders tended to be male. While women indeed participated in high-risk peasant struggles, such as invading lands or occupying government offices, only a few were recognized as local leaders (see Carbajal Ríos 1988; Stephen 1992).[48] The capitalists in my story were either white or mestizo men.

While Native American peasants were involved in land invasions in significant numbers, especially in those protests that occurred in the south of the country (Rubio 1987; Paré 1990; N. Harvey 1998), my efforts to identify specifically indigenist claims in these protests were anachronistic. Various native languages, social-political institutions, and customs and beliefs did survive the state's efforts to homogenize all native groups as mestizos, and indigenous cultural practices were integral to daily life at the community

---

48. On women's general marginalization in Mexico's political life, see Rodríguez (1998). This gender inequality in leadership is not unique to Mexico or Latin America. It has historically also been true in many nonwomen's movements in the United States (Morris and Staggenborg 2004).

level for millions of Mexicans (Hernández Navarro and Carlsen 2004).[49] However, this is not to say that Indians refrained from making extralocal political claims on the state. Indeed, they did, but until the 1990s, they tended to do so in the most politically effective way, by claiming rights as campesinos, landless farm workers,[50] and, after 1976, producers (in ejido unions) (N. Harvey 1998; Womack 1999, 165). Rubio specifies that unlike the protests of the first half of the 1970s, land invasions in the second half of the decade and during José López Portillo's administration sought to reclaim native lands taken by large landholders (1987, 32). In these struggles, Native Americans worked in broad coalitions with mestizos and, as I demonstrate throughout this book, were frequently led by ladino leftists transplanted from urban centers.

In other words, politically independent mobilization foregrounding Native American claims did not begin in earnest until the late 1980s and early 1990s, against the backdrop of the impending quincentennial anniversary of Columbus's arrival in the Americas (Hernández Navarro and Carlsen 2004, 444–45; Martin 2005, 210; Carton de Grammont and Mackinlay 2009, 31).[51] In anticipation of the 1992 anniversary, Mexico signed the ILO Convention on indigenous peoples' rights in 1991; it reformed Article 4 of its Constitution a

49. Estimates on the exact number of indigenous people in Mexico vary in part because it depends on whether one's definition of "indigenous" stresses culture (such as an indigenous language or traditional dress) or phenotypical signifiers of "race" (on the latter, see Mora 2008). Conservative estimates of the number of indigenous peoples range from 9 to 10 percent of the country's 111,211,789 people. The CIA World Factbook, however, estimates that about 30 percent of Mexico's population is of Amerindian, or predominantly Amerindian, ancestry.

50. Examples include the Independent Union of Peasants of Northern Chiapas circa 1977 and the Ejidal Unions and United Peasant Groups of Chiapas of the Lacandon jungle.

51. Although the Mexican government convened the first-ever National Congress of Indigenous Peoples in 1975, it was not politically independent from the government. Not even in Chiapas did distinct native groups organize in a pan-ethnic protest movement before 1974 (Womack 1999, 149). On October 13, 1974, Chols, Tzotzils, Tzeltals, and Tojolabals expressed solidarity with one another by agreeing to present their grievances about "land, commerce, education, and health" at a local congress in Chiapas (Womack 1999, 149). These were the issues around which the congress's leaders (including a Marxist sociologist) mobilized until their organization dissolved itself in March of 1977. Shortly thereafter, Maoists from Línea Proletaria arrived in the area and competed with organizers historically linked to the Central Independiente de Obreros Agrícolas y Campesinos (CIOAC), which had close ties to the PCM, and the government's National Peasants' Confederation (CNC) for hegemony among native groups there. The CIOAC organized peons, peasants, and the landless as unionists or peasants through the mid-1980s (Womack 1999, 163). According to Womack, by 1990, the "CIOAC remained the deepest and strongest organization in the region" (1999, 164). The Organización Campesina Emiliano Zapata (OCEZ) gained strength in the Tzotzil and Tzeltal areas, and in the late 1980s, it foregrounded indigenist claims (Womack 1999, 184).

year later to acknowledge the right of Indian peoples to their own "languages, cultures, customs, and resources" (Hernández Navarro and Carlsen 2004). What is more, the political capital of indigenist claims increased[52] at the very moment that the political capital of "campesino" claims decreased (with the state's loss of patronage resources, the end of land reform, and the withdrawal of the state from the economy). Finally, the success of the Zapatistas in Chiapas gave further momentum to the growth of a pan-Indian movement in Mexico (N. Harvey 1998; Stahler-Sholk 2008, 119) in the context of greater organization and communication among native groups across Latin America that had mobilized to protest the anniversary of Columbus's arrival.

This brings me to the subplot of this book. Two of the chapters concern unarmed peasant movements, but I also frequently mention the armed guerrilla movements of the 1960s and 1970s. The broad support that the guerrillas received from rural peoples helped them elude soldiers. This explains why the government intensified the dirty war against them and extended it to the unarmed left and, indeed, to entire rural communities. The evidence is clear that soldiers and lower-level police units not only violated the human rights of nonguerrilla rural activists but sometimes even killed such innocents as the elderly or young boys; they also raped women. But while the unarmed peasant movement clearly did not operate in a vacuum, I am unable to tell the story of the government's dirty war against the armed rural guerrilla movements of the 1960s and 1970s.[53] Instead, I concentrate on why and how some nonviolent rural movements operated in the context of increasing state repression, because these data, while difficult to assemble, were more available than data on the armed guerrillas or the army's actions.

52. For example, Native Americans from all over Mexico, as well as thousands of ladino leftists and students, participated in a massive demonstration in Mexico City to commemorate five hundred years of Indian resistance. When thousands of Indians chanted, "Se ve, se siente, el Indio esta Presente" (loosely translated as "Indians are present" [to speak truth to power]), they clearly appropriated and reinterpreted the term "Indio." For centuries, many Mexicans used the word derogatorily to signal ignorance, poverty, and backwardness. As evidenced by chants such as these during the 1990s, the term was recast in a positive light, reflecting a significant change in the cultural identity (akin to "black" in the black power movement in the United States) while also expressing pan-ethnic solidarity.

At the community level, JoAnn Martin describes the change as follows: "Everyday practices in Tepoztlán [Mexico] in the 1980s pointed to the indigenous past, but without being marked as such. . . . It was not until the 1990s, with the general resurgence of indigenous identity in Latin America, that Tepoztecans began to distinguish between indigenous practices and foreign imports" (2005, 208–9).

53. For the story of the EZLN, which began in the early 1980s, see Collier (1994), N. Harvey (1998), and Womack (1999).

For these reasons, I examine how nonviolent rural movements spawned by the events of 1968 contributed to Mexico's recent democratization. As unarmed social movements are more common than armed struggles,[54] my focus has broad implications for the scholarship on social movements and countermovements. These are developed in the following chapter.

---

54. The literature seems to be reaching a consensus that nonviolent struggles are more likely to be effective in achieving goals than are movements that rely on violence, especially in authoritarian societies (Drake 1996; Schock 2005; Sharp 2005; Stephan and Chenoweth 2008).

# 1

## Social Movements and Democratization

Notwithstanding work on recent Latin American transitions to democracy,[1] much scholarship has glossed over the relationship between nonrevolutionary social movements and institutional reforms of the national political arena.[2] While a burgeoning literature on Latin America explores how social movements since the 1980s secure or redefine citizenship rights,[3] influence electoral outcomes,[4] generate multiple public spheres, and otherwise democratize

---

1. The recent transitions to democracy in Latin America have generated a growing body of work that examines the relationship between social movements and the quality of newly democratized regimes (Escobar and Alvarez 1992). For a brief summary of this literature, see Avritzer (2002) and Vanden (2008, 55). For empirical discussions of the Bolivian, Chilean, Mexican, Paraguayan, and Venezuelan cases, see Arditi and Rodríguez (1987), De la Cruz (1989), Oporto (1991), Schild (1998), and Vanden (2008). See also Kuecker, Stahler-Sholk, and Vanden (2008) for a discussion of the relationship between social movements and progressive political change in Latin America.

2. The following have made similar observations: Foweraker (1990), J. Fox (1990), Markoff (1996), Giugni, McAdam, and Tilly (1998 and 1999), McAdam, Tarrow, and Tilly (2001), Andrews (2002), and Schock (2005).

3. For an excellent review of the literature, see Foweraker and Landman (1997).

4. In Bolivia, poor indigenous peasants and miners who had mobilized locally for centuries met with success when they worked in broad coalitions with other social movements. Through a broad national coalition, they supported Evo Morales and his Movimiento al Socialismo (MAS) party, propelling him to a near presidential victory in 2002; eventually toppled the Sánchez de Lozada government and forced the resignation of his successor; and voted Evo Morales into political power in late 2005 as Bolivia's first indigenous president (Vanden 2008; Becker 2008). Similarly, Brazil's militant landless rural workers' movement (Movimento dos Trabalhadores Rurais Sem Terra, MST), with more than one million members nationally, contributed to regime change by supporting "Lula" and the left-of-center government Workers' Party (Partido dos Trabalhadores) in the 2002 elections (Vanden 2008, 54; see also Ondetti 2008). As it is politically independent of the Workers' Party, the MST continues to protest for land reform.

political culture by challenging "social authoritarianism" (Escobar and Alvarez 1992; Alvarez, Dagnino, and Escobar 1998), there remains a pocket of theoretical and empirical neglect with respect to how protest movements may restructure the legal-institutional terrain of the political game itself. In other words, the possibility that nonrevolutionary[5] social movements may transform the political system, or significant institutional subparts, remains understudied.[6] Indeed, regarding Mexico, many scholars have considered the political action of politically autonomous organizations within a weak civil society to be "politically inconsequential and incapable of effecting social and political change" (Holzner 2006, 79).

This theoretical and empirical neglect is partly explained by the fact that the democratization literature tends to stress external, or global, processes. Further, the scholarship that focuses squarely on domestic processes tends to look at how political elites engage in legal reforms rather than at the role of grassroots movements in this process (for a summary, see Foweraker 1989; Foweraker and Landman 1997). This emphasis may have to do with the size and power of pretransition authoritarian states. The problem, however, is that not all political dissidents are disabled, and their grassroots opposition may well have an independent effect on the democratic transformation of the political arena. As Foweraker has shown of some authoritarian societies, civil society is indeed an important "site of political strategies and democratic projects. It is civil society where the battle is lost and won; and this political battle cannot be reduced to the binding imperatives of national or international economic orders" (1989, 248; see also Foweraker and Landman 1997). In other words, it is primarily through social movements—collective subjects in civil society—that the battle for democracy is waged and potentially won (Foweraker 1990; Munck 1990; Giugni, McAdam, and Tilly 1998; McAdam, Tarrow, and Tilly 2001; Schock 2005).

Even research on established democracies tends to treat normal institutionalized politics and social movements as alternatives (for a summary, see Goldstone 2003; Becker 2008). Further, the scholarship on the latter

5. Gamson (1990) argues that nonrevolutionary social movements are generally more likely to succeed than those with displacement goals (see also Ackerman and Kruegler 1994).
6. Three notable exceptions are Joe Foweraker's *Making Democracy in Spain: Grass-roots Struggle in the South, 1955–1975* (1989), Joe Foweraker and Ann L. Craig's *Popular Movements and Political Change in Mexico* (1990), and Leonardo Avritzer's *Democracy and the Public Space in Latin America* (2002).

has historically sought to explain why people make contentious political claims outside of normative or institutionalized avenues. The literature on social movement outcomes is not only relatively smaller, but since it is based primarily on Western democracies, there is a presumption that social movements are only successful in democratic polities because they confer greater political opportunity for exacting policy concessions (for a summary of the literature, see Giugni, McAdam, and Tilly 1998 and 1999). In addition to ignoring social movement outcomes in repressive political contexts, much of the social movement scholarship has glossed over the role of grassroots leaders at a micro-level of analysis (Barker, Johnson, and Lavalette 2001). Finally, my work contributes to the literature on the political outcomes of movement-countermovement dynamics, an emerging body of work at the meso-level of analysis (Meyer and Staggenborg 1996; Andrews 2002).

As noted in the introduction, my empirical analysis shows that a massacre of students in 1968 radicalized youth who, in turn, contributed to the protest cycle of the 1970s through the 1980s in Mexico. The nonviolent movements and countermovements in this cycle led to significant policy concessions and structural reforms despite the state's closed and increasingly repressive tendencies. Further, the leaders of these movements eventually drove their support bases into two opposition political parties, the right-of-center Partido Acción Nacional (PAN) and left-of-center Partido de la Revolución Democrática (PRD), which weakened the regime electorally. The PAN eventually unseated the Partido Revolucionario Institucional (PRI) regime after a seventy-one-year monopoly on power. Paradoxically, while students did not get what they wanted in 1968, they contributed to movements that would exact even greater democratizing reforms than they had originally demanded. Using Mexico as an example, I argue that despite seemingly impossible odds, social movements can promote legislative and structural reforms of the political arena over the medium to long term, and in unexpected ways, even in repressive political contexts.

This chapter examines the strengths of the globalization thesis before showing its limitations as applied to Mexico. I argue that a historical analysis of domestic movement-countermovement dynamics helps explain not only that country's democratic transformation but even the early adoption and ultimate viability of free market economic policies there. I conclude with a discussion of how the role of leadership, as well as movement-countermovement dynamics, matters to social movement outcomes in repressive political contexts.

## Social Movements and Democratization in the Global Context

As Markoff and others observe, the third wave of democratization that began in the mid-1970s and continued through the 1990s was an intercontinental phenomenon affecting Latin America and Eastern Europe (Markoff 1996, 9). Transnationalism, or globalization, is considered important to democratizing stories because social movements and governing elites are part of global information and communication networks that value democracy. With greater communication technologies (for example, television, phones, faxes, and the Internet), democratic ideas and values are disseminated. This is especially so with the aid of transnational or international social movement organizations, nongovernmental organizations (NGOs), and cross-national networks.[7] For these reasons, cultural and even political transformations are seen as accompanying greater global economic integration (Yúdice 1998). As Markoff put it, "Both social movements and governing elites pay attention to what other social movements and governing elites are doing elsewhere. The result is sometimes a transnational convergence of political transformations driven in some places by movements, in others by elite reforms, in still others by both" (1996, 20; see also Huntington 1991).

Beyond the cultural diffusion or cultural convergence argument, other "third wave" theorists stress that economic liberalization facilitates (but does not necessarily determine) political liberalization (see Huntington 1991; Lipset 1994). Some scholars hold that when states "relinquish control over economic and social progress to the market," they open the door for grassroots groups to enter the political arena in such a way as to revitalize civil society (Li and Reuveny 2003, 34; see also Yúdice 1998; Dixon 2008; Alcañiz and Scheier 2008, 278). Similarly, when states decentralize by giving local governments more administrative or fiscal autonomy (Rodríguez 1997), they create space that local actors from civil society politicize. Put differently, political decentralization creates new political opportunities for the articulation of

---

7. Please see Lins Ribeiro (1998), Yúdice (1998), Sikkink and Smith (2002, 31), Almeida and Johnston (2006), Carty (2006), Olesen (2006), Stewart (2006), and Dixon (2008).

grievances, political preferences, mobilization, and even conflict (Avritzer 2002, 80; Almeida and Johnston 2006).

While many scholars disagree that economic globalization favors democracy,[8] even those highly critical of neoliberalism agree that the confluence of economic restructuring and political decentralization has led to a sharp rise in anti-austerity protests (Almeida and Johnston 2006, 12; Shefner, Pasdirtz, and Blad 2006, 19; Stahler-Sholk, Vanden, and Kuecker 2008). This is so because the former increases economic hardship (Evrensel 2002; Shefner, Pasdirtz, and Blad 2006) while the latter results in both the loss of state legitimacy and greater political opportunity for mobilization (Shefner, Pasdirtz, and Blad 2006). Many studies have found that people resist inflation, cuts in social services, insecure employment or unemployment, wage cuts, poor working conditions, and inadequate housing and healthcare. Such protests explicitly link worsening economic conditions to the structural adjustment policies associated with global economic integration (Almeida and Johnston 2006). Some of these protests are also tied to movements for minority rights and cultural autonomy because racialized communities, already disproportionately poor, are further marginalized by structural adjustment programs (Dixon 2008; Becker 2008). According to Villalón, "All of the Latin American countries have witnessed grassroots resistance to economic and political abuses of power, particularly those related with neoliberal regimes and corporate globalization" (2008, 269; see also Almeida and Johnston 2006).

Many empirical studies have indeed documented mass protests against austerity measures since the 1980s in Latin America; these protests occurred in Argentina, Bolivia, Brazil, Chile, Columbia, Ecuador, Mexico, Peru, Uruguay, and Venezuela (Almeida and Johnston 2006; Stahler-Sholk, Vanden, and Kuecker 2008). Protests against privatization and other neoliberal development plans occurred in Costa Rica, El Salvador, Guatemala, Honduras, and Mexico (Almeida and Johnston 2006; Spalding 2008; Carton de Grammont and Mackinlay 2009). Peasants, workers, teachers, indigenous groups, blacks, the urban poor, the unemployed, the indebted, and women who once depended on state patronage, social services, state-related employment, or

---

8. Of course, much of the debate hinges on the definition of democracy. For some, democracy is strictly about fully competitive elections and the individual rights of citizens. Others stress that only social and/or participatory democracy empowers individuals to fully realize their de jure rights as citizens. For a review of this debate as applied to recent transitions, see Alvarez, Dagnino, and Escobar (1998), Li and Reuveny (2003), and Slater (2008).

production inputs have protested their deteriorating economic conditions in broad coalitions; many have done so with innovative strategies and tactics outside of traditional organizations (such as trade unions or political parties) (Almeida and Johnston 2006; Dagnino 1998; Villalón 2008; Spronk and Webber 2008; Kuecker 2008; Stahler-Sholk 2008; Dixon 2008). Some of these groups have mobilized at both the community and international level to reclaim indigenous or black identities (Yashar 2005; Dixon 2008; Mora 2008) and cultural-political autonomy (N. Harvey 1998; Stahler-Sholk 2008; Issa 2008) in a growing and increasingly influential indigenous peoples' movement (Yashar 2005).[9] Others assert local communal rights to land (in Mexico, Brazil, and Columbia) and other natural resources (natural gas and water in Bolivia, minerals in Ecuador, and rainforests in Brazil). As many rural communities are outraged by private sector development that destroys national resources and communities for the benefit of foreign capital (in other words, accumulation by dispossession), some organize both locally and in solidarity with transnational networks (D. Harvey 2003; Spronk and Webber 2008; Kuecker 2008).[10] Indeed, according to Almeida and Johnston, "since the 1980s, an anti-globalization master frame has become a powerful lens through which to view local grievances" in rural areas and especially in the urban centers (2006, 7; see also Holzner 2006).

Mexico's experience with economic globalization is comparable, even though most observers agree that political liberalism developed more slowly there than in most Latin American countries (excepting Cuba, of course). Mexicanists stress that international pressure, especially from the International Monetary Fund (IMF), was indeed an important mechanism for Mexico's neoliberal turn (Paré 1990; Shefner, Pasdirtz, and Blad 2006). According to this perspective, the oil and then debt crisis of 1982 not only underscored the problems with the state-led model of capitalist development but also gave the United States and especially the IMF leverage in their long-standing efforts to

9. Examples of such movements include the Zapatistas in Chiapas, Mexico; Ecuador's Confederación de Nacionalidades Indígenas del Ecuador (CONAIE), as well as its Movimiento Indígena Pachacutik; the San Blas Kuna rights mobilizations in Panama; mobilizations of the Yanomami in Brazil; mobilizations among the *altiplano* Aymara and Quechua groups in Bolivia; and the pan-Maya movement in Guatemala (Almeida and Johnston 2006; Warren 1998).

10. While struggles against foreign capital's tendency to accumulate through dispossession take various forms, some battles for national self-determination rely heavily on international networks of environmentalists for support. Others have helped create the Vía Campesina (on which see McMichael 2006; Martínez-Torres and Rosset 2008), while still others emphasize regional identities based on shared anticolonial histories, such as Foro Mesoamericano (Spalding 2008).

liberalize Mexico's economy. To negotiate the debt, Mexico had to establish its credibility vis-à-vis powerful global actors by liberalizing its economy. Neoliberalism was adopted precisely to establish credibility, and from the 1980s onward, presidents increasingly privatized state firms, imposed austerity measures, opened the economy to foreign investment, and, in 1992, signed the North American Free Trade Agreement (NAFTA).

According to Levy and Bruhn, political liberalization would follow, because "in some ways the liberalization of markets contributes to political liberalization" (2006, 149). Many scholars note that Mexico's political system eventually liberalized because when the PRI state divested from the economy, it had fewer resources for patronage and, thus, political co-optation. Further, the state retreated from the economic sphere precisely when poverty and economic insecurity increased among peasants, workers, and popular groups (McAdam, Tarrow, and Tilly 2001; Williams 2001). Luisa Paré explains, "The austerity program, implemented under International Monetary Fund dictates so as to pay the external debt, disproportionately affected peasants and industrial workers, lowering 1988 wages to 1960s levels and significantly reducing living standards, particularly in terms of health and nutrition" (1990, 84; see also 92).[11] Under these circumstances, the PRI and its corporatist organizations lost legitimacy; they would see a further decline in support among their traditional clients when the ruling party ended land reform and failed to otherwise respond to social needs (even after a devastating earthquake in 1985) (Williams 2001, 210, 220; Middlebrook 2004b, 17–18; Mackinlay 2004; Levy and Bruhn 2006, 69–70).

The crisis of corporatist representation, subsequent regime crises, and increasing income inequality opened the way to the mobilization of alternative peasant, ethnic, worker, urban, teacher, middle-class, and women's movements.[12] As the government had no patronage resources with which to buy support, it relied on repression to quell social unrest. This further eroded the legitimacy of the regime, leading to even more protest. But in addition to protesting their deteriorating economic circumstances, from the 1980s onward, Mexicans from multiple spheres increasingly articulated political demands in terms of individual citizenship rights rather than as clients (J. Fox

11. On the IMF, see Shefner, Pasdirtz, and Blad (2006).
12. For an overview of this literature, see Foweraker and Craig (1990), Serrano and Bulmer-Thomas (1996, 3), McAdam, Tarrow, and Tilly (2001, 291), Williams (2001), Avritzer (2002), Middlebrook (2004b, 17–18), and Stahler-Sholk (2008).

1994a; Foweraker and Landman 1997; Tamayo Flores-Alatorre 1999; Avritzer 2002; Wada 2006). In this context, electoral competition became more meaningful, as evidenced by the emergence, in the early 1990s, of civic organizations that would closely monitor elections and mobilize to protest electoral fraud (Avritzer 2002; Eisenstadt 2003; Middlebrook 2004b, 18–19; Shefner, Pasdirtz, and Blad 2006).

In sum, many scholars hold that Mexico's civil society blossomed in the 1980s because economic globalization led to political decentralization, and both led to a sharp rise in anti-austerity protests and cultural autonomy movements (Ramírez Sáiz 1992; Shefner, Pasdirtz, and Blad 2006; Holzner 2006; Stahler-Sholk 2008; Vanden 2008). The growth and vibrancy of Mexico's civil society is attributed to "social and demographic change" and the "internationalization of the economy and cultural life" that accompanied neoliberal restructuring in the context of the PRI government's decreasing ability to either silence the opposition or purchase political support with clientelistic favors (Levy and Bruhn 2006, 69–70). Some scholars add that Mexico would eventually democratize because the more international shareholders invested in the country, the more they cared about its political stability and its elections (Levy and Bruhn 2006, 89, 166, 171; Serrano and Bulmer-Thomas 1996, 12; see also Castells and Laserna 1994).

My historical analysis does not deny that the international arena influenced the economic strategies of Mexico's power holders as well as the lives of its challengers. Indeed, it did, but it did so even before the global oil and debt crises of 1982. For example, the dirty war took place against the backdrop of an international cold war that motivated (indeed underwrote) other dirty wars in South America. Further, the students' prodemocracy movement in 1968 was partly inspired by international youth movements that year. Peasants, too, reacted to the penetration of markets in the countryside well before the oil and debt crises of 1982. In this analysis, I focus on explaining how global processes mattered to Mexicans at the grassroots level. I specifically show how domestic social movements responded on the basis of their own internal history. Moreover, I look at whether their political responses were consequential.

To put this schematically, the globalization literature does a good job of identifying common catalysts that affect countries globally.[13] My study

---

13. For a critique of this literature as well as a critical analysis of political hybridization in Latin America resulting from globalization processes, see Avritzer (2002).

complements this work by focusing on *who* was catalyzed domestically and *how* their local actions mattered. I demonstrate that while an international student movement inspired Mexican students in 1968—and while Mexico's political elites certainly worked to make the country both credit and investment worthy, especially after the 1982 economic crisis—it was ultimately *domestic* social movements that forced changes in electoral and property laws and whose electoral and postelectoral mobilizations would eventually unseat the PRI.

My focus, then, brings agency back into the conversation about global waves of democratization. It also helps specify historically more of the actors involved in Mexico's democratic transformation than would be seen by focusing on the timing proposed by the global cultural convergence thesis. Even scholars who have linked global and local processes tend to miss rural actors and earlier movements.[14] Their analyses begin with the global oil and debt crises of the 1980s, given that multiple *urban* groups responded politically to the failure of corporatism in the face of neoliberalism's economic shock therapy, which included "hyper-urbanization" (Castells and Laserna 1994; Almeida and Johnston 2006; Holzner 2006). Although the 1980s were crucial to the formation and consolidation of an electoral opposition and to the (re)activation of old and new social movements, I show that pre-1985 social movements weakened corporatism and challenged presidentialism even before the period of political decentralization. In fact, the cycle of protest began immediately after the tragedy of 1968—during the 1970s, in the context of increasingly statist governance. This pretransition period saw not only a rise in the state's patronage of popular groups but also a sharp increase in political repression.

While not obvious at first, these earlier social movements transformed civil society to such a degree as to make possible the transition to democracy. Though slow, Mexico's transition was viable precisely because prior movements laid the organizational infrastructure and developed the political ideologies that strengthened civil society.[15] These earlier movements restructured entire classes, civic organizations, electoral law, political parties, and even some aspects of the country's political culture. They did so, moreover, despite increasing repression. Thus, this book not only offers a history that helps

14. An exception is Heather Williams's work (2001) on the El Barzón debtors' movement.
15. For a comparable analysis of Spain, see Foweraker (1989). For a discussion of deliberative public spheres, see Avritzer (2002).

account for what scholars have referred to as Mexico's "civic-electoral insurrection"[16] of the 1980s, but the historical analysis also reminds us that capitalism penetrated Mexico earlier than the global wave thesis suggests (Nun 1993). This happened, however, in a complex and incomplete way. Indeed, this early, if uneven, penetration of capital helps account for the rise of earlier pro- and anticapital movements in the 1970s. These earlier movements, in turn, help explain why political competition in contemporary Mexico continues to be structured around a right vs. left axis.[17]

My domestic focus, then, complements rather than refutes claims about Mexico's place in the global wave of democratization. I argue that in order to fully understand Mexico's transition to democracy, we must begin earlier than the 1980s and with a close examination of domestic actors in the aftermath of the 1968 student massacre. While students did not immediately get what they wanted, they, along with peasants and businessmen, contributed to significant legislative and structural reforms that paved the way for their country's ultimate democratization. In other words, protest movements—including, paradoxically, the student movement—proved consequential over the long haul by transforming civil society and electoral law despite an increasingly repressive political context. As compared to other Latin American countries, Mexico democratized slowly, yet it quickly passed seemingly viable neoliberal reforms, in part because of the outcomes of this earlier history. Movements during the pretransition period not only helped to slowly evolve electoral law but also created the organizational structures that would successfully exploit further political openings. The businessmen's countermovement, moreover, helps account for the rapid adoption of neoliberal reforms, as well as the strong internal support for neoliberalism among many economic elites and their political arm, the PAN.

## Social Movement Outcomes in Repressive Political Contexts

As noted, my analysis contributes to the literature on social movement outcomes, a body of work that emphasizes the opportunities for success conferred

---

16. This phrase is Aziz Nassif's, as quoted in Carr (1989, 381).
17. The 2006 presidential election is noteworthy because the former ruling party, accustomed to winning elections by landslides (with the exception of 1988 and, of course, 2000, when the party was defeated), appeared irrelevant in what was clearly a left vs. right political contest.

on movements by democratic polities. This scholarship holds that social movements have the opportunity to effect change in democracies, but that this is far less true in authoritarian settings. Piven and Cloward (1997), for example, specify that mass political disruption has the power to reform policy because legislators respond in order to reestablish political order, especially in election years (see also Banaszak 1996; Tilly 1999; Alcañiz and Scheier 2008, 274–75). Political opportunity theory is explicit that social movements are more likely to succeed in democratic societies, especially those with decentralized power structures and with association-based political parties, than in more closed political systems.[18] While most scholars agree that a country's policing strategy is an important "barometer of political opportunities available to social movements" (della Porta 1996, 90), some hold that social movements are unlikely to succeed in those societies where repression is probable or where it is severe enough to make a continuation of protest too costly (Muller and Weede 1990; Koopmans and Statham 1999; Kriesi 2004, 72).[19]

Our very definition of movement success precludes ways in which social movements may operate effectively in repressive contexts. In his now classic definition, for example, William Gamson defined social movement success as those instances in which the "targets" both accept the claimants as legitimate and offer them fundamental concessions (1990, 31–32). While limited concessions may either preempt or co-opt movements, outright movement failure occurs when targets refuse to offer movements any new benefits (see Piven and Cloward 1977). Defined in this way, political repression would seem to be a prima facie example of movement failure, since repression is evidence that government officials define the claimants and their demands not only as illegitimate but also as a political or economic threat to the nation. These officials frequently justify harsh political repression with frameworks about national security, whether the security threat is real, exaggerated, or even completely fabricated (Boudreau 2005, 34).[20]

---

18. The democratic institutions that are seen as being favorable to social movement claims are political parties based on association, rather than patronage, and real legislatures. These help decentralize power (Amenta, Carruthers, and Zylan 1992; Rummel 1995; Kriesi et al. 1995; Brockett 1991; Kitschelt 1986; Amenta and Caren 2004). According to Amenta, Carruthers, and Zylan, patronage parties structurally block "programmatic spending policies because discretionary and individualistic policies are the lifeblood of" patronage (1992, 313–14; see also 335–36).

19. Kriesi, for example, argues that "reform is never forthcoming" and repression is too great in "extremely closed" political systems (2004, 82).

20. While government officials have no choice but to attempt to justify mass and indiscriminate state violence that is difficult to cover up, even those violations that happen illegally and

To be clear about the phenomena, political repression refers to all acts in which the government violates the political and civil liberties of political actors in civil society either legally or illegally, overtly or covertly (Schock 2005). Such actions can be distributed along a continuum of severity, with the mass imprisonment of activists and/or indiscriminate state violence being located at the extreme upper end of that scale. According to Francisco, harsh repression refers to "overwhelming" and "one-sided" state force, and it is usually perpetrated by social control agents, such as military or police units, against nonviolent activists (2005, 59). This definition excludes atrocities committed in civil war because under those circumstances both sides are armed.

Without suggesting that the state and its propensity for political violence are irrelevant to movement outcomes, I argue that too narrow an analytic focus on state structures or government reaction will overlook how movements may operate effectively even in repressive contexts (see also Foweraker 1989; Sharp 2005; Stephan and Chenoweth 2008). While Amenta and Young (1999) also stress the importance of focusing on movement outcomes rather than on success or failure as historically defined, I add that the analytic lens needs to be wide enough to view not only how social movements interact with their political and cultural contexts but also how they do so over time (Jenkins 1995; Zwerman and Steinhoff 2005). By focusing on the dynamic relationship between social movements and states historically, one might see how political opportunities (or the opposite) are constructed by those who take political repression for granted. A wider analytic lens that follows the relationship over time might reveal that social movements can prove consequential in the long term even in authoritarian societies (Foweraker 1989). As noted, the following chapters show that social movements that were met with repression in Mexico still contributed to seemingly small policy shifts, which, over time, increased the opposition's leverage vis-à-vis the state and ultimately helped pave the road to that country's democratization.

My research also shows that while many activists demobilize in the face of massive state violence, others will commit more deeply to political struggle but develop clandestine tactics to avoid further repression (see also Foweraker 1989; Francisco 2005; Johnston 2005; Zwerman and Steinhoff

---

covertly require the cooperation of other government officials and military or police agents. As such, they require a justification.

2005).²¹ This finding seems well established in the literature. According to Kurt Schock, the repression-dissent paradox refers to the historical contradiction that repression sometimes ends social movements while at other times it encourages more political dissent regarding the illegitimacy of state repression (Hess and Martin 2006). The apparent radicalization that occurs can generate an immediate backlash or promote protest activity in the medium to long term.²² The backlash can take any form, from highly disruptive hit-and-run guerrilla tactics at one extreme to more subtle "everyday" forms of resistance at the other. Paul Drake, for example, argues that while labor movements and their parties failed to dethrone the dictators of Latin America's Southern Cone, they "devised creative ways to survive, to parry some of the worst abuses of these governments, to carve out niches for activity, to reassemble . . . ranks, and to prepare for future democratization" (1996, 47, see also 52; Schneider 1995).²³

In emphasizing the interaction of protest movements and government action, I help reintroduce agency into the conversation about how protest movements may matter in repressive contexts. As Schock observes, "The literature neglects to consider how characteristics of challengers affect the relationship between repression and dissent." This is problematic on many levels, not least of which is that too narrow a focus on state structures or political elites treats challengers as "passive objects," seemingly "powerless in the face of regime repression" (Schock 2005, 33–34; see also Davenport 2005, xix).

## Movement Resiliency and Effectiveness in Repressive Contexts

Kurt Schock argues that unarmed movements may succeed in repressive contexts because violence against unarmed citizens may undermine the legitimacy of government officials nationally and internationally (2005, 42–43; Francisco 2005; Stephan and Chenoweth 2008).²⁴ In Schock's words, "The

---

21. Some activists may seek to provoke repression so as to demonstrate to various audiences that the political system is repressive, closed, or both.
22. Please see Goldstein (1983), Munck (1990, 32), Brockett (1995), della Porta (1995), Loveman (1998, 485), Francisco (2005), Schock (2005, 42), Hess and Martin (2006), and Chang and Kim (2007).
23. Worker organizations, Drake further observes, frequently held power not long after the dictators left, and even if they could not implement many pro-labor reforms, they offered labor more freedom and ultimately helped rebuild democracy.
24. On external allies, see Drake (1996, 47).

key variable for the success of an unarmed insurrection is not the amount of violence that accompanies it, but rather the ability to remain resilient in a repressive context and to increase its leverage relative to the state, either by directly severing the state's sources of support or by mobilizing the crucial support of third parties that have leverage against the target state" (2005, 161). Schock maintains that how a movement is organized, what evasive strategies and tactics it chooses, who it targets, who countermobilizes, and how activists communicate with third parties all contribute to a movement's resiliency and long-term effectiveness in a repressive political context (2005, 157).

My analysis similarly emphasizes that movement characteristics interact with the political opportunity structure (POS) as well as the cultural context of the society in which protest occurs. The POS is usually defined by the institutional characteristics of the state that help shape some aspects of opportunity for mobilization success (Jenkins 1995, 17). It includes some, or all, of the following: the extent to which the institutionalized political system is open or closed to inputs from nonelites; the degree to which elite alignments produce political stability or instability; the extent to which social movements have elite allies, especially in the state; and the state's capacity and propensity for repression (Kitschelt 1986; McAdam 1996; Brockett 1991; Kriesi 1995). By cultural context, I specifically refer to the dominant political ideology, as well as the most widely accepted narratives and myths about the nation.

My research suggests that the movement characteristics necessary for effective mobilization in repressive contexts are leadership and organizational autonomy (see also Foweraker 1989). While these variables are important in all contexts, they are central to movement resiliency and long-term effectiveness in authoritarian societies. My empirical analysis of movements over time suggests that effective leaders in politically independent organizations help movements succeed over time by offering key cultural, social, and material resources, such as political ideology (a.k.a. political "propaganda," however disseminated), social networks, information, hiding locations, and culturally competent movement frames.

*Leadership*

Movement leaders are "strategic decision-makers who inspire and organize others to participate in social movements" (Morris and Staggenborg 2004,

171). While it may be true, as Williams writes, that an excessive concentration of leadership makes movements vulnerable to repression (2001), movements in authoritarian political contexts need leaders to survive in the long term. In addition to violence, authoritarian governments rely heavily on movement infiltration to identify dissidents, either to threaten or to co-opt them. Thus, while some would-be reformers retreat in the face of threats, others are co-optable. Some leaders, in contrast, are simply indomitable.[25] In other words, it is precisely because authoritarian governments rely heavily on repression and co-optation that it takes politically resolute characters to engage in the slow work of building both an opposition and the organizational infrastructure to support it. The leadership provided by dissidents is the first step toward extending the boundaries of civil society (Foweraker 1989).

Beyond being politically determined, leaders are also intellectuals (Morris and Staggenborg 2004), even if they are not all from privileged backgrounds (but are rather organic intellectuals). Leaders synthesize information and viewpoints, and they articulate goals, define strategy, and alter tactics. While strategic decisions are important to movement outcomes in all contexts, in repressive contexts the margin for error is smaller. Good leaders are especially attuned to the possibility of deadly decisions and are therefore intellectually nimble when working through strategy and tactics. Such leaders must also be flexible enough to experiment with organizational forms and especially movement frames. This suggests that ineffective leaders are rigid about their strategies and tactics and are culturally insensitive in their framing work.

Significantly, effective leaders in repressive contexts must have authority vis-à-vis a base of supporters, and/or trust among both followers and fellow leaders, so as to balance clandestine work with aboveground mobilization.[26] Further, while knowing when to mobilize involves calculating risk and perceived opportunity, being able to mobilize presupposes that there is a body of activists who will act collectively. For such a body to exist, leaders must have developed and disseminated counterhegemonic ideas, framed injustices in culturally competent ways, and articulated goals that seem actionable to those who are willing to follow (Morris and Staggenborg 2004, 183).

25. This could explain why Ronald Francisco's study of ten independent cases of state-involved massacres found that such massacres "appear to strengthen dissident leadership and mobilization" (2005, 78).
26. On trust, see Foweraker (1989).

To the extent that leaders are successful in cultivating an opposition, they extend the boundaries of civil society (see Bennett 1992, 255). As we saw earlier, Foweraker (1989) argues that in authoritarian contexts, it is in civil society that democratic projects emerge in the first place. Avritzer (2002) similarly argues that democratic impulses and political innovation happen in society rather than authoritarian states.[27] This is not to suggest, however, that civil society is itself without contradictions or nondemocratic cultural practices. While democratic projects are more likely to emerge there than in authoritarian states, some groups may indeed form autonomous associations for the sole purpose of redefining boundaries of exclusion and privilege. Even progressive social movements may struggle with problems of internal democracy, given that they undoubtedly reflect the various forms of "social authoritarianism" (for example, based on gender, race, ethnicity, and sexual orientation) of their broader social-cultural context. For these reasons, social movements in Latin America target not just states but also civil society and even their own internal practices (Alvarez, Dagnino, and Escobar 1998). They seek to transform both social-cultural and legal-political forms of authoritarianism (Alvarez, Dagnino, and Escobar 1998).

*Politically Autonomous Organization*

Like Schock (2005), I find that politically autonomous organizations are especially important in nondemocracies where governments rely on repression and/or co-optation to suppress or eliminate political dissent (Alvarez and Escobar 1992; J. Fox 1994a). While political autonomy is necessary to sustain an authentically oppositional stance, political independence from the government is, by itself, insufficient for movement resiliency. Social movements also need some form of organization (called "voluntary associations" in some traditions), whether highly centralized or somewhat decentralized (Avritzer 2002; Chang and Kim 2007). Examples of the former type from my research include radical opposition organizations that are nominally "parties" or are "peak associations." Less centralized organizations include

27. Avritzer (2002) adds that democracy can deepen in newly democratized regimes only if innovations from society are so institutionalized that they become a regular part of public deliberation. In his words, "Deliberative publics become the central arena for completing democratization due to the way they manage to connect renovations within the public culture to institutional designs capable of transforming non-public and hybrid practices into democratic forms of decision-making" (2002, 10).

umbrella organizations that bring together multiple groups into an alliance structure, however temporary. In Mexico, these organizations are called *coordinadoras, confederaciones, uniones,* or *frentes.* Temporary coalitions are a highly decentralized type of umbrella organization.

As noted earlier, while leaders function as intellectuals, in organizations they synergistically develop ideas and attempt to disseminate a more or less coherent political ideology (Brulle 1996; Zald 1996). Until recently, scholars have neglected the ideological work of organizations as well as the fact that organizations provide the context and frameworks for "political conversations" about what is possible and about strategies for generating social change (Clemens and Minkoff 2004, 157). Thus, whatever the organizational form, politically autonomous organizations are important in nondemocracies because they create space for alternative or dissident ideas. In other words, they strengthen civil society. In doing so, they help prepare the political conditions for meaningful transitions to democracy as well as long-term democratic consolidation (Foweraker 1989; Avritzer 2002).

As Oliver and Johnston make clear, ideologies are "theories of society coupled with value commitments and normative implications for promoting or resisting social change" (2000, abstract). Like frames, they are diagnostic and offer prognoses as well as arguments about the good society. While political ideas are less coherent at the individual level than what is articulated by formal organizations, long-term exposure to political ideology will impart, at a minimum, political intuition. Among those well socialized, exposure to ideology offers a perspective—what many refer to as a political consciousness.

Further, people who have received formal counterhegemonic training through such programs as "cadre schools" on the left or "training schools" on the right frequently develop deep value commitments alongside their political perspective (see Schneider 1992; Clemens and Minkoff 2004; Kuecker, Stahler-Sholk, and Vanden 2008, 342). Indeed, they may develop what Verta Taylor and Craig Calhoun refer to as "activist identities," which are held by people who commit to political struggle "regardless of personal rewards and sacrifices" (Taylor 1989, 766; see also Calhoun 1991; Schneider 1992). As Calhoun puts it, the self-conception of such radical activists "would be irretrievably violated by pulling back from the risk" of repression (1991, 51). Thus, rather than demobilize in the face of repression, such activists operate more intently, if more carefully, than the less committed. They immerse themselves in a culture and politics of resistance. Hank Johnston argues that even in extremely repressive political contexts, duplicitous organizations will form and nurture protest entrepreneurs while pretending to be apolitical (2005, 122). He adds that only some members of these duplicitous organizations will engage in what he calls "hit-and-run protests." These protest entrepreneurs thus differ from others for taking on the risk. As such, Johnston observes that their risk taking "gives them broader notoriety and situates them for leadership in the broad oppositional fronts that eventually form" (2005, 134).

The evidence from Mexico and the Southern Cone illustrates that the ideological commitment of those with activist identities survives long jail sentences and violent repression, and it will outlive the mobilization phase of movements. Indeed, the political values of the ideologically committed may provide continuity between movements, either in different sectors or in the same sector after a long period of political quiescence (Taylor 1989; Schneider 1992; Trevizo 2002; Alcañiz and Scheier 2008). Paul Drake, for example, found that the historical memories and consciousness of unionists in the Southern Cone drew them back to their original, if ultimately more moderate, political parties after the reinstatement of democracy in those countries (1996, 53, 191).[28]

Communist parties are examples of highly centralized organizations whose ideological work and practical training of cadres is carefully planned and executed. While my empirical analysis looks at how the formal organizational structures of both Communists and capitalists offered ideological and material resources to their loyalists, the organizational and ideological coherence of the Mexican Communist Party (PCM), along with its history of repression, made it especially adept at nurturing militants who would endure political repression and find ways to skirt state violence.[29] My research thus concurs with Paul Drake, who argued that communist parties appear to be especially resilient in the context of violence. He specifies that this is so because they seem "capable and most agile at operating in two modes—aboveground and underground—simultaneously" (1996, 54–56). Similarly, Joe Foweraker (1989) comments on the superior capacity of the Spanish Communist Party to survive instances of extreme repression during Franco's dictatorship. The Spanish Communist Party also offered key organizational resources (leadership, coordination, and logistical support), more so than either ideology or

---

28. Drake argues that the old left parties considerably tempered their ideological views, rejecting armed struggle and ultimately accepting social democracy, so as not to threaten newly restored civilian rule (1996, 53, 191).

29. On Chile, see Schneider (1995).

strategy, to grassroots activists that helped the labor movement combat Franco's regime. Foweraker argues that because the principle organization of clandestine resistance was the Spanish Communist Party, it directly (if paradoxically) contributed to Spain's liberal democracy (1989, 185).

Whether or not individuals remain affiliated with a communist party, their shared ideological training and/or experiences with militancy are enough to embed them in social networks that may function informally across distinct protest movements. Indeed, those communist parties in Latin America that emphasized grassroots community activism (as opposed to guerrilla work) nurtured and sustained a broad network of skilled militants who would continue organizing, informally and clandestinely, even when entire communist party leaderships were jailed (Schneider 1992; Trevizo 2002). For example, my research shows that former members and sympathizers of the PCM were early risers in peasant movements and continued to work in coalitions with known members of the PCM despite the fact that the party faced an organizational crisis, given state repression. Similarly, Alcañiz and Scheier (2008) note that radical *piquetero* protest networks (of unemployed workers) in Argentina during the 1990s were closely tied to networks of Communist Party militants, and some actually antedated the dictatorship (1976–83), although the piqueteros remained politically autonomous from the Communist Party. Schneider (1995) also found that anti-Pinochet protest in Chile was more forceful in shantytowns previously organized by the Communist Party.

The foregoing findings suggest that the ideological resources of formal organizations provide the glue that also links people *informally* through what are called conflict networks. Put differently, political ideas learned from organizations can connect like-minded people over time, through periods of heightened repression or political quiescence. Williams noted, for instance, that even ex-activist professionals, such as professors, lawyers, and doctors, in Mexico remained loyal to their old activist networks, with whom they continued to share a similar worldview (2001, 65).

My research further suggests that when communist parties encourage grassroots activism, they also indirectly socialize those without any direct ties to the party or even a coherent commitment to its ideology. Foweraker (1989) and Schneider (1992) have similarly shown that communist parties may indirectly and inadvertently train others in the art of being an opposition without necessarily persuading them to adopt the communist ideological perspective. It follows that centralized organizations such as communist parties go a long way toward creating both formal and informal networks of activists whose political views may range from the very coherent to the incoherent.

*Informal Conflict Networks*

In contrast to highly centralized organizations, informal conflict networks do not take direction from a centralized leader or set of leaders. In high-risk contexts, those who independently take the initiative to attempt to mobilize others are frequently (but not exclusively) people with intense ideological commitments, or activist identities. They often work underground in their efforts to raise consciousness and sometimes even join communities with the goal of converting people to their political views. If they build a base of like-minded supporters, they may opt to work cooperatively in temporary coalitions to mobilize a protest aboveground.

Although informal networks "guide the flow of collective action" everywhere (McAdam, Tarrow, and Tilly 2001, 49), dispersed conflict networks contribute to movement resiliency in authoritarian contexts because they evade social control forces more easily than highly centralized associations (see Foweraker 1989). According to Williams, by decentralizing administrative and leadership functions, opposition groups raise the cost of political repression for the state (2001, 82, 216–17). The very fact that they are decentralized and diffused makes them less vulnerable to annihilation, since some people are likely to escape police dragnets; those who do escape continue to struggle and recruit others. Indeed, as I have argued elsewhere, in situations where the state targets specific groups by jailing the entire leadership, future mobilization depends on the operation of decentralized and informal conflict networks.

Informal networks not only find it easier to regroup after instances of violence, but the very fact that they do not follow orders from above facilitates tactical innovation and the discovery of new strategies. Experimenting with tactics, deciding on targets at the local level, and finding ways to skirt repression all contribute to turning activists into informal "grassroots" leaders in their own right (Foweraker 1989). Additionally, informal networks rely heavily on interpersonal trust. This trust is especially important in the recruitment of new actors in authoritarian settings or in taking on especially high-risk tactics, because interpersonal relations can help sustain commitment to the seemingly impossible (Foweraker 1989).

However, to gain momentum and prove consequential in the long term, decentralized conflict networks need to find ways to regroup or to have regular cooperative relations with some form of formal centralized organization. The latter facilitates long-term resiliency in that centralized organizations provide resources. Whether as clandestine opposition parties or as front or umbrella organizations, formal organizational structures offer grassroots leaders information about tactics, strategy, and the armed forces; general moral support; material resources; and connections to other activists. Centralized organizations may raise money for prisoners and their families as well as supply food and safe houses (Foweraker 1989). The extralocal connections they offer activists are especially important in helping a movement expand beyond the local or regional level. According to Foweraker, "Networks become both tighter and more extensive as they find more permanent forms of political organization, and even the stray threads tend to tie in sooner or later" (1989, 25).

While many highly centralized organizations may want to control their grassroots political allies, they may also develop egalitarian alliances and facilitate other horizontal links between genuinely grassroots networks. Without necessarily losing their political autonomy, grassroots networks may, in turn, help their own cause by working strategically with a highly centralized organization, such as an opposition political party (Hellman 1992; Williams 2001, 59–62; Alcañiz and Scheier 2008).[30] The outcome of negotiating the tension between absorption and political autonomy is not predetermined. As Williams observes, "The split between political parties and grassroots organizations should not be exaggerated. . . . Despite friction between political parties and many social movements in Mexico, there is also substantial convergence between party activists and social movements in high-profile protests and electoral campaigns. Political parties ultimately play an important part in bolstering social movement campaigns in many localities" (2001, 79; see also Tamayo 1990). Hellman agrees, arguing that "the encounter between movement and party is a dialectical one in which the movement is altered but so, too, is the party" (1992, 58).

My research concurs with Schock's conclusion that dispersed and informal protest networks may survive violence by coordinating with more formal, but

---

30. Williams (2001) also observes that political dissidents in Mexico may draw support from the kindness of neighbors and strangers because of a deep reservoir of antistate, specifically anti-PRI, sentiment.

politically independent, organizations (Trevizo 2002; Schock 2005). To do so, they may create temporary coalitions or simply connect with more formal organizations at conferences and *asambleas* to share information and resources, as well as to coordinate action beyond the local level. In short, I argue that both formal organizations with centralized leaderships and informal conflict networks composed of unofficial, independent grassroots leaders are necessary for movement resiliency and thus long-term effectiveness in repressive contexts.

*Framing*

Beyond their deep ideological commitment to activism, formal or grassroots leaders may also experiment with different ways of framing their demands so that they resonate broadly and are less vulnerable to repression. This emphasis draws from Benford, Snow, and colleagues, who argue that the ways that social movements assign culpability ("diagnostic" frame) and propose solutions ("prognostic" frame) also matter to movement outcomes (Benford and Snow 2000). While Jean Franco (1998) and others (see Swidler 1986) similarly stress that struggles over language speak to the power of interpretation and appropriation, Benford and Snow specify that frame resonance is a function of the frame's credibility and salience.[31] Salient frames are those that are consistent with the values and beliefs of nonactivists, are "commensurate" with the lived experiences of their audiences, and are congruent with the cultural narratives, myths, and ideologies of their society (that is, they have "narrative fidelity") (Benford and Snow 2000, 619–20; Snow and Benford 1988).[32]

Noonan (1995) argues that strategic framing is especially important in societies with authoritarian states because social movements *may* avoid repression by using the same discourse and frame as government officials (see also Wada 2006). I illustrate this point by showing that peasants were

---

31. Whereas credibility depends partly on the frame's disseminators, as well as the logical-empirical quality of the frame itself, "salience" refers to the cultural characteristics of the audiences.

32. While using a different concept, Charles Tilly also agrees that there are cultural dimensions to how political disruption matters. He argues, for example, that movement strength derives from the interaction of "worthiness x unity x numbers x commitment" (or WUNC). Worthy movements are those that claim cultural legitimacy by their "sobriety, propriety of dress, endorsement of moral authorities, and evidence of previous undeserved suffering" (1999, 261).

more successful in terms of achieving their demands (for land redistribution) than were 1968 students because peasants employed nationalistic symbols and arguments. Students, in contrast, misframed a moderate, prodemocracy movement as a communist one. The peasantry's co-optation of the regime's nationalist discourse helped them both avoid repression and create indirect alliances with public officials. Williams similarly found that "where challenger movements successfully co-opt the concept and rhetoric of revolutionary nationalism and gain wide visibility, agencies of the [Mexican] state will often back down from frontal attacks, refraining, for example, from arresting a group's leadership or evicting a group forcefully from an occupied area" (2001, 67–68).

Meyer and Staggenborg note that even people who mobilize in response to threatened economic interests will sustain themselves beyond the resolution of the narrow conflict by framing their grievances in ways that speak to broader cultural values (1996, 1640). My research on Mexico's businessmen indeed illustrates that when the business leaders reframed their grievances to address broadly held concerns about the lack of democracy, they were able to forge political alliances with the middle class and thus mobilize across class lines to an ultimate electoral victory.

My empirical chapters show when, why, and how some leaders dropped, or tried to drop, ineffective ideological frames so as to employ frames that resonated more broadly. I demonstrate that while the students' frames were unsuccessful in 1968, the framing successes of peasant and business leaders mobilized new and old activists and forged political alliances with unexpected forces. These divergent outcomes support the view that social movements can build support for their causes by strategically framing their grievances and demands in ways that resonate with disinterested audiences, or even with officials of nondemocratic states. While, as we know, positive public opinion depends on favorable media coverage, it is also achieved through strategic framing and counterframing efforts.

The foregoing discussion suggests that whether or not social movements, or their mobilized opposition, are effective in nondemocracies depends in part on the magnitude of their organized disruption and on the cultural relevance, or resonance, of the frames that movement leaders deploy. This is true even if states are repressive (see Wada 2006). While this work is consistent with Mayer Zald's (1996) claim that centralized organizations are key to defining ideologies and framing grievances, I add that leadership strategies interact with the general political and cultural contexts to determine whether or not activists are able to bring about favorable political change.

At the empirical level, I demonstrate that whether they were on the left or on the right of the ideological spectrum, the protest movements of peasants and businessmen proved consequential in nondemocratic Mexico despite considerable political repression. Specifically, while strong activist identities and/or deep ideological beliefs about what was good for Mexico motivated activists on the left and on the right, the way that leaders framed their issues inspired the less committed and opened, or closed, alliances with others, including political elites.

Clearly aligned with an earlier scholarship emphasizing the interaction of organizing structures, informal networks, framing processes, and political and cultural contexts, my work also emphasizes the role of leadership. I show that leaders not only experiment with movement frames but also create and recreate organizational structures, develop political ideologies and movement strategy, sustain networks, and, consequently, contribute to movement outcomes. Illuminating the role of leadership in long-term political organizing, institution building, and movement outcomes contributes to a social movement scholarship that has tended to neglect the role of individuals (Barker, Johnson, and Lavalette 2001, 1).

While there are multiple reasons for this neglect, some have to do with the effort by scholars not to reduce complex social-political processes to the role of "great men" (Barker, Johnson, and Lavalette 2001). In addition, the work of leaders tends to be obscured at the empirical level by the drama and power of collective contention. This neglect potentially depicts movements as erupting from nowhere and frames as static, as if derived from preexisting menus. But, as Gramsci argued, movements do not erupt from nowhere (1971, 196). Even seemingly spontaneous movements mobilized because leaders initiated action by organizing their networks around a specific political ideology (see also Barker, Johnson, and Lavalette 2001). Nor are frames preestablished. Movement leaders experiment with framing, responding to the feedback that they receive in their efforts to mobilize others and win support from bystander audiences, or from government officials. They may experiment, moreover, in response to the frameworks of their political opponents.

I hope to demonstrate that a look at leaders and their actions is not necessarily atomistic at a methodological level, nor is it an expression of historical volunteerism. Throughout my analyses, I emphasize that just as collective action interacts with its political and cultural environments, so does leadership. In other words, I do not suggest that great leaders can create movements and achieve their goals in the absence of political and cultural opportunities. Rather, I concur with Morris and Staggenborg's conclusion that leaders interpret their political and cultural contexts and make strategic choices on the basis of how they read (or misread) political and cultural opportunities (2004, 191).

## Movement-Countermovement Dynamics

Beyond exploring the role of social movement leaders, my work sheds light on meso-level movement-countermovement dynamics. As noted in the introduction, when a movement mobilizes to oppose the specific claims or newly won benefits of another movement, it is a countermovement (Meyer and Staggenborg 1996; Andrews 2002, 918). While rising levels of mobilization influence other movements (Whittier 2004), the concept of the countermovement also signals intermovement contention. As I focus on the organizational and political outcomes of such contention, this analysis contributes to a body of work that has only recently begun to theorize the short- and long-term, intended and unintended, consequences of movement-countermovement dynamics (see Meyer and Staggenborg 1996; Andrews 2002).

Specifically, my research illustrates that movements operate in a multi-organizational environment *within* civil society that includes supporters, political opponents, and, of course, bystander audiences. I show that the short- and long-term outcomes of a movement depend not only on its political allies and state responses but also on what its political opponents do. This contributes to the scholarship on movement outcomes because, as Andrews observes, movement-countermovement dynamics are frequently obscured, given that it is the state that mediates their relationship by responding to their opposing claims (2002, 918). In sum, when and how countermovements respond, what concessions they win or lose, what frames they use, and what organizational forms they adopt matter to the course and outcomes of initial movement challengers (Meyer and Staggenborg 1996, 1654).

Further, this research offers specific support for Meyer and Staggenborg's (1996) observation that when a countermovement opposes a movement, it frequently adopts similar tactics. Over time, their organizational structures may even resemble each other. I illustrate this claim by showing that agribusinessmen followed peasants into the streets with disruptive political protest that at first culminated in a politically independent peak association. Eventually, both businessmen and peasant movements created politically autonomous, umbrella-style organizational structures that represented other organizations at the national level. The leaderships of these broad movements ultimately followed each other into the electoral arena by revitalizing an old party or supporting a new one. Many left organizations involved in peasant movements would eventually converge in the new Partido de la Revolución Democrática (PRD). For their part, promarket, antistatist, "neoliberal" agribusinessmen would revitalize the right-of-center Partido Acción Nacional (PAN) to also compete in the electoral arena.

The specific political struggles on which I focus have broader implications than a mere restatement of Marx's classic thesis that groups contend over threatened economic interests. The historical analysis shows that the narrow interclass conflict over land turned into a businessmen's movement about the rights of private property, culminating in a politically autonomous organization allied with a broader peak association that promoted neoliberalism in a society with a mixed economy. Eventually, free market advocates would build electoral alliances with the middle class by reframing their economic grievances about property rights—and their political grievances about a potentially totalitarian state—as a broader concern about electoral democracy. Leftist leaders would also shine a greater spotlight on electoral fraud and the absence of democracy in Mexico than they had in the past. In other words, earlier interclass struggles over material interests developed into broader political struggles that, paradoxically, converged on similar prodemocracy demands.[33]

## Conclusion

According to Vanden, some politically contentious social movements are "strengthening participatory democratic practice substantially and altering the way politics are conducted in Latin America" (2008, 55). The same is true

---

33. For a comparable analysis of urban labor movements, see Foweraker and Landman (1997).

for Mexico, although the transition to democracy there was protracted and contradictory given that the state responded to earlier social movements with both concessions and political repression (Foweraker and Landman 1997). The empirical chapters that follow illustrate that while the protest cycle after 1968 through the 1980s was met with repression, these pretransition social movements nevertheless strengthened civil society and prepared the organizational infrastructure and political ideologies for the transition at the end of the twentieth century. Thus, earlier nonviolent social movements succeeded in altering the legal-institutional terrain of the official political game. As such, the empirical analysis provides evidence for the argument that social movements as collective subjects of civil society contribute to democratic transitions (Foweraker 1989 and 1990; Munck 1990; Giugni, McAdam, and Tilly 1998; and McAdam, Tarrow, and Tilly 2001; Schock 2005).

The evidence from Mexico and some of its hemispheric neighbors, such as Bolivia and Brazil, thus suggests that the structure and politics of states are dialectically related not only to international forces but also to the social forces within civil society. Social movements from within civil society influence state policy and can even constrain the actions of political elites who, for their part, also engage in politics in the global arena. Put another way, if, as Theda Skocpol once argued, states "influence the meanings and methods of politics for all groups and classes in society" (1985, 28; see also 21–22), states are themselves subject to being reshaped and, indeed, interpenetrated by social struggles in civil society (see also Zeitlin 1984, xi; Zeitlin and Ratcliff 1988, 189; Goldfield 1989, 1277; Goldstone 2003). To quote Goldstone, "We ... cannot understand the normal, institutionalized workings of courts, legislatures, executives, or parties without understanding their intimate and ongoing shaping by social movements. . . . State institutions and parties are interpenetrated by social movements, often developing out of movements, in response to movements, or in close association with movements" (2003, 2).

In sum, this research focuses on how movement-countermovement dynamics reshaped the legal-institutional terrain of political power in Mexico prior to its adoption of neoliberal economic policies and democratizing reforms. The political struggles studied in this book restructured entire classes, civic organizations, electoral law, political parties, and even some aspects of Mexico's political culture; this happened, moreover, in the context of increasing repression. In extending and strengthening civil society, opposition movements and their countermovements laid the organizational foundation necessary for Mexico's transition to democracy and its subsequent consolidation. As Foweraker points out, the consolidation of newly established democratic states depends on "the democratic maturation of actors within civil society; and democracy is thus to be defined as a practice of citizenship, or the achievement of an increasingly autonomous control of the political conditions of social life" (1989, 247).

# 2

## The "Banner of 1968"

*The Student Movement's Democratizing Effects*

This chapter focuses on the 1968 student movement in Mexico City. This urban detour in the story of the rural roots of Mexico's democratization is necessary because the student massacre at Tlatelolco in 1968 was a historical turning point to the degree that it created a legitimacy crisis of the state (Basáñez 1990). I argue that while repression ended the prodemocracy movement, students still contributed to democracy in the medium to long term. After the massacre, ex-student radicals helped spawn a cycle of protest in the 1970s and 1980s, not only in the urban centers but also in the countryside, where they contributed to the rise of peasant protest. As such, they helped reorganize civil society independently of the state. While state officials responded to the increasing organization and contention of civil society with moments of political tolerance, they also carried out what is now officially deemed a dirty war against leftists (CNDH 2001). As of 2006, the Mexican government has admitted that presidents Gustavo Díaz Ordaz, Luis Echeverría, and José López Portillo sustained policies of violence against political dissidents. This violence included two student massacres (1968 and 1971), political torture, extrajudicial detentions in clandestine prisons, extrajudicial executions, and the disappearance of hundreds of victims.

The inconsistent management of political dissidence, coupled with a low-level but sustained dirty war, undermined state corporatism even further. In response to the growing legitimacy crisis of the state, administrations since that of Echeverría continually reformed the electoral rules of the game so as to channel their political opposition into the electoral arena. The slow evolution of a more pluralistic political system is thus an indirect and unintended medium-term outcome of the student movement. The paradox, then, is that Mexico democratized in response to the very political crises created by some of the most authoritarian moments in the country's twentieth-century history.

Beyond reorganizing civil society and catalyzing electoral reforms, the massacre of unarmed students on October 2, 1968, altered Mexican political culture to the extent that it spotlighted Mexican authoritarianism. Human rights activists from the 1970s onward kept the memory of 1968 alive in their ongoing demands that the government release political prisoners and/or acknowledge those who had permanently disappeared (*desaparecidos*), whether killed or imprisoned. The events of 1968, in other words, haunted subsequent administrations as well as activists in civil society. As such, the massacre contributed to the creation of a movement within Mexico that has insisted on the inalienability of human rights. That this demand became a formal public charge in 1990, when the state created the National Commission on Human Rights (Comisión Nacional de Derechos Humanos, CNDH), was a long-term, if unintended, outcome of the 1968 student movement. In what follows, I briefly describe the students' oppositional political identity before explaining the massacre and the ultimate democratizing outcomes of a seemingly failed movement.

## The Students' Oppositional Political Identity

Despite various efforts to organize college campuses since 1939, the ruling party never gained hegemony among students. On the contrary, the large number of leftist and rightist political parties competing for student support at the National Autonomous University (UNAM) made it "one of the chief oppositionist centers to the national government" (Mabry 1982, ix; see also Babb 2001, 66). Consequently, pro-PRI student organizations tended to operate clandestinely (Zermeño 1978, 59).

At an institutional level, moreover, UNAM and its affiliated preparatory schools had claimed political and academic autonomy from the state since 1929. These claims were made through frequent struggles in which students and faculty militantly struck out against the encroachment of the state on UNAM's academic and administrative jurisdiction. While students and faculty demanded financial resources from the state, they were uncompromising about academic freedom (for example, they rejected former president Cuauhtémoc Cárdenas's attempt to offer guidelines for the university's curriculum). As such, they succeeded in limiting the state's involvement in UNAM to finances (Mabry 1982).[1] Thus, although the university did ultimately pledge loyalty to the Revolution, it was one of the only publicly funded institutions to remain politically autonomous (Mabry 1982, ix; see also Stevens 1974, 188; Levy 1980, 77; Babb 2001, 66; Levy and Bruhn 2006, 58).

At a cultural level, UNAM's hard-won autonomy was part of its students' political identity. UNAM students cherished the autonomy of their university, while students from the more working-class, vocationally oriented, and state-controlled Polytechnic Institute (IPN) envied it.[2] According to Mabry, for much of the twentieth century, the very "independence of the university and its self definition . . . brought it into conflict with the state" (1982, 14). This was especially the case in the 1960s and early 1970s. Thus, when soldiers entered university campuses in 1968, student claims to university autonomy became one of their most important organizing principles.

## The 1968 Student Movement

Local instances of police abuse gave birth to the largest prodemocracy movement that had ever been seen by the postrevolutionary state up to 1968. A student movement mushroomed in Mexico City that summer when the mayor of the Federal District, General Alfonso Corona del Rosal, deployed *granaderos,* or riot police, to manage extramural student conflict and leftist student demonstrations. When, on July 29, students barricaded themselves inside their high school to protest police abuse, infantry troops used a bazooka to blast through the eighteenth-century baroque doors; they proceeded to beat and ultimately arrest one thousand students (Riding 1986, 84).

Student grievances quickly expanded from police abuse and the violation of university autonomy to demands regarding political prisoners, state

---

1. This compromise was acceptable to the nation's political leaders, who were satisfied to recruit government personnel from the ranks of university graduates and faculty (Levy and Bruhn 2006, 58–59; see also Mabry 1982, 195).
2. The government ended student protest by shutting down the IPN and its affiliated high schools in 1956 (Guevara Niebla 1988). When it reopened the campus two years later, the government organized students into the Federación Nacional de Estudiantes Técnicos (Stevens 1974, 194).

repression, and authoritarianism in general. Adopting the countercultural symbolism of 1968 student movements internationally, and especially the leftist "master frame" of revolutionary movements, the students in Mexico articulated a critique of their country's political system. They zeroed in on the extreme centralization of decision-making powers, the country's lack of civil liberties, the PRI monopoly on power, corporatism, and the loyal press, and they even demanded a more equitable distribution of income (Stevens 1974; Shapira 1977; Guevara Niebla 1988; Gilabert 1993).

Hundreds of thousands of middle-class mothers, office workers, and lower-level public officials participated in student demonstrations. According to Gilberto Guevara Niebla, a 1968 student leader, the massiveness of these challenges constituted an "unprecedented political crisis" (1988, 39–41). There is, however, little to indicate that there was a real political crisis of the state. The Constitution of 1917 was not questioned, nor did students or elites challenge the incumbency of those in power. As Zermeño argues, in the absence of a coherent utopia, the students' prodemocracy movement amounted to a small number of reformist demands concentrated around administrative concerns that were to be negotiated publicly with the existing government (1978, 51). Finally, while the student movement was massive, it was limited to Mexico City's middle class (Imaz Bayona 1975) and university students in the provinces. President Díaz Ordaz consequently understood that his hold on power was not at stake, and he even believed that public opinion was unsympathetic to students, given their riots (CIA Weekly Review, 8/23/68, in National Security Archive).

However, as suggested by table 1, the students won a moral victory when the state pulled back its repressive forces at the end of July, after the bazooka incident. This suggested that excessively violent policing norms could improve, and it appeared to affirm the students' demand for democratic liberties. The point here is that in this special conjuncture, government officials directly addressed the students' critique that the government violated the country's constitutional guarantees of civil liberties by temporarily creating just that—the appearance of democratic liberties.

The state's conciliatory gestures came at the very moment that the movement received political support from faculty and UNAM's rector. Consequently, the movement's political opportunities at the end of July seemed golden. By early August, students had organized a democratic, multiuniversity coalition called the National Student Strike Committee (Consejo Nacional de Huelga, CNH). A small leadership quickly centralized decision-making authority over 250 CNH members who, in turn, represented more than 100,000 students nationwide (Guevara Niebla 1988, 47). Beyond these vast human resources, the CNH had a highly effective division of labor with specialized functions in external relations, propaganda, finances, information, and juridical matters (Zermeño 1978, 109). The financial commission coordinated 150 "people-to-people brigades" that circulated in the streets, informing the citizenry about the movement and asking for financial donations. This degree of organization was replicated, in turn, in each department and school on various campuses. In addition to this internal organizational coherence, the CNH had the external support of various faculty coalitions (Zermeño 1978, 110).

The CNH's organizational, human, and financial resources facilitated massive demonstrations at UNAM, at the IPN, and in the central square, or Zócalo, in front of the National Palace. Students dramatized the lack of democracy by appropriating the Zócalo for performances of "people's power" and ingeniously drew audiences by insisting that negotiations with government officials be broadcast on television or radio. These highly disciplined and creative demonstrations were extremely disruptive by virtue of their size, their symbolism, their demands for public accountability, and, as we shall see, their revolutionary frames and symbols.

Despite its organizational coherence and substantial resources, the CNH never embodied a single political vision (Zermeño 1978), nor did it control all activists. The movement represented students from multiple political orientations, ranging from hard-left Trotskyists, Maoists, Guevarists, and members of the Mexican Communist Party (PCM) to a soft "new" left composed of countercultural students. That is, to the right of the PCM was a mass of ideologically less dogmatic radical youth who, despite appearances, were neither Communists nor Socialists (Poniatowska 1977, 68–69; Zermeño 1978; Guevara Niebla 1988, 46).

The evidence is clear that members of the PCM and especially its youth wing wielded great political influence inside the CNH. According to CNH leader González de Alba, "After the top CNH leaders were captured, and other delegates retreated, the CNH's direction came to be almost completely in the hands of the PCM's Juventud Comunista." González de Alba explains that the PCM led the movement in these circumstances "not because they had the most delegates, but because they happened to be the best known and with the

Table 1  Chronology of events in the 1968 organized student movement

| Date (1968) | Significant events | Movement status/ government response |
|---|---|---|
| July 23 | Grenadier forces end an intramural fight between high school students. | Movement not organized |
| July 26 | Grenadiers stop a pro–Cuban Revolution student demonstration. | |
| July 27 | Students from the IPN declare an indefinite strike. | Emergence of movement organization |
| July 28 | Student representatives from the IPN, UNAM, Chapingo, and the normal schools form a strike committee and issue six demands. | |
| July 29–30 | Army bazookas blast their way into the Preparatoria de San Ildefonso. Many students are injured, and many more are jailed. | Government repression continues |
| July 31 | At a UNAM rally, the university rector tells students that the army has violated the university's autonomy. The Mexican flag flies at half-mast. | Repression ends; movement demands defined |
| Aug. 1 | UNAM's rector leads a demonstration of 100,000 to defend university autonomy. President Díaz Ordaz makes a conciliatory extended-hand speech. | Movement heyday |
| Aug. 5–9 | IPN students lead a demonstration of 100,000 in the Zócalo. IPN students insist on public dialogues and get support from their teachers. A multi-university coalition of students creates the CNH. | |
| Aug. 13 | 150,000–300,000 students march from the Casco de Santo Tomás to the Zócalo to demand the release of political prisoners. | |

|  |  | |
|---|---|---|
| Aug. 18 | 20,000 students organize for a mass public debate with government officials. | |
| Aug. 22 | Luis Echeverría, in charge of security as the head of Gobernación, agrees to a meeting with students but not to a public dialogue. | |
| Aug. 27 | 500,000 demonstrate in a five-hour march to the Zócalo. | Movement zenith |
| | 5,000 volunteers form a brigade to remain in the Zócalo after the march and hold an iconoclastic rally. While demanding "public dialogues" with the president, some students hoist a red and black flag on the flagpole used for the Mexican flag; others make "incendiary" speeches and chant insults to and about the president. At 1:00 A.M., army tanks, police, and the fire department disperse the crowd. | |
| Aug. 28 | The government organizes a rally of public employees and official unions to compensate for the students' iconoclasm the night before. The government represses the rally when many support students. | "Climate of terror" |
| Sept. 1 | President Díaz Ordaz makes minor concessions to the liberal wing of the student movement in a presidential speech but threatens that the government will use all means at its disposal to restore social order. | |
| Sept. 7 | 25,000 students attend a CNH rally in Tlatelolco. | Movement declines |
| Sept. 13 | 300,000 participate in a "silent march." Nationalist symbols replace foreign ones. | |
| Sept. 15–16 | Nonofficial independence day student festivals are held at UNAM and IPN. | |
| Sept. 18 | The army occupies UNAM's Ciudad Universitaria campus for fifteen days and makes mass arrests. | |
| Sept. 22 | 20,000 people rally at the Plaza de las Tres Culturas. | |
| Sept. 23–24 | Soldiers end a street battle between students and granaderos at the Casco de Santo Tomás. | |
| Oct. 1 | Government officials agree to meet with CNH leaders the next day. | |
| Oct. 2 | 300+ students are massacred and 2,000 detained; hundreds disappear. | Movement ends |

most political influence" (quoted in Gilabert 1993, 194; see also Zermeño 1978, 151). The PCM's influence is also evident in the six demands on which all students agreed. These included liberty for political prisoners; the dismissal of two chiefs of police as well as the riot police chief; the disbanding of the granaderos; the derogation of the "crime of social dissolution," referring to the violation of the antisubversion laws of the 1940s that stipulated the political crimes codified in Articles 145 and 145 bis of the Federal Penal Codes; compensation for the families of those students injured or killed; and the identification of those police, granaderos, and soldiers responsible for excessive force (Guevara Niebla 1988, 39, 49). Since 1958, the PCM had demanded liberty for political prisoners as well as the elimination of antisubversion laws. Given the fact that no student had been arrested under antisubversion laws, it seems fair to infer that the centrality of this demand was due to the PCM's influence on the student movement (Zermeño 1978, 31; Mabry 1982, 243).

Not only did communist youth help articulate the demands listed above, but they also influenced the students' street performances. Demonstration banners and flyers decrying "the climate of oppression" and the taking of "political prisoners" were as omnipresent as those bearing Che Guevara's likeness. In their efforts to build alliances with peasants and especially workers, far-left students multiplied the issues with banners against "co-opted" unionism (called *charro* unions),[3] the "sold-out press," and progovernment student organizations (*El Día*, 8/6/68; Zermeño 1978; Babb 2001). Some created so-called factory brigades, while others indeed hoped to "provoke a revolutionary crisis" as the "only way for bringing about a socialist future" (Zermeño 1978, 46). According to one of the most important CNH student leaders, Raúl Álaverez Garín, Trotskyists and other far leftists initiated interminable debates about "whether or not the movement was revolutionary" (quoted in Poniatowska 1977, 68–69; Gilabert 1993, 188). While the CNH made the important logistical decisions about demonstrations, rallies, dates, and times, it could not stop some students from discrediting the movement with frequent and destructive riots, the estimated property damage of which totaled eight million U.S. dollars in 1968 terms (Department of Defense Intelligence Information Report, 10/18/68, in National Security Archive).

3. A *charro* is, literally, a Mexican cowboy. Unions led by progovernment leaders were called charro unions. This unusual name originated when, during a railroad workers' union struggle, then-president Miguel Alemán successfully imposed a leader who dressed as a cowboy and "went by his nickname of 'The Cowboy,' or 'El Charro'" (Foweraker 1993, 28).

Thus, while the vast majority of students were ideologically moderate, the radical flank's "revolutionary" frames and symbols eclipsed the more reformist goals of the student movement. Moderate "new" left students embraced the symbols of the "old" left not because they were Communists but because they identified them as the symbols of 1968's youth movements internationally. Student activist Claudia Cortés González explains the students' sentiments as follows: "I never really thought of Zapata as a student symbol, an emblem. Zapata has become part of the bourgeois ideology; the PRI has appropriated him. Maybe that's why we chose Che as our symbol at demonstrations from the very beginning. Che was our link with student movements all over the world! We never considered Pancho Villa. His name never even crossed our minds!" (quoted in Poniatowska 1977, 40; Gilabert 1993, 201).

In borrowing the symbolism of international radical youth movements, students unwittingly communicated displacement goals and, as such, provoked repression. In a videotaped interview thirty years later, 1968 student leader "Tita" suggested that the radicalism of the speeches and actions at an evening rally on August 27 constituted a turning point for the government (see also Zermeño 1978, 125–27; Mabry 1982, 259; Gilabert 1993, 191, 205; Guevara Niebla 1988, 42). By 1:00 A.M., soldiers had cleared out a "permanent guard" brigade of three to five thousand students who intended to occupy the Zócalo until the government conceded to public negotiations. The government readopted repression even though the largest demonstration in Mexican history had ended without incident the previous day. According to participants, it did so because squatters that evening made "incendiary" speeches at the ceremonial site of power (the Zócalo) while crowds cried, in reference to the Olympic Games to be held in Mexico City that October, "We don't want Olympics! We want a revolution!"

After a botched progovernment counter-rally (the *mitin del desagravio*) on August 28, Díaz Ordaz moved to contain the radical flank. CIA intelligence reported that from late August through September, he had three gunboats and two minesweepers patrolling the Yucatán. Díaz Ordaz based these orders, according to a skeptical CIA report, on possibly fabricated Mexican intelligence that the Cuban government planned to smuggle arms into Mexico (CIA Intelligence Information Cables 81569, distributed 8/30/68, and 87410, distributed 8/30/68, in National Security Archive).

Regardless of whether or not the Mexican government fabricated information about Cuban and Soviet involvement, officials had been engaged in a cold war against Communists since Cuba's revolution. For example, the Mexican government used army troops against striking students in Mérida (1955) as well as Puebla and Oaxaca (1959), and even stationed police on the IPN campus for two years after a "Communist-inspired" student strike in 1956 (Mabry 1982, 209). It incarcerated PCM organizers of the 1958 militant railroad workers' strike for more than a decade. The government also deployed soldiers to the University of Morelia in 1966 and then to the University of Sonora in 1967 to stamp out the left-wing students. In February 1968, approximately six months before the eruption of the student movement, the government began to jail the leadership of the PCM.

As I show below, the Mexican state's efforts to contain communism at home turned into a dirty war. Once they became genuinely concerned with national security, government officials approved of using whatever force necessary to extinguish what they believed was a revolutionary opposition. In the words of Congressman Octavio Hernández, "extremists" operating within the student movement "threatened" the nation (Zermeño 1978, 144; Stevens 1974, 198–99; Shapira 1977; Mabry 1982; see also American Embassy telegram to U.S. secretary of state, 7/30/68, in National Security Archive). The government believed that the student movement's radical flank was increasing in influence, as hundreds of thousands of people now marched through the streets denouncing repression, demanding things unrelated to campus issues, and sometimes even triumphantly calling for revolution. Thus, the government's cry of subversion became "hysterical" (Mabry 1982; Gilabert 1993; Stevens 1974). As noted by Shapira, the government claimed to have evidence that the PCM's student front "had sent 'shock units' to provoke disorder and to aggravate student-police clashes" (1977, 565–66). The Communists' supposed threat to national security ultimately became the basis for the government's legal cases against students (and its illegal war against guerrillas). The hysteria leading up to the massacre is illustrated by the following editorial published on August 14, 1968, in *El Heraldo*, whose progovernment reporters were on the government's payroll: "The images of 'Che' Guevara and banners openly glorifying Cuba's communist regime and other doctrines foreign to our people were the flags of the demonstrators.... [They were] shouting with impunity insults against the authorities, offensive phrases aimed at the armed forces and police.... Large posters with provocative messages brought about the proliferating disorder" (quoted in Gilabert 1993, 219).

In response to the criticism of the movement's iconoclasm, CNH leaders instructed their base to refrain from insulting chants and violence. They added, "Do not take red flags [to the demonstration]. Do not take Che banners! Do not take Mao banners! Take banners with images of Hidalgo, Morelos, Zapata, so that they can say, 'Those are our Heroes! Viva Zapata. Viva!'" (Poniatowska 1977, 48; see also Gilabert 1993, 307).

This nationalist reframing occurred too late, however. Just days after the most iconoclastic rally had sparked repression, President Díaz Ordaz announced a military strategy for restoring domestic order in his September 1 address to the nation. He argued that "pseudo-students" with "foreign" ideas had manipulated authentic students to riot as part of a conspiracy against the Olympiad and Mexico. Strategically, he stated that it was his "solemn obligation to heed the will of the people" and would, if congressional hearings mandated it, repeal the laws pertaining to political prisoners (Díaz Ordaz 1968, 82). Nevertheless, he also threatened violence against the "small" but intransigent group of "un-Mexican" subversives, warning that the government would "use all of the legal means at our disposal to maintain domestic order and tranquility so that nationals and foreigners have the necessary guarantees" during the Olympic Games (Díaz Ordaz 1968, 76). Díaz Ordaz explicitly justified military force on the grounds that citizens were indignant over student demonstrations, riots, the destruction of property, and the disruption of the Olympiad.

Within days of this speech, the Mexican Senate empowered Díaz Ordaz to use the army, navy, and air force for either national or international "security" (Stevens 1974, 228). Díaz Ordaz refrained from repressing the "silent" demonstration on September 13, most likely because three hundred thousand students participated. But on September 18, he ordered ten thousand soldiers onto the UNAM campus and thousands more to other universities, including those in other states. Soldiers occupied UNAM for two weeks, where they arrested roughly five hundred students. A few days later, an army unit shot its way into the Casco de Santo Tomás campus of the IPN after students held granaderos at bay for several hours with Molotov cocktails and a small arsenal of firearms (CIA Weekly Review, 9/27/68; Department of Defense Intelligence Information Report, 10/18/68). Four students were killed and an additional three hundred arrested (Riding 1986, 85; Department of Defense Intelligence Information Report, 10/18/68, in National Security Archive).

With hundreds of students behind bars and with riots growing more violent, the massive demonstrations of August were replaced by significantly smaller rallies and riots between mid-September and October 2, 1968. As public support for students waned with the increasing number of riots (Poniatowska 1977; Gilabert 1993, 248–49), Díaz Ordaz undoubtedly believed that he had succeeded in isolating the radical flank purportedly threatening the country's national security and the upcoming Olympic Games.

It was thus that he approved the use of massive force at the October 2, 1968, rally in the Plaza de las Tres Culturas in the district of Tlatelolco. There, a dramatically smaller crowd of an estimated five to ten thousand students was met by at least three hundred sixty snipers from multiple, and uncoordinated, units of the armed forces (Boudreaux 2003). Soldiers, cavalry troops, police units, federal security and intelligence officers, members of the army's Olympic Battalion, and a secret police battalion infiltrated the student rally, some in plain clothes. On an official signal, they fired high-caliber machine guns and other automatic weapons indiscriminately into the crowd at short range from rooftops and residential windows; this lasted for over an hour.

Testimonials support the theory that rank-and-file soldiers accepted the government's frame that students were revolutionary. For example, student Ignacio Galván recalled the following about the night of the massacre, when he and other students were being transported to the Campo Militar Número 1: "The sergeant [on the vehicle transporting the students] was furious. . . . He gave us a long speech; [he stated] that we were idiots for thinking that we could overthrow the government because they [the armed forces] also had machine-guns" (Poniatowska 1977, 228). Similarly, a group of CNH students reported that when a plainclothes social control agent detained them that same evening, he ordered, "Up against the wall, you sons of bitches, we're about to give you your revolution!" (Poniatowska 1977, 238).

Other testimonials indicate that those who were branded Communists were treated more severely than non-Communists. In his memoir, one of the CNH's most important leaders, Guevara Niebla, recounted that as soon as a soldier (perhaps wrongly) singled him out as a Communist, "an official and three soldiers separated me from my [student] companions [also detained at Campo Militar Número 1]. Then they beat me again. . . . I believed they were going to kill me. . . . [They said,] 'If you don't tell us where you've hidden the firearms you're fucked [*te va a cargar la chingada*]. You will not leave here alive.' . . . After they faked my execution, they took me back to my cell" (1993, 38).

Similarly, another student, Luís Tomás Cervantes Cabeza de Vaca, recalled an exchange with a solider who interrogated him by torture. When the student, whose head was hooded, either could not or would not answer his interrogator, the soldier threatened, "Either you talk or we'll kill you. . . . You traitor, son of a whore. What do you bastards want? What are you trying to accomplish?" The student remembers, "He [his torturer] then called over another who was very likely a sergeant because he said, 'Sergeant, refresh the memory of this son-of-a-bitch traitor who wants to turn us into Communists. I'll send for the death squad.' . . . The torture continued, but it was more brutal, it lasted longer. . . . When the torture ended the soldier said to me, 'Do not give yourself any illusions! Communist pigs! If you won't talk, we have *gringos* nearby'" (quoted in Poniatowska 1977, 106, 115).

The evidence thus supports the view that at all levels of the state, government officials, rank-and-file soldiers, and various police forces acted against what they believed were communist youth who conspired against the Mexican state and, more immediately, planned on disrupting the Olympic Games. The paradox is that the vast majority of students were not Communists. Their revolutionary symbols and rhetoric simply echoed the international insignia of 1968 youth. However, in the context of Mexico's ongoing cold war, the radical flank's leftist master frame overshadowed the meaning of the student frames. Thus, students misframed a movement that essentially sought moderate democratic reforms, and Díaz Ordaz and the hawks of his administration exploited their rhetoric and symbols to justify repression through violence (see Gilabert 1993, 168).

Put differently, the tragedy at Tlatelolco is partly explained by the fact that Mexico's authoritarian government defined the supposedly revolutionary wing of the student movement as a threat to national security, but the students' own frames made this interpretation plausible and precluded the possibility of creating alliances with public officials. State agents adopted grossly repressive tactics for dealing with politically dispensable students, already defined as ungovernable given their combative history, because students misframed their movement as revolutionary. In doing so, the students unwittingly discredited their prodemocracy political agenda. In other words, it was not just the left flank's radicalism that discredited the movement but also the revolutionary frames of the nonradical students. It is reasonable to assume that in a more democratic society, a comparable student movement would not have paid so dearly for such tactical errors. However, if, as William

Gamson argued, movements with displacement goals tend to be repressed even in democratic societies (1990, 39–40), Mexico's version of authoritarianism ensured that the repression would be bloodier than most.

This explanation implies the counterfactual that if students had been more strategic about their frames, they would have constrained extreme forms of authoritarianism. That Díaz Ordaz had been uncharacteristically concessionary toward them throughout most of August supports the idea that students could constrain political repression. In the pre-Olympic conjuncture in which the international media had descended on Mexico City, he ordered federal troops, local police, and granaderos to refrain from violence even as three to five hundred thousand students triumphantly demonstrated in the streets; yet he did this to strategically counter the claim that Mexico lacked civil liberties. Additionally, his government returned some preparatory and vocational schools to their academic authorities and released hundreds of students from jail. Meanwhile, the mayor of Mexico City announced concessions for progovernment students and promised to investigate "conciliatory and friendly forms" of policing. On August 8, the government offered to create a multilateral commission that would include IPN students as well as other "sectors of public opinion" (Zermeño 1978, 14–18).

Despite the tragic end to their movement, students forced the issue of democratic liberties onto the national political agenda. When the minister of the Interior, Luis Echeverría, offered to meet with student representatives during the movement's heyday, he stated that the "irrefutable respect with which the government had treated peaceful student demonstrations was evidence of the [country's] atmosphere of democratic liberties" (quoted in Zermeño 1978, 17). Even Díaz Ordaz was forced into rhetorically affirming the value of consultative policy making (recall that in his presidential address he spoke of his "solemn obligation to heed the will of the people"). Although Díaz Ordaz had no serious intention of promoting civil or political rights,[4]

---

4. This is evidenced by the fact that in November 1968 he approved of the military operations against armed guerrilla movements that led to illegal detentions, interrogation by means of torture, and extrajudicial executions, as documented in a special prosecutor's report (Comisión Nacional de Derechos Humanos 2006, 314–18). It further states that Díaz Ordaz began a dirty war against guerrilla movements led by Genaro Vázquez and Lucio Cabañas in the state of Guerrero. Near the end of his term (1969), army units began to detain even family members of suspected guerrillas. This report documents at least three extrajudicial executions, one in which the victim was forced to dig his own grave, as well as multiple cases in which interrogation by torture resulted in the death of the victims. In one instance, the wife of a detained peasant was raped by both an army captain and his subordinate in the presence of her husband.

he delivered on his promise to work with Congress to investigate the issue of political prisoners and even repealed the social dissolution federal penal codes (Articles 145 and 145 bis). But his government then passed more effective "antiterrorism" laws in 1970. That said, Díaz Ordaz did take concrete steps toward lowering the voting age from twenty-one to eighteen.

Although the students did not immediately get what they wanted, the sections that follow show that those who survived or witnessed state violence contributed to democracy in significant ways in the medium and long term. They did so by continuing to carry the political banner of 1968 in their subsequent political struggles.

## The Student Movement's Medium- to Long-Term Democratizing Outcomes

Although the government tried to cover it up, the October 2, 1968, massacre was documented by journalists, some of them from the international press, who had personally been beaten at the scene. Consequently, 1968 proved to be a historical turning point. Not only did it create a legitimacy crisis for the state, but the government's responses created still other political crises (Basáñez 1990). In this post-1968 dynamic, the country slowly convulsed into a more pluralistic and democratic political system.

When he began his term in 1970, Luis Echeverría sought to rebuild the political legitimacy of the Mexican state (Shapira 1977; Fox and Gordillo 1989, 140; Schryer 1990). According to Shapira, the "PRI showing in the 1970 presidential elections was alarming ... with 34% of the eligible voters abstaining, 25% of the ballots cast annulled, and another 20% given to other parties" (1977, 566–67). Echeverría, moreover, had a personal stake in rebuilding legitimacy because, as he had been secretary of the Interior under Díaz Ordaz, he was widely believed to have pressed for a military solution to student protests. Echeverría distanced himself from his predecessor by pledging a democratic opening (*apertura democrática*) and by promising to spread the benefits of economic development via redistribution (Shapira 1977).

While Echeverría delivered on this populist stance by increasing public expenditures as a proportion of the gross domestic product (Chislett 1985, 2),[5]

 5. As Chislett writes, he "pushed public expenditure as a proportion of GDP up to 27 per cent in 1973, after averaging 21 per cent during 1966–1970" (1985, 2).

his political reforms were shallow and contradictory. Though he passed a general amnesty law that released political prisoners from jail within his first year in office (1971), his promises to increase freedoms of the press proved hollow. In his final year as president, Echeverría orchestrated the purging of journalists from the newspaper *Excelsior* for its critical coverage. Still, his moderate political reforms of the rules governing party representation in the Chamber of Deputies (in 1973) unwittingly began a long but ultimately profound process of electoral reform.[6]

Crucially, while Echeverría tolerated some politically autonomous nonguerrilla peasant and worker protests early in his administration, he intensified the dirty war against guerrillas and eventually extended it to nonguerrillas, especially Communists.[7] Although political repression, torture, disappearances, and executions were not new to Mexican regimes, Echeverría extended the use of these tactics geographically and to nonrevolutionary movements. For example, in addition to fully militarizing the state of Guerrero, Echeverría depended heavily on paramilitary groups (such as the so-called Halcones) that functioned both as movement provocateurs and assassins while, at the same time, they coordinated intelligence and even action with the police and military. The evidence is clear that Echeverría himself was informed that Halcones and riot police were responsible for a small massacre of students on June 10, 1971, when armed Halcones attacked a demonstration of 8,000 to 10,000 people—mostly students and some workers—who demanded freedom for political prisoners and politically independent unions, and generally denounced antidemocratic and bourgeois educational reforms. In the attack, 18 to 23 people died, 120 to 169 were injured, and somewhere between 150 and 300 were detained.[8]

---

6. Luis Echeverría lowered the threshold for party representation in Congress to 1.5 percent of the total vote. For a complete explanation of why his reforms were ineffective, see Molinar Horcasitas (1991, 87–89).

7. The evidence is categorical that, upon assuming power on December, 1, 1970, Luis Echeverría intensified the dirty war as a counterinsurgency strategy against both ongoing and new armed guerrilla movements. For example, 1974 marked the largest number of proven cases of disappeared people from Guerrero (Comisión Nacional de Derechos Humanos 2006, 521). Further, as Lucio Cabañas's Poor People's Party (El Partido de Los Pobres) gained influence in other states, the number of armed guerrilla movements across Mexico also grew (in such states as Aguascalientes, Sonora, Veracruz, Chihuahua, Oaxaca, Chiapas, and Jalisco). The dirty war expanded accordingly.

8. These numbers are based on the unofficial draft report (the "White Book") that was leaked to some print media outlets and prominent human rights figures, such as Elena Poniatowska, in 2006 (Comisión Nacional de Derechos Humanos 2006). It was produced by twenty-seven investigators hired by Mexico's *fiscalía especial para movimientos sociales y políticos del pasado* (special

For their part, the students' initial experience with movement success, followed by instances of brutal repression along with a permanent climate of political harassment, deepened their commitments to social justice and opposition politics. In the aftermath of 1968 (and, for some, 1971), there was a general ideological shift to the left among youth. Those who had not been socialist became so (Gutmann 2002, 69–70); still others joined armed groupings, such as the Comandos Armados del Pueblo (CAP; this organization worked with the Frente Urbano Zapatista, FUZ) (Ulloa Bornemann 2007). Further, as we shall see in greater detail in the next chapter, those who were already communist broke with the PCM on the grounds that it was not radical enough in the context of growing state violence. Some former Communists thought that they had to defend themselves from violence with violence and took up arms in such groups as the Frente Revolucionario Armado del Pueblo (FRAP), the Lacandones, and the Movimiento de Acción Revolucionaria (MAR) (Ulloa Bornemann 2007). Other former students and moderately socialistic youth joined Maoist groupings (such as the Liga Comunista Espartaco, LCE) in a growing number of armed guerrilla groups and mini-groups (Procuraduría General de la República 2006; see also Ulloa Bornemann 2007). To connect to both peasant and workers' movements, some of these groups organized cells in both the countryside and the urban centers.[9] In his memoir, Alberto Ulloa Bornemann describes a fluid movement between peasant and union activities among guerrilla Maoist activists, and he identifies at least one such activist as having been a university student from 1968. Nicknamed "El Indio" (the Indian), this young activist was "a former political prisoner of the popular student movement of 1968 . . . [and]

---

prosecutor for social and political movements of the past, or FEMOSPP), and it was given to President Vicente Fox in December 2005. The draft report indicates that between 1968 and 1971 the Halcones worked with local police from the Dirección General de Servicios Generales del Departamento del Distrito Federal. While the Mexican government never made the unofficial draft public, the documents are available on the National Security Archive Web site (see Procuraduría General de la República 2006).

9. See Mexico's 2006 *Informe histórico a la Sociedad Mexicana* (Procuraduría General de la República 2006) for a detailed analysis of the various types of armed guerrilla groups, their goals, their methods, and their ideologies. The Liga Comunista 23 de Septiembre (23rd of September Communist League, LC23S) managed to unify a large number of these groups. During Echeverría's administration, armed groups in the urban centers managed a few well-publicized armed bank robberies and kidnappings for ransom, the money from which was funneled back to the armed peasant movements in Guerrero (to support the families of *guerrilleros*, buy arms, and otherwise finance their activities).

had studied philosophy at the UNAM. He was committed to securing a job as a rail worker... where the LCE had a sectional cell. El Indio wanted to keep faith with the Maoist slogans of 'serving the people' and 'be like the people, uniting with them'" (Ulloa Bornemann 2007, 46).

As noted by Shapira, "The new guerrilla challenge, sustained in some cases by extremists among students and even young university lecturers, culminated with the kidnapping from August 28 to September 8, 1974 of the president's father-in-law, José Guadalupe Zuno. The FRAP, a guerrilla group that claimed responsibility for the kidnapping, called its operation 'Operación Tlatelolco, 2 de Octubre de 1968'" (1977, 567). This suggests that the guerrillas were not only geographically dispersed but also deeply entrenched in, and a well-organized part of, opposition politics that threatened even the president's family.

Not all students radicalized by the 1968 (or 1971) massacre took up arms. Some simply turned to trade-union work in the hopes of building a politically autonomous, antiregime workers' movement (Shapira 1977; Pérez Arce 1990). Many youth who abandoned the PCM founded new, nonviolent left political parties, such as the Mexican Workers' Party (PMT) led by Heberto Castillo and Demetrio Vallejo (the latter was a former member of the PCM). Another group once closely allied with Castillo and Vallejo formed the Socialist Workers' Party (PST) in 1973. Still others formed far-left parties, such as the Trotskyists' Revolutionary Workers' Party (PRT) (Foweraker 1993, 88).

That politically alienated youth and others proliferated a large number of nonviolent left political parties did not immediately alter the electoral arena (Molinar Horcasitas 1991). This is because these so-called political "parties" were that in name only. The 1946 electoral law had made it difficult for opposition parties to register with the state (that is, to attain their *registro*) to actually compete in elections. The fact that state officials did not recognize these parties as interlocutors meant that they functioned more like nonviolent social movement organizations. And this was as young leftists preferred it. The majority had adopted a principled antiparliamentarian stance on the grounds that electoral competition merely legitimated a corrupt political system. Many ex-student radicals preferred nonviolent direct action to electoral politics and immersed themselves in nascent social struggles or in ongoing social movements in the cities and the countryside.

In the context of Echeverría's dirty war, ex-student radicals mobilized in clandestine and loose networks that helped spawn the nonviolent protest cycle of the 1970s and 1980s (Monsiváis 1987; see also Foweraker 1990, 9).[10] As fig. 1 clearly shows, this cycle of protest was composed mostly of peasant and poor people's movements in the mid-1970s, but ex-student radicals certainly played a key role. According to Joe Foweraker, "If 1968 is a historical watershed, then the subsequent popular movements can be seen as a rising tide of popular organization, with the thousands of leaders of the generation of 1968 providing the principle of continuity between tens of apparently separate movements (the leaders going from movement to movement and even galvanizing Indian and municipal struggles)" (1990, 9).

Because they immersed themselves in nonviolent movement work in the countryside and urban centers, ex-student radicals should be given some credit for leading parts of civil society to shake off the shackles of corporatism to become both politically independent and contentious. As the following chapter will show, the escalation of nonguerrilla peasant protest eventually incited both state repression and state concessions, the combination of which further undermined state corporatism among rank-and-file peasants. A similar dynamic occurred in the urban centers, prompting even middle-class mothers and family members to join human rights groups (see table 3 for a list of select human rights organizations). In short, civil society reorganized and grew strong in part because of the former students who, radicalized by their involvement in the 1968 student movement, spurred a protest cycle.

The increasing organizational strength and political independence of civil society combined with the declining legitimacy of the political system to force administrations after Echeverría to accelerate the pace of electoral reform (Molinar Horcasitas 1991, 95–98; see also Lomelí Meillon 2006, 44). In the 1976 election, for example, the PRI candidate, José López Portillo, ran without a real opposition (see Molinar Horcasitas 1991). Partly in response to his unopposed candidacy, President López Portillo (1976–82) altered the Constitution to pass the Federal Law of Political Organizations and Electoral Processes (Ley Federal de Organizaciones Políticas y Procesos Electorales, LFOPPE) on December 31, 1977 (Luna 1992; Crespo 2004). While there had been other important electoral reforms prior to 1977 (such as the one in 1953 that gave women the franchise), none opened the electoral arena to interparty competition as much as LFOPPE. Indeed, it is widely seen as the first in a

10. On unions, see Pérez Arce (1990) and Bennett (1993).

series of significant institutional reforms (between 1977 and 1996) that liberalized a previously closed electoral system (see table 2).

The LFOPPE took a decisive step toward making Mexico's political system more pluralistic. It did so by creating multiple incentives for opposition groups to become political parties and actually compete in elections (Molinar Horcasitas 1991). Since it was better for the government to have the opposition advance policy alternatives according to the institutional rules of the game, rather than through disruptive and perhaps violent social movement tactics, LFOPPE recognized political associations and eased the restrictions on new party registration. Todd Eisenstadt observes that part of the LFOPPE motivation was to "defuse tensions on the left . . . and . . . channel guerrilla participation by guaranteeing the safety of opposition-party poll watchers" (2003, 49n7; see also Gómez Tagle 2004, 84–86).[11] Indeed, this is practically what then secretary of the Interior (secretario de Gobernación) Jesús Reyes Heroles argued when he announced the public hearings proposing the constitutional amendments necessary for the new electoral law. He stated that "intolerance is the sure path to return to a wild and violent Mexico" (quoted in Preston and Dillon 2004, 91).

Then-president José López Portillo was also explicit about his government's efforts to channel and discipline the left. He argued that with electoral reforms "we want to make it understood that dissidence is not synonymous with violence, and opposition should not be associated with crime" (quoted in Preston and Dillon 2004, 92). In addressing a human rights group (the organizational precursor to the Comité Político de Familiares) in 1977, López Portillo further promised that amnesty would be a part of a political reform package, clarifying that with such reforms all parties, including ideologically left ones, could register for elections. But at this gathering he is also quoted as having warned that elections "would be the legal avenues by which to participate in politics and that he would not be responsible for those [groups] which continued to function illegally" (CNDH 2006, 711). The new law was thus designed not only as democratic window dressing; it was also clearly intended to channel both armed and unarmed dissidents into the electoral

11. While Eisenstadt emphasizes that the PRI passed these historic reforms because the regime's claim to democracy was called into question by López Portillo's unopposed presidential candidacy, the two points are not mutually exclusive (as clearly indicated in Eisenstadt 2003, 49n7). Channeling the left opposition into the electoral arena would solve the problem of political disruption and violence as well as offer much-needed democratic window dressing. LFOPPE was a reasonable policy solution to the regime's legitimacy crisis on multiple levels.

arena, where they could participate "legally" (that is, peacefully and not disruptively) in politics.

Under the new law, parties would no longer have to compile lists of notarized signatures of supporters before being allowed to compete in elections. Instead, parties were given "conditional registry"; this allowed them to first compete in elections and provide proof of support afterward. In order to keep their registry, parties simply had to attain a minimum of 1.5 percent of the *total* votes in three consecutive elections. Further, conditional registry did not "require any particular geographic distribution of the vote" (Bruhn 1997, 59).

The LFOPPE also increased the size of Mexico's Congress (Camara de Diputados) by one hundred seats and further stipulated that 25 percent of the total (of four hundred seats) would be distributed among minority parties according to proportional representation (Molinar Horcasitas 1991; Gómez Tagle 2004, 86). In other words, the new law created a mixed electoral structure wherein three hundred seats were distributed to the majority while the remaining one hundred seats were held by the minority via proportional distribution. This created an incentive for parties to compete in elections rather than use them as mere platforms to denounce the ruling party. The more votes parties received, the greater the number of congressional seats for which they qualified (Bruhn 1997, 60). Crucially, the greater the representation of opposition parties in the Chamber of Deputies, the greater the political pressure for continued electoral reform (García Díez 2001, 21).

To increase party competition, LFOPPE also gave public campaign money to registered parties and offered public funds for parliamentary staff and for party presses. Additionally, registered political parties were guaranteed limited time on television and radio. With greater public resources and real incentives to compete, a large number of left parties, including the PCM (in 1979), registered and began to compete in the electoral arena (Molinar Horcasitas 1991, 103). Whereas prior to LFOPPE there had only been four registered political parties, there were seven by 1979 and nine by 1982 (Molinar Horcasitas 1991, 102). While the PRI initially benefited from fragmenting the left opposition in what was clearly an overcrowded electoral field (see Diaz-Cayeros and Magaloni 2001), over time the growing electoral experience of left parties contributed to the unified left's competitiveness from the 1990s through the present.

Not only did the LFOPPE create multiple incentives even for radicals to operate legally in the electoral arena, but it also created institutions that at

Table 2 Key institutional reforms to Mexico's electoral authority

| | LFOPPE (1977) | CFE (1986) | COFIPE (1990) | COFIPE (1994) | COFIPE (1996) |
|---|---|---|---|---|---|
| Electoral authority | Comisión Federal Electoral | Comisión Federal Electoral | Instituto Federal Electoral (IFE) | Instituto Federal Electoral (IFE) | Instituto Federal Electoral (IFE) |
| Deciding authority | Government "comisión" | Government "comisión" | General Council | General Council | General Council |
| Composition | Minister of the Interior | Minister of the Interior | Minister of the Interior | Minister of the Interior (vote) | Congressional representitives (non-voting) |
| | Congressional representatives | Congressional representatives | Congressional representatives | Congressional representatives (vote) | Nonpartisan citizen councilors nominated and approved by Chamber of Deputies (vote) |
| | One representative per registered national party | Proportional representation of national registered parties | Proportional representation of national registered parties | Nonpartisan citizen councilors nominated and approved by Chamber of Deputies (vote) | Representatives from registered national national parties (non-voting) |
| | Public notary as acting secretary | | Nonpartisan magistrate councilors voted in by Chamber of Deputies | Representatives from registered national parties (non-voting) | |
| Government control vs. political autonomy | Ministry of the Interior chairs the Comisión Federal Electoral | Ministry of the Interior chairs the Comisión Federal Electoral | Ministry of the Interior chairs the General Council | Ministry of the Interior chairs the General Council | Parliament nominates individuals and Chamber of Deputies elects president |

| Democratizing changes | Constitutional recognition of political parties granted, extending rights to register to the opposition<br><br>Comisión Federal Electoral given power to register parties and candidates, administer public finances, create an electoral formula for proportional representation, and count proportional votes | Proportional representation of political parties in the Comisión established<br><br>Tribunals created to investigate party complaints of electoral irregularities<br><br>Opposition can help supervise the electoral register | IFE defined as a separate public institution responsible for electoral processes<br><br>Professionalization of electoral civil service<br><br>Citizens can operate in *casillas* | Professionalization of electoral civil service<br><br>Political parties lose capacity to influence the General Council's decisions<br><br>International election observers allowed | Full political autonomy of electoral authority<br><br>IFE is to organize and oversee elections |
|---|---|---|---|---|---|

SOURCE: Adapted from Lomelí Meillon (2006, tables 1, 2, and 3); Prud'home (1998); Crespo (2004); Gómez Tagle (2004).
NOTE: LFOPPE stands for the Ley Federal de Organizaciones Políticas y Procesos Electorales; CFE for the Código Federal Electoral; and COFIPE for the Código Federal de Instituciones y Procedimientos Electorales.

least gave the appearance of electoral oversight. It did this by giving registered opposition parties the right to vote in the Comisión Federal Electoral, which had been newly charged with organizing and overseeing elections (see column 1 of table 2). Minority parties also gained the right to sit on various supervisory committees, including at the polls (Molinar Horcasitas 1991, 97–148). While it was true, as opposition parties argued, that the new electoral oversight rules could not prevent electoral fraud (Molinar Horcasitas 1991, 97), the Comisión Federal Electoral's new mandate proved to be a first step toward democratizing elections. The power to register/unregister political parties and to organize elections was officially transferred from the Ministry of the Interior (Secretaría de Gobernación) to the Comisión Federal Electoral. While PRI officials initially dominated the latter, they were outnumbered by the opposition, once opposition parties registered and got the vote (see Molinar Horcasitas 1991, 107). Further, the Comisión Federal Electoral did appear to promise electoral oversight.

With this new institution in place came growing expectations about clean and fair elections. As Molinar Horcasitas (1991) put it, as a result of such successful reforms as LFOPPE, the PRI began to justify its uninterrupted rule with a new discourse about electoral legitimacy, rather than with its traditional rhetoric about their trusteeship of the Revolution. For their part, opposition parties appropriated the regime's new framework of electoral oversight and legality in their postelectoral protests. They cleverly grafted "electoral code rules onto" informal negotiations aimed at settling postelectoral confrontations and otherwise partly "'vested' themselves in the regime's illusion of legality" (Eisenstadt 2003, 41).[12] Eisenstadt emphasizes that at the subnational level the opposition, especially the Partido Acción Nacional (PAN), evoked the institutional rules of the game while, at the same time, it relied on informal bargaining to gain political posts as concessions to its postelectoral mobilizations.

In other words, opposition leaders responded to LFOPPE by successfully exploiting both the new rhetoric and the new institutional codes that appeared to ensure electoral justice (Eisenstadt 2003). From the mid-1980s onward, opposition leaders mobilized massive and highly disruptive postelectoral protests by carefully framing the demand for electoral justice using the government's legalistic frames about, and institutions designated for, overseeing elections. While both opposition parties strategically prioritized postelectoral

12. According to Eisenstadt, the opposition also created alternative (informal) "people's courts," dramatizing the idea that its courts were no more biased than the official ones (2003, 40).

mobilization, between 1989 and 2000 the Partido de la Revolución Democrática's (PRD's) postelectoral conflicts were more numerous than those of the PAN (735 compared to 203); they lasted longer, and many even threatened local-level governability (and came with a high price, including the 153 deaths reported by Eisenstadt 2003, 36–37).

In their efforts to defuse the growing political unrest and to promote trust in the legitimacy of elections, the official party passed a decisive electoral reform in 1990 that made the Comisión Federal Electoral almost completely independent of the party state (but for the fact that the minister of the Interior would chair the General Council for six more years). In the process, the Comisión Federal Electoral became the Instituto Federal Electoral (IFE) about thirteen years after López Portillo introduced the historic LFOPPE reforms (see table 2, per Lomelí Meillon 2006, 46–48; see also Domínguez and Lawson 2004, 336; Eisenstadt 2003). Further pressure from roughly eighteen thousand citizens calling for clean elections in a nationwide civic movement called the Alianza Cívica (Civic Alliance) led to other significant reforms in 1996, when the IFE became completely autonomous from the federal government (Avritzer 2002; see also García Díez 2001; J. Fox 1994a, 163). Until the minister of the Interior ceased to chair its General Council that year, the IFE was not free of presidential influence (see Crespo 2004, 58).

Political struggles, in short, can be credited with having "institutionalized a 'panoptic regime' of surveillance that allows them to monitor closely the entire electoral process . . . from voter registration to vote counting" (Schedler 2000, 8). But while the incessant pressure of pre- and postelectoral rallies, blockades, and even hunger strikes was behind many of the historically significant legal reforms outlined in table 2, it is clear that the 1977 electoral laws were a crucial initiating force (Gómez Tagle 2004).[13] While they did not evolve unilinearly, the 1977 LFOPPE reforms created both an electoral opening for the opposition and the institutional terrain on which many prodemocracy struggles would be fought and ultimately won (Eisenstadt 2003; Gómez Tagle 2004).[14]

13. For an analysis of how the Alianza Cívica was instrumental in securing the role of citizens in, and consequently the political autonomy of, the IFE, see Avritzer (2002). For a discussion of how the Ejército Zapatista de Liberación Nacional's (EZLN's) 1994 uprising unwittingly contributed to the progressive democratizing electoral reform of 1994, see Crespo (2004) and Gómez Tagle (2004).

14. According to both Gómez Tagle (2004) and Crespo (2004), some electoral reforms after 1977 were regressive to the extent that they intended to weaken the political opposition. Crespo makes it clear, for example, that the electoral reforms in 1987, 1990, and 1993 were meant to preserve the ruling party's majority in the Chamber of Deputies as well as its "control over electoral authorities" (2004, 72).

## The Long-Term Struggle for Human Rights in Mexico and the Emergence of the CNDH

Mexico's post-1968 legitimacy crisis democratized more than the laws on and the discourse about how the political opposition would influence policy making. The student massacre directly influenced Mexico's political culture beyond the issues of electoral oversight and justice. Tlatelolco came to signify the worst side of Mexico's version of authoritarianism, offering concrete evidence of the state's role in the mass violation of human rights. As I argue elsewhere (Trevizo 2006), 1968 marked the beginning of Mexico's dirty war against the left, and the massacre of upward of three hundred unarmed students was its most visible manifestation. Significantly, the events at Tlatelolco put into clear relief the power of the president; they demonstrated that he could take lives by fiat.

Not only did the massacre outrage Mexico's intelligentsia and left, but it also came to represent everything wrong with the party state in the view of many right-wing businessmen. While some progovernment business organizations (such as the Confederación de Cámaras Nacionales de Comercio [CONCANACO], the Confederación de Cámaras Industriales [CONCAMIN], and the Knights of Columbus) approved of the use of deadly force to stop disruptive students, many businessmen did not. According to one businessman who joined the right-wing PAN, "in Mexico, [it was] not to our pride" but a source of "shame" that some businessmen "applauded the government's actions" (quoted in Shirk 2005, 79). Decades later, a businessman and member of the right-wing opposition explained, "After 1968 we experienced a civic awakening and a desire to participate. The people are searching for leaders, and they obviously have begun to prefer the political vision advanced by the PAN. . . . The crisis has created an entrepreneurial leadership" (José Luis Coindreau, quoted in Luna, Tirado, and Valdés 1987, 30).

The full meaning of this argument will become apparent in chapter 4. The point here is that the repression of middle-class leftist students even moved some right-wing businessmen to take a stance against authoritarianism. But, as table 3 suggests, it was the family members of disappeared leftists who did the most to bring attention to the issue of Mexico's massive and ongoing human rights violations. Throughout the 1970s, they formed various human rights organizations that demanded amnesty for political prisoners as well as the reappearance of those who had disappeared at the hands of the military or the police. Two of these organizations—the Comité Político de Familiares and ¡Eureka!—became national-level social movement organizations, frequently engaging in such politically disruptive tactics as rallies, demonstrations, and vigils to make their claims. They held events in Mexico and abroad to demand human rights in their country. Despite the fact that the mothers who led ¡Eureka! were middle-class *doñas*, this organization was especially disruptive, as evidenced by the fact that one of its hunger strikes was met with police violence (¡Eureka! 1989).[15] At their demonstrations, the so-called doñas frequently linked the massacre of 1968 to the ongoing disappearances of their children. As one of their 1988 demonstration banners stated, "Our disappeared children are the heirs of 1968" (Nuestros hijos desaparecidos son los herederos del 68).

Tlatelolco thus became a part of the nation's collective memory as movement survivors, sympathizers, and human rights activists chanted, "The second of October will not be forgotten!" (¡El dos de Octubre, no se olvida!) on every major anniversary publicly commemorating the massacre of 1968 (including in Los Angeles, California, in 1988). The work of collective remembrance can be attributed to the left as well as to the human rights organizations that were sympathetic to them. In 1975, Gómez Villanueva, secretary for the Ministry of Agrarian Reform, accused groups of "anarchists," by which he meant the left, of "carrying the banner of 1968" into the countryside to incite peasants to confront the state (*Excelsior*, 9/3/75). Less disruptive human rights organizations succeeded in working with a rather large number of lawyers and legal organizations to press their cases of human rights violations in Mexico's courts. For their part, academic intellectuals created the Mexican Academy for Human Rights in 1984 to help train human rights advocates and promote research on the subject (Sikkink 1993). After decades of official amnesia about 1968, the local government of Mexico City and UNAM created a cultural center (the Centro Cultural Universitario Tlatelolco) housing a multimedia exhibit on the tragedy near the very site of the massacre (Johnson 2008).

In other words, 1968 created a movement within Mexico that has insisted on the inalienability of human rights. This demand became a formal public charge when, in 1990, the state created the National Commission on Human

---

15. In fact, ¡Eureka!'s main leader, Rosario Ibarra de Piedra, ran for president on the Trotskyist party ticket (the PRT) twice.

Table 3  Select human rights organizations that emerged as a direct result of Mexico's dirty war

| Organization and dates of operation | Demand/objective | Composition and membership | Tactics | Number of meetings with Special Prosecutor's Office, 2002–5 |
|---|---|---|---|---|
| Comité Político de Familiares* (1974–present) | Demands amnesty for political prisoners | Family members | Rallies, demonstrations, hunger strikes, national and international information tours about Mexico's political prisoners | |
| ¡Eureka! (1977–present)** | Searches for those who disappeared | Mothers play leading role | Rallies, demonstrations, hunger strikes, national and international information tours about Mexico's political prisoners | 69 (only local chapters from Sinaloa and Jalisco have met) |
| Comité 68 Pro Libertades Democráticas (1978–present) | Seeks justice for 1968 and 1971 student victims | Former 1968 students who were released from prison | Commemoration of the massacre in Tlatelolco, legal battles in court (including Mexico's Supreme Court) | 157 |
| Asociación de Familiares de Detenidos, Desaparecidos, y Víctimas de Violaciones a los Derechos Humanos en México (AFADEM) (1978–present) | Researches and denounces human rights violations in Mexico, especially in Guerrero State | Family members | Legal battles | 66 |

| Fundación Diego Lucero (1977?–present) | Demands the appearance of those who disappeared, as well as human rights in Mexico | Ex-guerrilleros and family members | Presentation of research and demands for justice to government officials |

SOURCE: Data from Procuraduría General de la República (2006, 711–22).
NOTE: The Special Prosecutor's Office is the Oficina del Fiscal Especial para Movimientos Sociales y Políticos del Pasado.

* The work of this committee resulted in the reappearance of one hundred of those who had previously disappeared; it forced the release of dozens of political prisoners and made possible the return to Mexico of some who had been exiled (Procuraduría General de la República 2006, 712). By 1977, families were joined by organizations on the left to demand the whereabouts of disappeared persons who had been detained. The name of this organization changed several times, from its founding Comité de Familiares de Presos, Perseguidos y Exiliados Políticos in 1974 to the Comité de Familiares de Presos, Perseguidos, Exiliados y Desaparecidos Políticos in 1976. It also came to be known as ¡Eureka!

** In an interview, Ibarra de Piedra said that ¡Eureka! was formally founded in 1978. María Santoyo-Borjas, phone interview, Mexico City, 12 January 2011.

Rights (Comisión Nacional de Derechos Humanos, CNDH).[16] The CNDH's mandate to "protect, observe, promote, study, and disseminate the human rights protected by the Mexican legal system" is a progressive step forward (Human Rights Watch 2008, 12). Since its emergence, the CNDH has documented tens of thousands of complaints of past and present human rights abuse, issued hundreds of recommendations regarding torture, and uncovered hundreds of cases of human rights violations implicating the military and even government personnel (U.S. Department of State 2004). However, as Human Rights Watch (2008) observes, because the CNDH has not aggressively followed up on the implementation of its recommendations, it fails to protect Mexico's citizens.[17] So while politically motivated human rights abuses by the military have declined, other abuses by undertrained and underpaid police forces persist at the local and state level where recently there have been guerrilla peasant movements, such as in Guerrero and Chiapas, and a radical teachers' movement, such as in Oaxaca.

To be clear, my point is that the 1968 massacre spawned a human rights movement within Mexico that, over the long haul, contributed to the emergence of the CNDH. Despite its significant limitations, its very existence indicates progress in the realm of human rights, as it constitutes a radical departure from the history of secrecy about military and policing practices. For example, it was instrumental in the passage of legislation that protects journalists from disclosing their sources (2006) and that decriminalized defamation (2007) (Human Rights Watch 2008). In a recent and highly critical report, even Human Rights Watch recognized that the CNDH represents a step forward. The report argues, "When it comes to actually securing remedies and promoting reforms to improve Mexico's dismal human rights record, the CNDH's performance has been disappointing." Nevertheless, it admits, the

---

16. Through constitutional reforms, the CNDH first attained administrative independence in 1992 and then attainted full autonomy from the executive branch in 1999. The Senate appoints its president and members after consulting with organizations from civil society (Human Rights Watch 2008, 11).

17. For example, despite the CNDH's efforts to professionalize the Federal Judicial Police and to make confessions extracted by torture inadmissible in court (Sikkink 1993), such problems and others remain. Not only are coerced confessions still admissible in trial, but police also engage in arbitrary and prolonged detentions, and prison conditions are inhumane. Worse still, damning evidence points to police involvement in narco-trafficking, kidnapping for ransom, and human trafficking (including the trafficking of women and children for sexual abuse) (U.S. Department of State 2004). The evident corruption and cruelty of the police could explain why many citizens believe that they are involved in the disappearances of women in Ciudad Juárez.

"CNDH has made some valuable contributions to human rights promotion in Mexico over the years, providing detailed and authoritative information on specific human rights cases and usefully documenting some systematic obstacles to human rights progress" (Human Rights Watch 2008, 1).

Thus, however significant the CNDH's limitations, the Mexican state and civil society are now institutionally better positioned to take greater steps toward protecting citizens from authoritarian governmental practices than they were prior to its emergence. As noted by Human Rights Watch, "The CNDH is often the only meaningful recourse available to victims seeking redress for past abuses. It is also, potentially, the most important catalyst for the changes that are urgently needed in Mexico to prevent future human rights violations" (2008, 1). Given its mandate, the ongoing scrutiny to which the CNDH is subjected will hopefully encourage the evolution of both its practices and institutions to more effectively protect Mexico's citizens.[18]

But rather than attempt to forecast the future, my point here is historical: after decades of political and legal struggles, the impressive array of post-1968 human rights organizations put the issue of human rights on the national political agenda. They also achieved one of their primary goals when the state acknowledged their long-standing claim that PRI governments had violated the human rights of political dissidents. This recognition came when the conservative PAN government finally wrested power from the PRI in 2000. Shortly after his election, then-president Vicente Fox attempted a reckoning with Mexico's authoritarian past by appointing to his cabinet human rights advocates (such as Jorge G. Castañeda and National Security Adviser Adolfo Aguilar Zínser), inviting international human rights monitors to Mexico, and creating official human rights posts.[19] The special prosecutor's office was specifically charged with investigating the PRI's history of human rights abuses of student activists and other dissidents (Enriquez 2006). While in existence, this office actually worked with Mexico's human rights movement by documenting human rights violations (see the last column of table 3). On the basis of secret military, police, and intelligence records, their official report concludes that presidents Díaz Ordaz, Echeverría, and López Portillo sustained a

---

18. Some evidence suggests that the CNDH is growing in its institutional capacity. For example, since 2005, it has opened special offices to focus on the human rights violations suffered by migrants.
19. While Fox's government ultimately failed to aggressively prosecute former government officials and military personnel, an official acknowledgment of human rights violations broke with prior presidential practice.

dirty war against the left. This report is significant because it documents presidential complicity in issuing orders to the defense secretary and the Ministry of the Interior, and in receiving reports with evidence of abuse.[20]

That it took decades of struggle before there was a real investigation into the decision to use military force in 1968 speaks to dirty PRI politics but also to the tenacity of Mexico's human rights organizations, which would not let 1968 fade from the nation's collective memory. Put another way, the special prosecutor's report and the "genocide" case brought against Luis Echeverría in the twenty-first century reveals two things at once. First, it shows that the PRI's prior arbitrary acts against Mexico's citizens were tolerated by political elites, progovernment business associations, progovernment unions, and progovernment peasant confederations. This suggests that authoritarianism was a part of Mexico's normative political order. Second, the demand for retroactive justice shows that political authoritarianism gave birth to a tenacious human rights movement that delivered on the promise not to let the memory of October 2, 1968, die. Human rights activists both kept the memory of Tlatelolco alive and, by insisting in Mexico's courts that Echeverría had committed genocide, introduced a new normative framework for governance and politics that insists that human rights are inalienable.

## Conclusion

I have argued that public officials brutally repressed a nonviolent movement because students misframed their prodemocracy movement as a revolutionary one. Their revolutionary frames made credible the government's view that the student movement was a threat to national security. But while the students' ideological adventurism discredited their movement, the government's response discredited the PRI state. The massacre brought to light the most repressive tendencies of Mexico's version of authoritarianism and consequently spawned multiple opposition movements that took up the banner of 1968 in making their claims. Because the state's management of a growing number of protests combined some tolerance with extreme repression, politically independent movements gained strength, radicalized, and, as we shall see in the following chapters, ultimately undermined corporatism.

20. For the official report, see http://www.gwu.edu/~nsarchiv/NSAEBB/NSAEBB209/index.htm (accessed June 25, 2010).

The growing organizational and political strength of these social movements, coupled with their capacity for disruption, forced elites to reform the rules of electoral competition. Since it was preferable that the opposition advance policy alternatives according to the institutional rules of the game rather than through disruptive social movements, the LFOPPE laws in 1977 channeled the left into political parties and electoral competition. This was a decisive step toward pluralism.

Finally, the human rights now promised by the CNDH are the long-term outcome of 1968 student survivors and the families of student victims. If human rights organizations, along with international monitors, continue to pressure the CNDH to live up to its mandate to protect human rights—and if the CNDH acts more aggressively to do so—such protection could deepen Mexico's nascent democracy. According to McAdam, Tarrow, and Tilly (2001), the protection of citizens from arbitrary government action is a sine qua non of democracy, and Mexico's progress in this area is due to the efforts of post-1968 human rights organizations.

# 3

## State Repression and the Dispersal of Radicals into Mexico's Countryside, 1970–1975

This chapter focuses on the *nonguerrilla* peasant movements of the first half of the 1970s. These unarmed peasant struggles are, in and of themselves, noteworthy for having constituted the most widespread series of rural protests since the 1930s (A. Bartra 1977, 157). On the basis of the national daily newspaper *Excelsior*,[1] I estimate that peasants from nearly every state of the Republic mobilized for land between 1970 and 1975.[2] Because more than half of these protests were land invasions of local private estates, most scholars agree with Fox and Gordillo's contention that the "mobilization was less 'national' than the simultaneous convergence of many regional movements" (1989, 140). That said, their simultaneity calls for an explanation given that land squatting is frequently met with violence from the affected landed proprietors and/or agents of the state.

Scholars have traditionally held that the convergence of these local land invasions was motivated by the interaction of a nationwide subsistence crisis and what has been described as the favorable political opportunity structure of the period. Specifically, many Mexicanists argue that peasants spontaneously mobilized for land independently of official or opposition organizations when the political "space" favored it (A. Bartra 1977, 166–67, 177; Canabal

---

1. As noted in the introduction, *Excelsior* was the only politically independent national press in Mexico at the time. It remained so until 1975 when President Echeverría orchestrated a purging of its editor and journalists for their critical coverage.
2. For a view of the states in which peasants protested by year, see the maps in Trevizo (2002), which can be viewed at http://caliber.ucpress.net/doi/abs/10.1525/sop.2002.45.3.285.

Cristiani 1984, 249-50; Montes de Oca Luján 1977, 64-65; Paré Ouellet 1992, 127). According to this view, the presidential succession of 1970 created mobilization opportunities at the historical juncture in which the government's corporatist peasant association, the National Peasants' Confederation (CNC), was losing legitimacy for failing to resolve peasant grievances in the face of an agricultural production crisis (Lúa, Paré, and Sarmiento 1988, 36). The new president, Luis Echeverría (1970-76), is seen as having made way for mobilization through his attempts to rebuild political legitimacy for the Mexican state (Fox and Gordillo 1989, 140; Schryer 1990). His promise of rural development programs and apparent tolerance of some land squatting early in his administration exemplify these legitimacy-building efforts in the countryside (Fox and Gordillo 1989, 140-41; Schryer 1990, 194; Paré Ouellet 1992, 127). Some scholars and most pundits believe that Echeverría even directly encouraged land invasions by rewarding them with land reform (Canabal Cristiani 1984, 249; S. E. Sanderson 1979; *Excelsior*, 12/2/75).

In this chapter, I explore whether the unarmed peasant struggles were as spontaneous as they appeared or whether there was continuity between previous movements and subsequent peasant protest. The Mexican Communist Party (PCM), for example, had been organizing peasants since the late 1920s. Did this matter to later struggles for land? Further, as Joe Foweraker argues, thousands of leaders from the 1968 generation went "from movement to movement and even galvaniz[ed] Indian and municipal struggles" (1990, 9; see also Collier 1994). It is well known that many former students radicalized by 1968 joined armed peasant movements (Shapira 1977; Ulloa Bornemann 2007). Were they also involved with the unarmed peasant struggles for land?

This chapter demonstrates both that the political opportunity structure was not as favorable to peasant protest as has been assumed and that the land revolts were not as spontaneous as they appeared. Luis Echeverría's government not only intensified the dirty war against armed guerrilla movements (especially a peasant movement in the state of Guerrerro), but he frequently deployed army troops to dislodge *unarmed* peasants from the lands they invaded. Only in the face of massive rural unrest and a national public outcry about the government's repression of peasant squatters did Echeverría scale back on military repression. However, this happened near the end of his administration, in November 1975. By that time, a cycle of local peasant land invasions had already been initiated and had affected nearly every state of the country (Trevizo 2002).

Further, I find that members and ex-members of the PCM, including previously affiliated youth radicalized by 1968, were among the *early risers* in the growing unarmed peasant struggles of 1970-75. While the historical record is clear that other Marxist currents, such as Maoists and later Trotskyists, also mobilized with peasants, chapter 5 of this book demonstrates that the majority of the left groups leading the *unarmed* peasant protests from 1979 on were either directly or indirectly affiliated with the PCM. It is reasonable to assume that this pattern was established early on—in the first half of the 1970s—because the PCM was the oldest and largest left party among the opposition. Hence my focus on the PCM.

The role that the PCM played in Mexico's countryside is significant not just historically but also theoretically. Leftists organized political contention in the face of increasing repression; moreover, the PCM had been previously smashed by state repression in the late 1960s and through Echeverría's dirty war in the early 1970s. Despite this repression, I show that fragmented networks of PCM militants, former militants, mere sympathizers, and even ex-student radicals were consistently among the early risers of peasant protests in the early 1970s. I specifically find that individual PCM cadre and ex-members previously associated with the PCM's youth wing protested in the context of state violence because they had developed ideological and organizational resources to cope with repression. As targets in an expanding dirty war, PCM militants redefined the state as unreformable and committed to political struggle, irrespective of jail sentences and possibly death. Additionally, the communist master frame of human liberation via a workers' and peasants' revolution resonated with former students from the 1968 generation. Even those who remained nonpartisan involved themselves in peasant struggles. Finally, the qualitative analysis shows that party militants, former PCM members, and 1968 youth operated through the PCM's organizational fronts or simply in informal networks.

The foregoing overview suggests that the PCM's history of formally organizing peasants mattered organizationally, ideologically, and even practically to subsequent peasant protests. The thesis to be demonstrated in this chapter is that the temporal convergence of the local land revolts is partly explained by the explicit communications among leftist networks, and not by a significant or unambiguous improvement in the political opportunity structure. This argument does not imply that the PCM's networks led all, or even most, of the land invasions, nor that they were hegemonic among the peasantry. As noted, other Marxist currents, especially Maoists, were also active in the countryside, and not just in the armed guerrilla movements. Línea Proletaria, for example, was influential among peasants in Durango, Coahuila, Nuevo León (La Botz 1995, 33), and, from 1974 onward, Chiapas (Foweraker 1993, 88–89). A quantitative analysis will tease out where the PCM was influential between 1970 and 1975. It will show that peasants were significantly more likely to participate in early land invasions (1970–75) in those states where the PCM had previously organized formal bases of support than in the states where it had not.

Consistent with resource mobilization theory, this finding illustrates how social movement organizations may enhance the "mobilization potential" of the people they organize. It specifically offers evidence in support of Mayer Zald's (1996) contention that the willingness to engage in particular forms of protest on the basis of specific forms of consciousness does not emerge from nowhere. Rather, Zald notes that social movement organizations define ideologies, frame grievances, and develop tactics (1996, 269). I show that the PCM did just that in the countryside, and that its history of organizing mattered over the long term, even after the organization had been smashed by state repression. For example, some of the rural structures that it had once created would be revivified in peasant struggles, and the ideological framework that it deployed would continue to exert influence even after the national organization lost contact with grassroots activists.

This chapter speaks not only to the importance of formal organization but also to some of its less tangible legacies; these include informal networks, ideology, and political identity. The research suggests that an organization's ideology is crucial to such processes as "reading" state signals, imagining political opportunity, and creating political identity. I show, for example, that those groups with ideological frameworks expecting state repression will seek mobilization strategies to skirt it. Some ideological frameworks, moreover, help develop radical "activist identities." According to Taylor (1989, 766) and Calhoun (1991), those with radical activist identities mobilize irrespective of horrific personal sacrifices, including the possibility of death. Thus, even where states succeed in dissolving the organizational capacity of a movement, they may not completely extinguish its mobilization potential because repression may harden the ideological views and deepen the activist identities of its survivors and even observers. Such like-minded people may, in turn, organize informally and clandestinely.

In short, the evidence suggests that social movement organizations can leave a legacy of both material and cultural resources that may be important for subsequent struggles. Specifically, a social movement organization's prior cultivation of political values, activist identities, and justice and injustice frames may survive its structural dissolution to become cultural resources aiding movement resurgence, even of other movements. This may be especially the case when political repression is the cause of organizational dismemberment. As I will show, those who survive or witness repression may become the activists who help determine the forms and breadth of subsequent struggles (della Porta 1988, 166).

The next section offers a brief history of the political economy of peasant production in postrevolutionary Mexico. I then provide a history of the PCM's organizing in the countryside, as documented in the independent scholarship about the party, internal PCM documents, PCM publications (such as its bimonthly magazine *Oposición* and its weekly magazine *La Voz de Mexico*), and accounts published by members and ex-members of the PCM. A quantitative analysis of peasant protests follows. Based on an original random sample of 221 cases of peasant protest (see appendix B), I present an ordinary least squares regression of the net differences among all peasant protests between 1970 and 1975 using key independent variables.

## The Political Economy of Peasant Production in Postrevolutionary Mexico

While antedating the Revolution, Mexican agrarianism was deepened by the constitutional promise of land to the landless and by the substantive land reform of the 1930s (see Wilke 1967). Not only did official nationalist discourse identify Francisco Villa and Emiliano Zapata as national heroes, but it also defined the peasantry as one of the most important clients of the state (along with workers). Constitutional law, moreover, adopted a significant social justice principle opposing the private monopoly of natural resources by stipulating that rural proprietors were subject to expropriation for purposes of redistribution if they concentrated land beyond some very specific land caps.[3] Through such land redistribution, the state created and sustained

---

3. During Echeverría's presidency, land was subject to expropriation if it exceeded the following: one hundred hectares for irrigated land or wet farmlands; two hundred hectares for rain-fed

a sizeable class of *ejidatario* (social proprietor) campesinos for much of the twentieth century.[4] Table 4 presents a snapshot of Mexico's agrarian classes and other social strata in 1970. It shows that while 30 percent of the peasantry owned private parcels, 69 percent of 2,212,406 peasants were ejidatarios. At the close of the twentieth century, ejidos accounted for about half of the country's arable land.[5]

Despite the constitutional laws designed to protect communal land and to limit the size of private rustic estates, Mexico's countryside could not "resist the market's pressure" (Gutelman 1971, 165). The development of capitalism in the countryside since World War II[6] led both to the covert concentration

---

(*temporal*) or cattle-grazing lands susceptible to cultivation; four hundred hectares for good-quality cattle-grazing lands; eight hundred hectares for hillside or arid cattle-grazing lands; one hundred fifty hectares for land used for cotton production or that had fluvial or pump irrigation systems; and three hundred hectares for land used for the production of bananas, sugarcane, coffee, sisal, rubber, coco palms, grapevines, olive trees, *quinoa*, cocoa, *agave*, prickly pears, vineyards, *vides*, and vanilla. Further, animal-grazing lands could have the capacity to feed up to five hundred animals.

4. Until 1992, the Ministry of Land Reform created ejidos by redistributing land to villages (not individuals) in four ways: (1) outright land grants (*dotación*); (2) restitutions (*restitución*); (3) new population centers (*nuevos centros de población*); or (4) ejido enlargements. Outright land grants were given to villages that did not have a historical claim to the land or were unable to prove such a claim. Restitutions were granted to villages, typically indigenous ones, that proved that their lands had been usurped. New population centers were created so that peasants residing in one location could be eligible to receive land in another part of the country (where land was "available" for redistribution). An ejido enlargement was granted to those villages that could prove that they held an insufficient amount of land to secure a living.

The state granted particular individuals (ejidatarios) usufruct rights over specific parcels and over the commons area (meadows segregated for collective exploitation, usually animal grazing). Males over sixteen years of age or heads of household of any age or gender were eligible to receive such rights if they were Mexican citizens by birthright (i.e., not naturalized) and were full-time agriculturalists (S. E. Sanderson 1986, 44). Ejidatarios had rights to their parcels until death unless they stopped working the land for two or more consecutive years. Beneficiaries were able to bequeath their usufruct rights to their children.

5. As noted earlier, ejidos and comunidades are a form of social property that, because they were theoretically owned by the village as a whole, were legally inalienable until 1992. That year, then-president Carlos Salinas de Gortari reformed the Constitution to legalize the privatization of ejidos if the village majority agreed to such privatization by majority vote.

While juridically similar to ejidos, indigenous comunidades possess land through custom or by legal title antedating the 1915 Constitution. Postrevolutionary (1917) governments also created comunidades via the restitution law. In practice, however, some ejidos were composed of indigenous peoples and some comunidades were home to ladinos (nonindigenous peoples). Since the vast majority of operative communal farms were ejidos, I follow the custom of speaking of Mexico's social proprietors as ejidatarios and of the communal farms as ejidos.

6. World War II and the Korean War increased the demand for Mexican agrarian products. Between 1940 and 1944 the average annual rate of such exports was 8.7 percent, nearly twice the growth rate of agricultural production (Ortíz Mena et al. 1953; de la Peña and Morales Ibarra 1989).

Table 4  Mexico's agrarian classes, class segments, and other social strata, 1970

| Class or strata | Total number of individuals | Percent of total |
|---|---|---|
| Agrarian producers | | |
| Private capitalist agriculturalists | 15,084 | 0.58 |
|   Medium (hired ≤ 1,250 days of work p/y) | 7,402 | 0.28 |
|   Large (hired > 2,500 days of work p/y) | 7,682 | 0.30 |
| Private capitalist cattlemen | 19,347 | 0.74 |
|   Medium | 15,154 | 0.58 |
|   Large | 4,193 | 0.16 |
| Middle strata | 353,694 | 13.60 |
|   Private transitional producers[a] | 106,977 | 4.11 |
|   Ejido transitional producers | 240,744 | 9.25 |
|   Ejido sector capitalists[b] | 5,973 | 0.23 |
| Peasants | 2,212,406 | 85.10 |
|   Ejidatarios | 608,927 | 23.42 |
|   Ejido sector peasant-workers[c] | 922,294 | 35.46 |
|   Private smallholders | 180,583 | 6.94 |
|   Private sector peasant-workers[c] | 500,602 | 19.23 |
| Total | 2,600,531 | 99.00 |
| Other strata (non-agrarian producers) | | |
| Full-time agricultural workers | 433,788 | 52.00 |
| Unemployed landless | 400,000 | 48.00 |
| Total | 833,788 | 100.00 |

SOURCE: The data on agrarian producers are from CEPAL (1982). The data on other rural strata are from censuses (appendix D explains the nomenclature of the direct rural producers).

[a] Transitional producers hire fewer than four full-time wage workers per year and continue to employ family labor on their estates. To arrive at this estimate, I collapsed CEPAL's transitional agriculturalists and small businesses categories (*pequeños empresarios agrícolas* and *pequeñas empresas pecuarias*) (1982, table 2).
[b] Ejido sector capitalists hire at least four permanent wage laborers or have at least fifty young cows.
[c] The number of peasant-workers is estimated from CEPAL's "sub-subsistence" peasant producers category.

of land (Gutelman 1971, 282)[7] and to the displacement of peasants. In addition to buying land on the open market, some proprietors amassed land by illegally renting or buying ejido parcels on the black market. Still others stole ejido parcels through extralegal coercion (via strongmen or *pistoleros* [gunmen]).

Regardless of the strategy, the result was the same: a small number of landed proprietors tended to control, rather than legally own, large plots of land. In 1970, agrarian capitalists constituted just over 1 percent of all the

---

7. For the case of Sonora, see Sevilla Mascareñas (1977, 46–47).

agrarian producers but legally owned close to 20 percent of all the arable land (CEPAL 1982, 122).[8] The historical evidence is irrefutable that they illegally controlled more than that. The illegal concentration of land explains why peasants called them *neolatifundistas*. While not all agrarian capitalists were neolatifundistas,[9] agrarian law made concentrating land beyond the legal caps less risky than investing capital for the business's development.[10] Their increasing control of social and private rural property[11] explains why agrarian capitalists were the principle target of peasant land invasions. Even though large landowners did not employ many agricultural workers, peasants concluded that their increasingly difficult economic circumstances were a direct outcome of land concentration.

The growth of large commercial estates not only displaced peasants via the commercialization of ejidal and private plots but also slowed the pace of additional land reform. Large proprietors had the financial and political power to circumvent the law on land size restrictions on rustic property. For example, many agrarian capitalists fictitiously subdivided their farms, titling subdivisions in the names of children or using *prestanombres* (borrowed names). In

---

8. I define capitalists as those who produce for markets to profit and who also hire labor. Among agricultural capitalists, this definition included those who hired for at least 1,250 days of work per year, or the equivalent of four permanent workers. The main crops that they sold on the domestic market were corn, beans, rice, and wheat—basic staples of the Mexican diet (CEPAL 1982, 303). The government's food-buying agency, the Compañía Nacional de Subsistencias Populares (CONASUPO), created a guaranteed market for such crops.

Because cattle ranching does not require much labor, the size of a cattle-ranching estate can be determined by the number of young cattle (*novillos*) (CEPAL 1982, 110). According to CEPAL's categorization, medium and large cattle-ranching estates (*empresas pecuarias*) are comparable in terms of capital investment to medium and large agricultural enterprises. In the 1970s, there were little more than nineteen thousand capitalist cattlemen.

9. Likewise, not all neolatifundistas were agrarian capitalists. Some were merely unproductive landholders who owned large ranches for either social status or speculative reasons. Some of these unproductive neolatifundistas were foreigners who simply vacationed at their Mexican ranches.

10. Intensive capital investment was not a viable option prior to 1992 because upgrading the land subjected it to official reclassification and, hence, made it vulnerable to expropriation. To illustrate, if a proprietor installed an irrigation system on land classified for cattle grazing, the property would be reclassified as "irrigated land," for which the permissible size is much smaller (Cornelius 1992, 3).

11. Roger Bartra argued that two "modes of production" articulated to such a degree that they were becoming a single economic structure of exploitation (1974, 96). He specifically assumed that the capitalist mode of production was increasingly "proletarianizing" peasants (see also Gutelman 1971, 259). Armando Bartra, in contrast, argued that "capitalist development in the countryside exploits and partly ruins the peasant economy, but it can neither radically displace it nor proletarianize the rural masses . . . as they, those with and without land, struggle in defense and reconstruction of peasant economies [*condición campesina*]" (cited in CEPAL 1982, 55).

this way, land did not appear to be "available" for redistribution by the state, as thousands of hectares owned by one family were held under the names of hundreds of individuals. If these strategies failed, agrarian capitalists could drag out the process of expropriation through complicated appeals, even if they were proven to have concentrated land beyond the legal limits.

Consequently, by 1970, 64 percent of the ejidatarios and 71 percent of all private smallholders were *minifundistas,* cultivating plots of five hectares or less (CEPAL 1982, 292–93). Minifundistas are always on the verge of producing less than is necessary for their subsistence because their soil is usually exhausted, or eroded, from being overworked. Indeed, spiraling production costs in the late 1960s and early 1970s forced fully 90 percent of all minifundistas to scale back on their production to the degree that they could not even meet their subsistence needs (A. Bartra 1985, 98–100; see also CEPAL 1982, 292–93).[12]

At the same time, between 1950 and 1970, Mexico's population doubled, and this demographic explosion dramatically increased the pressure on the land. Whereas the population density per square kilometer of arable land had been thirty-six persons in 1960, it was fifty-two in 1970 and sixty-seven by 1977 (S. R. W. Sanderson 1984, 3). As a result, the number of eligible land reform beneficiaries rose to an estimated three million, more than double the 1.4 million landless of 1950 (A. Bartra 1985, 99).

Adding to the pressure for land was the fact that the actual distribution of previously decreed parcels was backlogged. Specifically, about thirty million hectares of land officially "granted" to peasants by previous presidential decrees had never actually been received by the people whose names were published in the *Diario Oficial* as land reform beneficiaries (*Excelsior,* 10/3/75). Perhaps equally frustrating was the fact that there were an additional sixty thousand pending land reform solicitations in this period (*Excelsior,* 5/6/75).

Worse still, many of the landless were unemployed. Table 4 shows that nearly four hundred thousand people, twelve years of age or older, were unemployed at some point in 1969 and were actively looking for work in agriculture, ranching, mining, fishing, or hunting. While the unemployed landless typically survived by working odd agricultural jobs or a craft, in the early 1970s, agrarian capitalists increasingly turned to labor-saving machinery. In

---

12. A national government survey in 1975 found that roughly one-third of the rural population never ate meat, eggs, or bread; fully 59 percent never drank milk (S. E. Sanderson 1986, 10). See also table 5.

Table 5 Characteristics of rural vs. urban population, select census years

| Variable and census year | % rural respondents | % urban respondents | Total % / N (all weighted cases) |
|---|---|---|---|
| Indigenous population (2000) | 63 | 37 | 100 (5,298,670) |
| Never attended school or had less than elementary school education[a] (1960) | 72 | 28 | 100 (7,008,736) |
| Never attended school or had less than elementary school education[a] (1970) | 58 | 42 | 100 (8,012,400) |
| Illiterate[a] (1960) | 74 | 26 | 100 (5,727,495) |
| Illiterate[a] (1970) | 61 | 39 | 100 (6,537,400) |
| Ate NO meat last week (1960) | 60 | 40 | 100 (33,687,600) |
| Ate NO meat last week (1970) | 66 | 34 | 100 (9,868,900) |
| Employment status[b] (1970) | | | |
| Employed at work | 42 | 58 | 100 (9,040,800) |
| Unemployed | 30 | 70 | 100 (261,500) |
| Inactive, other reasons | 31 | 69 | 100 (1,409,500) |

SOURCE: Data from Minnesota Population Center 2007.

[a] Age is greater than or equal to sixteen.
[b] Employed at work means that the person either worked for an employer or was self-employed. The employment sample was restricted to people whom we might reasonably expect to be employed at this time—i.e., males at least sixteen years of age but younger than sixty-five.

1970 alone, roughly one hundred thousand agricultural workers were suddenly unemployed (Páramo 1983, 38, table 7), and an estimated thirty thousand agricultural workers were unemployed each year thereafter in the first part of the decade (*Excelsior*, 7/14/75).

It is not surprising, then, that many rural dwellers suddenly migrated to the urban centers in the late 1960s.[13] But as is evident from the unemployment figures for males at least sixteen years of age near the bottom of table 5, Mexico's urban centers could not absorb the ballooning labor force. The percentages in table 5 also indicate that rural migrants would be the least competitive in tight labor markets given that their illiteracy rate was 1.5 times

13. As a consequence, between 1960 and 1970, the country transitioned from a predominantly rural to a predominantly urban society. According to census data, whereas the population had been 60 percent rural in 1960, it was 40 percent rural in 1970 and 29 percent rural in 1990; by 2000, about one quarter of the population lived in the countryside (Minnesota Population Center 2007).

greater than that of urban dwellers.[14] Indeed, for the period between 1940 and 1970, only 30 percent of displaced agrarians who were on the labor market for the first time actually found work in cities (A. Bartra 1985, 99). Since urban industry could not sufficiently absorb those displaced by the expansion of land and labor markets in the countryside and since the U.S. Bracero Program[15] ended in 1964, many landless rural dwellers, near-landless minifundistas, and rural unemployed were forced to remain in or return to their villages (Canabal Cristiani 1984, 239).

By all accounts, the countryside was undergoing an acute crisis of agricultural production that culminated in what scholars have described as a subsistence crisis during this period. As Jack A. Goldstone (1991) rightly notes, the type of sustained demographic pressure that leads to mass urban migration and overflowing labor markets also generates political unrest. Mexico was no exception (see fig. 1).[16] Then-president Luis Echeverría responded to this crisis with innovative policies aimed at increasing rural production by capitalizing the peasant sector. His administration introduced the Programa de Inversiones para el Desarrollo Rural Integrado (PIDER),[17] an "integrated rural development" policy aimed at integrating peasants into the modern economy.[18] This policy temporarily replaced land reform as a viable political option for the countryside because the latter was "seen by state elites as a risky, expensive, and politically volatile policy, difficult to implement and often unrewarding in terms of increases in production or political support" (Grindle 1986, 153; see also Fox and Gordillo 1989, 140). Other policies consistent with the integrated rural development approach included the ejido collectivization plan, infrastructural development for the countryside, and the

14. As indicated in table 5, the illiteracy rates nearly matched the rates of those people, sixteen years of age or older, who had never attended school or had never gone beyond primary school.

15. This program granted temporary work visas to Mexican nationals to work on U.S. farms.

16. The 1970s and 1980s witnessed not only the rise of traditional interclass conflict but also nontraditional urban movements comprising urban squatters, students, and women (Foweraker and Craig 1990; Foweraker and Landman 1997). After the 1985 earthquake, many *chilangos* from Mexico City mobilized as *damnificados*. They had been forced to live in the tent communities that they built when the state failed to offer the earthquake victims permanent shelter.

17. PIDER distributed green revolution technologies, increased both credit and price supports for basic staples, and planned on providing numerous services to peasants (these included technical, educational, and medical services, as well as short-term nonfarm employment) (Grindle 1986; Fox and Gordillo 1989, 140–41).

18. Less ambitious integrated development programs included the Programa Nacional de Alimentación (Heath 1985, 97) and the Unidad Agrícola-Industrial de la Mujer. The former sought to promote self-sufficiency in grains; the latter hoped to create space for women's industry (i.e., canning or sewing cooperatives) on the ejidos (Arizpe 1985, 213).

state marketing of peasant produce.[19] The ejido collectivization plan sought to unify (or reunify) plots to create economies of scale[20] and introduce tractors and other machinery (S. E. Sanderson 1979, 1192).

By 1974, the government's expenditure on agricultural development had increased to 17 percent of all public expenses; by the end of 1975, it was 20 percent, nearly twice the previous administration's average of 11 percent. Luis Echeverría clearly signaled to peasants that he was interested in rural welfare. But, as we shall see, these policies neither mollified peasants nor explain the widespread series of land revolts that seemed to have mushroomed at the start of the 1970s.

## Peasant Protest in the Echeverría Years

Despite Luis Echeverría's populism, his propeasant populist stance does not fully account for the widespread and quasi-simultaneous expansion of peasant protest. As indicated in fig. 4, peasant protests for land not only preceded 1973, the year that Echeverría began to implement new rural policies, but actually declined precipitously that very year. Toward the end of Echeverría's administration, the secretary for the Ministry of Agrarian Reform, Augusto Gómez Villanueva, argued that the government was unable to execute one of its programs, ejido collectivization, *because* of mounting peasant unrest.[21] In his words, the government failed "to collectivize peasant parcels because previous administrations left a great backlog of unfulfilled presidential resolutions to distribute land. This resulted in strong, potentially violent, social tensions from the *beginning* of this government" (*Excelsior*, 9/3/75; emphasis added). "There were pressures from provocateurs," asserted Gómez Villanueva, "anarchists who carried the banner of 1968 in an attempt to incite

---

19. In the 1970s, the state tried to increase its economic role in the countryside by buying, storing, and distributing peasant produce directly (Mackinlay 2004). The problem, however, was that the rural outlets for the National Popular Foods Company (Compañía Nacional de Subsistencias Populares, CONASUPO) did not extend to every village or even region. Further, CONASUPO did not always have the resources to buy the peasants' entire harvest, even in the regions where there were such outlets. As the price that the government paid for crops could vary from state to state (Gutelman 1971, 253), many peasants felt cheated by this state firm.

20. Plots were disjointed because individual families enjoyed usufruct rights over small parcels even though the law stipulated that the village as a whole is the land reform beneficiary.

21. Echeverría reunified less than 6 percent of the ejidos that he had hoped to reunify, mostly in the last few weeks of his term (S. E. Sanderson 1979, 1204; Montes de Oca Luján 1977, 66).

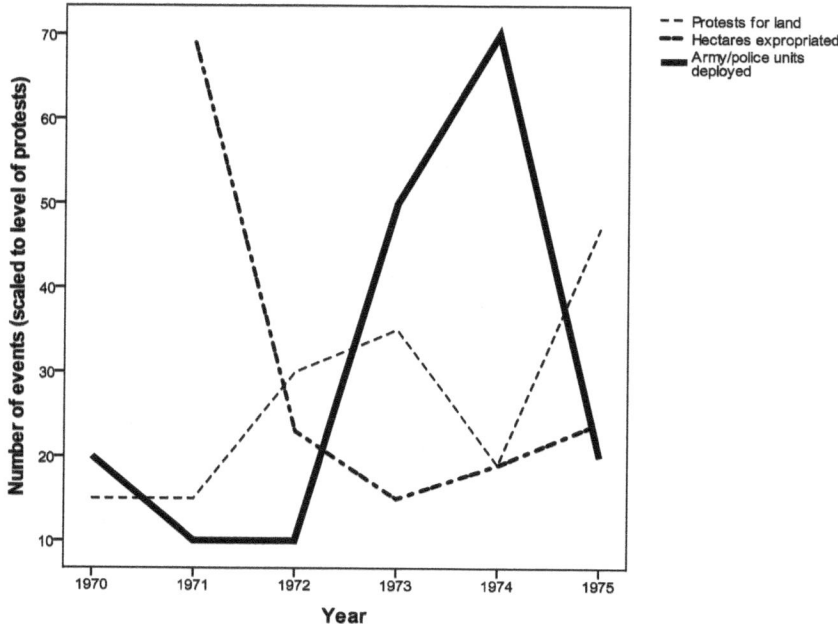

*Fig. 4* Peasant protests and government responses
SOURCE: *Excelsior* and the *Diario Oficial*
NOTE: Hundreds of thousands of hectares were expropriated in Mexico per year. I rescaled the variable to the level of peasant insurgency by dividing the raw values by ten thousand. Similarly, the number of army/police units deployed to a protest event per year was rescaled to the level of peasant insurgency by multiplying the raw values by ten.

peasants into a confrontation with the government. . . . We faced a mountain of peasant petitions, solicitations, plans that reflected pressures from all fronts, from land solicitations, accusations of disguised latifundios, petitions to execute prior presidential orders" (*Excelsior*, 9/3/75).

Thus, in contrast to the view that Echeverría's rural development policies "opened" the political space for peasant protests, it appears that rural development policies followed, rather than preceded, the protests for land. To put this another way, land invasions appear to have usurped the regime's plans for the countryside. From a slightly different point of view, some scholars hold that the government may have lowered the costs of peasant protest by tolerating land invasions "in a handful of highland states in 1972." According to Fox and Gordillo, "Government reformists tried to limit official repression, even encouraging land invasions in some cases" (1989, 140).

Despite his rhetoric, the historical record shows that Luis Echeverría was highly repressive, not only because he intensified the dirty war against revolutionaries and armed guerrillas[22] but also because he deployed the army against *unarmed peasant movements*. For example, just eight months after Echeverría announced that his government would not use the army to dislodge peasant squatters, the Ministry of National Defense released an official statement explaining that the army had been used for such purposes. This public statement further warned that the army would continue to eject peasants from the lands they invaded so as to "maintain the peace and tranquility necessary for the country's agricultural development as well as guarantee the legal possession of lands by small proprietors, ejidatarios, and comuneros" (*Excelsior*, 6/23/73). A random sample of *Excelsior* newspaper reports shows that army troops were occasionally sent to dislodge peasants from lands they had seized illegally. My sample of 221 incidents of peasant protest yielded sixty-seven cases in which the state forcibly dislodged unarmed peasants from such lands; army troops were used in twenty-six of these cases (see fig. 4).[23]

As suggested by fig. 4, Luis Echeverría followed the Mexican presidential tradition of *pan y palo* (bread and stick); he tolerated some protests but repressed those movements that could not be co-opted. Echeverría's double-edged strategy of combining political co-optation and low-intensity warfare

22. Early in his administration, in 1971, Echeverría committed roughly twenty-four thousand soldiers to the state of Guerrero to combat two ongoing guerrilla movements. It was under Echeverría's administration that the army began to use helicopters and other aircraft to bomb guerrilla camps. In June 1974, Echeverría dispatched an additional ten thousand troops to Guerrero when Lucio Cabañas's guerrillas held hostage then senator and gubernatorial candidate Rubén Figueroa Figueroa. As a result of Echeverría's militarization of Guerrero, a greater number of guerrillas and innocent civilians, among them elderly men, were detained (sometimes en masse), tortured, made to disappear, and/or executed extrajudicially (Procuraduría General de la República 2006, 330–428). During Echeverría's administration, the army harassed entire communities, sometimes holding them hostage, and, in at least once instance in 1972, set a village on fire for allegedly aiding and abetting *guerrilleros* (Procuraduría General de la República 2006, 342, 371). The years between 1973 and 1975 saw the highest number of people tortured by military personnel (more than 550 proven cases of torture, out of a total of 2,141 cases between 1956 and 1985). Finally, newspaper sources claim that during Echeverría's final year in power, the military carried out "death flights" in which executed prisoners were dumped into the sea, twelve cadavers at a time (Procuraduría General de la República 2006, 427–28).

23. This is a conservative estimate. Schmidt, for example, reported that the army dislodged peasant squatters from fully twenty-nine invasions that occurred in seven distinct states (Colima, Guanajuato, Michoacán, San Luis Potosí, Tamaulipas, Tlaxcala, and Querétaro) in June 1973. He generally concluded that "military and police intervention used a high level of violence to put down peasant unrest" (1991, 76).

backfired when the media spotlighted the deaths of six unarmed peasants in late October 1975. The army killed these peasants while it, along with state police troops, was ejecting over four hundred land invaders from a ranch in Guaymas, Sonora.[24] Because the media's attention to this event deepened the state's legitimacy crisis during an impending presidential succession, Echeverría responded dramatically: he forced Sonora's governor to resign from power[25] and made a radical 180 degree turn both in his agrarian policies and in his management of rural protest. In response to the media's outcry, his government not only promised to "uncover all of the disguised latifundios in the country" (*Excelsior*, 11/1/75) but even committed the resources necessary to do it.[26] Despite his initial rejection of land reform, massive land expropriations of large landed proprietors followed, and land was redistributed in direct proportion to the level of peasant disruption (Trevizo 2006).

While it is possible that the land reform that Echeverría adopted during his last year in office further encouraged land invasions, land reform departed from his earlier integrated development policies. As fig. 4 shows, the political context of his first five years in office was clearly less favorable to the unarmed peasant movements than has previously been assumed. Indeed, this analysis shows that even unarmed peasants faced repression. What follows is an explanation of how the "anarchists who carried the banner of 1968" operated politically in the context of increasing state repression.

## The PCM's Organized Bases of Rural Support

The PCM started to build a peasant base as soon as the party abandoned its workerist third-period dogma (which lasted from 1928 to 1935).[27] From the

---

24. Peasants had been demanding the redistribution of 250 acres from this estate for more than twenty-five years.

25. Echeverría also fired the governor's top aides and the head of the PRI in Sonora.

26. On the day that Echeverría forced Biebrich Torres out of the governorship, he created a special commission to implement all previous presidential land reform resolutions (some spanning several decades) and to settle the more than nine hundred pending solicitations for land in that state (many of which had been pending for more than thirty years). Although the government would claim to have investigated fictitious subdivisions of land since 1973, Echeverría did not commit the functionaries and technicians necessary to this task (fully one hundred of them) until November 1975.

27. Despite the ways in which agrarianism challenged the PCM's workerist ideology, the party developed deep roots in the countryside early in its organizational history (Carr 1992, 32).

mid-1930s on, the PCM began supporting all forms of land reform. This new stance increased its peasant ranks to 20 percent of all registered members (Carr 1992, 53), and the PCM ultimately won the leadership of significant peasant movements in at least four regional states.[28] Further, in 1949, the PCM joined forces with the nationalist Popular Party, led by Vicente Lombardo Toledano, to found the General Union of Mexican Workers and Peasants (Unión General de Obreros y Campesinos de México, UGOCM). The UGOCM's demands for land, higher wages, and improved credit won it so much mass rural support[29] that it threatened the government's official peasants' confederation (the CNC). But when, in 1958, the Popular Party's Lombardo Toledano adopted the view that the state had fulfilled its revolutionary goals, including land reform, the PCM became the only nationally organized force to promote a radical agrarianist stance (Carton de Grammont 1989, 231). Against Lombardo Toledano's explicit admonitions to the contrary, Communists led large land invasions in February 1958 in Baja California, Sonora, and Sinaloa that were ultimately repressed by federal troops (Schmitt 1965, 180).

The ideological incompatibility between these two parties split the UGOCM into three factions, two of which ultimately came to be controlled directly by the federal government.[30] In contrast, the PCM led a faction out of the UGOCM and in 1961 began to work closely with the Movement for National Liberation (MLN), which sought to unify Mexico's left. While former president Lázaro Cárdenas helped form this movement, the radical left, including leaders of the PCM, also defined the radical agrarianist program that it adopted (see Garza 1964, 450, 454-55). According to Garza, "Many among the thirty-odd organizations which it [the MLN] claims within its fold are frankly communistic in their leadership if not their total membership." He

---

Within a year of helping to found the National Peasant League in 1926, the PCM began to call for "the creation and development of individual peasant land holdings (pequeña propiedad)" (Carr 1992, 34). But then, in response to the Comintern's "third-period" policy (1928-35), the PCM denounced all forms of agrarian reform as "bourgeois." Although the party called for land invasions and for land expropriations of private proprietors without compensation (Carr 1992, 35), it broke with the National Peasant League in 1929, thus weakening its relationship to the peasantry in this period (Craig 1990, 69).

28. These were Veracruz, Michoacán, Coahuila, and Durango (Craig 1990).

29. Including from the procommunist National Miners' Union (SITMMSRM) (Besserer, Novelo, and Sariego 1983, 33).

30. In 1973 and 1974, both factions of the UGOCM signed "unity pacts" with the CNC (Esteva 1983, 90; Montes de Oca Luján 1977, 64-65).

adds, "What is perhaps most revealing about the political orientation of the Movement of National Liberation is the inclusion of Communists in the ranks of its National Committee" (1964, 451). The PCM and other radical leftists were already part of the leadership of the MLN when it founded the Central Campesina Independiente (CCI) in 1963 (Martínez Verdugo 1985; Lúa, Paré, and Sarmiento 1988).[31] Indeed, the CCI's principle reforms were "outlined by the CCI's general secretaries Arturo Orona, Ramón Danzós Palomino [both of the PCM] and Alfonso Garzón, [an] agrarian leader of Baja California" (Garza 1964, 451).

Although the CCI was successful in challenging the government's control over peasants, ideological divisions over autonomy from the federal government and direct action tactics occasioned the CCI's splintering in the mid-1960s and then twice in 1970 (for example, the factions around former president Lázaro Cárdenas and Braulio Maldonado [a Castroist] promoted an electoral alliance with the PRI in 1964) (Garza 1964, 459; Lúa, Paré, and Sarmiento 1988, 34). However, the core surrounding the communist leader Ramón Danzós Palomino remained staunchly independent of the federal government when it founded the communist peasant front called the Central Campesina Independiente–Danzós (CCI-Danzós) (see, for example, *Oposición*, 10/5/70, 10–12; see also *Oposición*, 2/1/72, 19–22).

To distinguish it from those sectors of the CCI that would eventually be controlled by the PRI, the CCI-Danzós was sometimes called the CCI-Roja (or the CCI-Red), signaling that it was led by PCM member Palomino. According to PCM documents, the CCI-Danzós was intended to "politicize, organize, as well as direct the true, independent, democratic, and revolutionary class struggle of the poor, exploited and oppressed in the countryside" (*Oposición*, 10/5/70, 11; see also 10–12). While not all peasants affiliated with the CCI-Danzós were Communists, the local leadership tended to be made up of individual Communists and ex-communist youth who had been recruited in the late 1960s from the country's rural and agronomy schools

31. The CCI was formally founded on January 6, 1963, by two thousand delegates representing half a million agricultural workers. The impetus for the CCI began earlier, in 1961, when former president Lázaro Cárdenas initiated the MLN in an effort to reach out to peasants alienated from the official CNC. According to Lúa, Paré, and Sarmiento, some of the peasant sectors that originally formed the CCI had indeed worked with the PCM and were, in fact, led by Ramón Danzós Palomino, a member of the PCM. Not all of its members, however, were Communists. Others were either dissidents from the UGOCM or *cardenistas* from Michoacán, Guanajuato, and Mexico State (1988, 34).

(Condés Lara 1990, 12; PCM 1977, 64). Further, key PCM national leaders not only doubled as the national leaders of the CCI-Danzós but also continued to lead invasions through the late 1960s and, as I will show, the 1970s and 1980s (see chapter 5 in this book).

In short, from the mid-1960s on, the CCI-Danzós was the only geographically dispersed nonguerrilla movement in the countryside that insisted on organizational independence from the federal government and promoted both the expropriation of latifundios and the radical and illegal tactic, the land invasion, to achieve land reform. The PCM made land reform via land invasion a high priority until 1975. That year, it began to prioritize the unionization of agricultural workers and changed its name to the Central Independiente de Obreros Agrícolas y Campesinos (CIOAC). As we shall see in chapter five, four years later, the CIOAC reprioritized the struggle for land and, along with the Coordinadora Nacional Plan de Ayala (CNPA), accounted for one-third of all the peasant struggles in the nation (Rubio 1987, 168).

## The Dismemberment of the PCM: 1968–

Such radicalism made the PCM a central target for state repression. Deeply concerned about communism, Díaz Ordaz's government (1964–70) began to jail PCM cadre *well before* the student movement erupted in Mexico City in the summer of 1968 (Peláez 1980, 135–36).[32] In May 1967, for example, Ramón Danzós Palomino was jailed for leading a land invasion in Sonora (Martínez Verdugo 1985, 456). According to recently declassified documents, the PRI state persecuted Palomino for his political views, and we now know that he was arrested in 1967 on the basis of evidence fabricated by the police (Procuraduría General de la República 2006, 542). By the end of Díaz Ordaz's administration in 1970, most members of the PCM's national leadership had been jailed, making it difficult for them to maintain direct communications with all nonjailed PCM members.

The repression of Communists combined with the generalized repression of the 1968 student movement to create a widespread political crisis of confidence within the PCM that culminated either in the mass desertion or mass expulsion of party cadre, especially its youth (Condés Lara 1990,

32. On February 6, 1968, government agents raided a PCM Central Committee meeting and jailed seven of its members, one of whom was Rafael Jacobo García, a peasant leader.

6). For example, the party appears to have lost half of its militants in 1970. According to Arturo Martínez Nateras, the PCM's secretary from 1974 to 1978, at that time there were only about eight hundred real dues-paying members out of the PCM's list of roughly fifteen hundred paper members (quoted in Condés Lara 1990, 11). Further, about five thousand communist youth abandoned the PCM's youth auxiliary organization (the Juventud Comunista Mexicana, JCM) (Martínez Nateras 1980, 10) on the grounds that the party had failed to provide coherent leadership during the tumultuous events of 1968. It follows that some of the youth who left the party had been student activists in 1968.

Arturo Martínez Nateras described the party's organizational crisis between 1968 and 1974 as follows: "The PCM did not have organized local cells, [and] the number of paid staff was barely twenty (some of whom worked for half-pay); we organized fund-drives, but those initiated between 1968 and 1974 did not raise any money" (quoted in Condés Lara 1990, 11). Local PCM leaders from the Puebla Tlaxcala region corroborated this description of organizational crisis in an internal document when they called the party in the post-1968 period "almost nonexistent" (PCM 1977, 77). According to the document, their "movement was defeated, [and] the Party was dismembered [*desmembrado*]; without organization, the left was divided, and the killings and repression were too recent" (1977, 60).

Despite this dismemberment, PCM newspapers provide evidence that some rural cells not only survived but continued to mobilize peasants in the face of state repression. For example, an anonymous *Oposición* correspondent wrote, "Civil and military officials of the state of Zacatecas have organized . . . an intense persecutory campaign against the well-known peasant leader J. Dolores López, the first secretary of the State Committee of the PCM." The correspondent maintained that soldiers were used to "'convince' peasants to abandon the CCI and the PCM so as to join the PRI and [its official peasants' confederation] the CNC" (*Oposición*, 4/15/70, 30). One month later, *Oposición* reported that in the state of Chihuahua local leaders of the CCI-Danzós and the PCM led two hundred peasants in land invasions. According to the report, "The militant peasants have received moral and material support from the State Committee of the CCI as well as the State Committee of the PCM and the Juventud Comunista de México, from the Electricians' sections XXV and XXXI, the Parral's Civic Union" (*Oposición*, 6/1/70, 14–16).

Thus, while the state's combined strategy of co-optation of the nationalist left and repression of Communists disabled the UGOCM and seriously undermined the PCM's national organizational capacity, it radicalized committed Communists. The PCM reacted to persecution by redefining Mexican society as "fully" capitalist and by calling for a "new revolution." This was a qualitative change from its previous stance that the domestic bourgeoisie was divided into two camps, a comprador bourgeoisie (allied with imperialist interests) and a progressive nationalist bourgeoisie (with vested national interests). The evidence further shows that party militants continued to mobilize during Luis Echeverría's dirty war against the Communists because they had a preexisting ideological model that led them to conclude that there was no longer a progressive faction of the bourgeoisie. As such, the state's repression dispersed and fragmented the PCM's organizing, rather than abolishing it completely.

## Semiformal and Informal Communist Networks Under Luis Echeverría

Despite the risk of being jailed or killed, and despite the party's prior organizational "dismemberment," the following anecdotes suggest that PCM militants played a grassroots leadership role in many of the early peasant movements between 1970 and 1975. At times, they even did this from behind bars.[33] For example, Ramón Danzós Palomino wrote the following "call to action" from his jail cell in Mexico's notorious Lecumberri prison in April 1970:

> We, like many other progressive forces in Mexico, argue that Agrarian Reform has not reached the end of its first phase. Despite what Zapata's detractors who are currently in power say in their efforts to . . . disorient, placate, and demobilize the peasant masses, . . . there are lands that can be redistributed to peasants. Many of these lands are in the

---

33. From jail, for example, CCI Secretary-General Ramón Danzós Palomino, Secretary Rafael Jacobo García, and Press Secretary Fernando Granados Cortes wrote a manifesto demanding (1) land and liberty; (2) the redistribution of large properties; (3) an end to government repression of peasants; and (4) constitutional reforms (*Oposición*, 5/1/70, 44). Similarly, in March 1971, Palomino published a special *Oposición* supplement from prison that purported to identify latifundistas by name and by the size of their illegal holdings in the states of Chihuahua, Sonora, Coahuila, and Guanajuato.

> irrigated districts as well as in the productive rain-fed zones. . . . For these reasons, let us honor Zapata's memory by making the 10th of April [1970] a date of revolutionary and combative struggle against those who would detract from his [Zapata's] ideals. . . . Let's also make this a date of struggle against governmental repression because the persecution of those who struggle for democracy affects the peasants' struggles for land. (*Oposición*, 4/1/70, 20)

Significantly, the evidence also indicates that PCM militants mobilized locally and semi-autonomously through debilitated local structures previously created by the party, or in new, supposedly apolitical, ones. The former is suggested by a pamphlet published in 1971 by a PCM cell in Torreón, Coahuila: "The Mexican Communist Party calls on the peasants, ejidatarios, and agricultural peons [*peones agrícolas*] to free themselves of the illusions planted by the bourgeoisie and its government. We enjoin them to organize independently to fight against the capitalist class, against the rich . . . for the liquidation of the system of oppression and exploitation to which we are subjected" (PCM, Comité Regional en La Comarca Lagunera 1971, 6).

This brash approach, however, was atypical of the period. Since Communists continued to face repression, the majority preferred to obscure their movement work with peasants in a number of ways. One way was to create local nonaffiliated movement organizations. Such was the case with Samuel Sánchez, a Communist from the state of Michoacán who was interviewed in *Oposición* just after his release from jail. Sánchez had been imprisoned in June 1973 when local authorities in Michoacán ended a rally that demanded the release of two other peasant leaders who had been taken into custody the previous day. He explained that he, along with former members of the CCI, faced governmental repression for organizing a local nonaffiliated peasant organization called the Comité de Defensa del Valle de Zamora. According to Sánchez, the government was threatened because the Comité competed with the local chapter of the CNC, leaving the latter "with virtually no base of support" (*Oposición*, 7/10/74). At that point in the early 1970s, the clandestine leadership of Communists in the Comité was unknown even to scholars of Mexico's peasant movement.[34]

---

34. Armando Bartra, for example, lists this organization among the many independent associations that emerged from "basically spontaneous" peasant struggles in the early 1970s (1977, 166–67).

Communists obscured their involvement in local peasant movements in other ways as well. According to internal party documents from the Puebla/Tlaxcala region, from 1967 through 1974, "Communists functioned in the bosom of the [peasant] movement organizations; [but] only a few retained their Party affiliation" (PCM 1977, 77). The politically independent press offers anecdotes consistent with this analysis. For example, *Excelsior* reported on a large Communist-led caravan from the Puebla/Tlaxcala region to Mexico City. About one thousand peasants and students representing seventy-two villages set out on the "Caravan for Justice and Land" in April 1972 but were stopped by army troops. *Excelsior*'s correspondent reported that a marcher angrily shouted the following demands at the tense standoff between soldiers and protestors:

> We want guarantees. We want the army to allow us to continue our caravan. For years they [state functionaries] have lied to us; we spin our wheels yet nothing comes from it. We don't have land and they rob us even when we go to the cities to sell our goods. Latifundistas title their properties under the names of family members and leave us with nothing. Their jobs pay ten to fifteen pesos for a thirteen- to fourteen-hour workday.... We are not armed. Why is the army stopping us with rifles and guns? The National Peasant Confederation protects landowners; we are not Communists.... Viva Zapata! (*Excelsior*, 4/13/72)

That Ramón Danzós Palomino headed this caravan clearly did not make all of its participants Communists, as the defensive claim that "we are not Communists" forcefully contended. However, that he and his comrades were able to lead such a large caravan with the representation of so many villages shortly after being released from jail suggests a strong following at the village level. Other examples from the independent press include that of a local CCI-Danzós peasant leader who said that he had led a land invasion in 1973 so as "to protest the agrarian authorities' negligence and bureaucratization. They [state actors] neither resolve old agrarian conflicts nor do they redistribute the lands concentrated by the rich" (*Excelsior*, 7/21/73). An *Excelsior* report a few months later quotes a peasant leader, Natalia Teniza, as maintaining that she led a land invasion because the "hacienda was a latifundio held by political elites protected by the Ministry of Agrarian Reform" and "because the Ministry of Agrarian Reform ignores our petitions [for land]" (*Excelsior*,

1/3/74). Although the journalist did not report Teniza's political sympathies, an interview that I conducted with a former leader of peasant movements identified the now deceased Teniza as having been a member of the PCM in the early 1970s (author interview, Cortez 2000).[35]

With the obvious exception of Palomino, the above examples reflect direct PCM leadership of local, but geographically dispersed, peasant movements. Because they were led by grassroots leaders, the national office offered them little by way of strategy and nothing by way of financial support. These movements, therefore, were semi-autonomous in relation to one another as well as to the national organization. This explains why Samuel Sánchez of the Comité de Defensa del Valle de Zamora remained in jail for a year until poor ejidatarios (communal farmers) from ten credit collectives raised nine thousand Mexican pesos (or about US$720) to post his bail (*Oposición*, 7/10/74). Sánchez had obviously earned the respect and loyalty of many poor peasants in Zamora, Michoacán. Remarkably, Sánchez asserted that the "primary lesson" he learned while behind bars was that "there is no other road that will help to resolve the overwhelming problems that Mexico's peasantry faces than to persist in [politically] independent struggle and organization" (*Oposición*, 7/10/74). This statement clearly illustrates Sánchez's commitment to activism regardless of the potential risks, a sentiment shared by some of his comrades upon their release from jail.

The party's dispersed militants and even its ex-cadre not only shared similar activist identities but also tended to retain the party's ideological commitment to "liberate" workers and peasants (as opposed to other subalterns, such as women, homosexuals, the disabled, etc.). Even those who joined armed guerrillas generally shared this perspective, differing from the PCM primarily on strategy and tactics rather than on the role of peasants and workers in building a better Mexico. Consequently, many guerrilla fighters eventually "made their way back into the PCM or founded new legal groupings of the left like the Corriente Socialista" (Carr 1992) or other left parties (Condés Lara 1990, 16).[36] A former PCM member who had become a leader of peasant struggles and eventually joined the now defunct Trotskyist Party explained, "Many members and ex-members of the Partido Comunista Mexicano participated

---

35. Rosario Cortez is a pseudonym.
36. The party nearly fell apart in the aftermath of 1968, mostly over strategic differences rather than ideological ones. These differences included the debates about the Mexico City student strike and whether or not to resist state repression via armed guerrilla warfare.

in the peasant movement [of the early 1970s]. While most of the youth who exited the PCM after 1968 became involved in the urban guerrilla movement, many others worked in the countryside. I was one of those who immersed myself in peasant work" (author interview, Cortez 2000).

The communist/socialist master frame insisting on the liberation of workers and peasants was shared by other left currents, such as Maoists, Trotskyists, and nonpartisan former students from the 1968 period. For example, George Collier reports that a UNAM student, Adolfo Orive Berlinguer, wrote a rather influential pamphlet in 1968 entitled *Hacia una política popular* (Toward a politics of the people). In his view, the pamphlet influenced the student movement that "decided, after 1968, to live and work with the masses to help them organize in a nonviolent struggle for socialism" (1994, 74). According to Collier,

> Former students turned to the poor in the urban neighborhoods and rural communities of central and northern Mexico, and to the rank and file of teachers' and workers' unions, to build movements that would seek [to] improve . . . [the] living and working conditions for people who had previously been ignored by society. In its rural efforts, the movement met with particular success in collective ejidos among the Yaqui and Mayo Indians of Sinaloa and Sonora and by establishing member-run credit and marketing organizations to circumvent exploitation by merchants, middlemen, and usurers. (1994, 74)

La Botz corroborates the importance of Orive Berlinguer's pamphlet for UNAM students, adding that the young author was a Maoist leader (1995, 32–33). According to La Botz, "The followers of Orive, known as the Popular Politics or later the Proletarian Line tendency, spread through Mexico building grassroots organizations. Maoist organizers succeeded in establishing political groups in rural communities, urban slums, and labor unions throughout Mexico. . . . In Monterrey, Durango and Zacatecas, Maoist activists led demonstrations and land seizures" (La Botz 1995, 33).

Since the ideological divide between PCM cadre, ex-cadre, and partisan and nonpartisan leftists was not great, the left sometimes overcame its factionalism to work together around specific mobilizations. Indeed, according to Luisa Paré, "one of the most important developments in this period was the emergence of regional coalitions ('fronts'), composed of students, workers, and peasants" (1990, 84–85). So, when the PCM's national peasant leaders were released from jail in the early 1970s, they quickly mobilized to link the various conflict networks to which they were connected. Ramón Danzós Palomino was especially well connected to other leftists given the leadership role he played in the left unity movement MLN in the 1960s. In July 1972, for example, *Oposición* organized a one-day conference (*reunión*) on the growing peasant conflicts throughout the country. Twenty-six "authentic" peasant leaders representing small and large villages from more than eight states (Sinaloa, Chihuahua, Durango, Coahuila, Tamaulipas, Michoacán, Tlaxcala, and Oaxaca, among others) attended. During this conference, Rafael Jacobo García exclaimed,

> They [the government] charge us with instigating peasant actions. This is the truth. Peasants have every right to act in this way and we to support them. . . . In the short time since our release from jail, *we have traveled throughout the country to create unity among millions of peasants as well as other forces to resolve the land problem*; it is known that we led the Puebla/Tlaxcala as well as Mexico City marches. We're also negotiating with peasant leaders, some of whom are UGOCM members, so that we can organize joint actions to help solve these [land] problems. (*Oposición*, 7/15/72, 8; emphasis added)

At the conference, Palomino was likewise quoted as saying, "The current struggles help backward groups to organize and struggle; our task is to motivate such groups to participate [in the struggle]. We need to convince them that only independent, organized, and combative struggles can provide solutions" (*Oposición*, 7/15/72, 8).

Thus, between 1967 and 1973, PCM militants worked with their networks of ex-cadre youth as well as politically independent, but sympathetic, peasants and former students from the 1968 generation. Together, they led land invasions at the grassroots level in eleven of the country's thirty states:[37] Sonora, Sinaloa, Chihuahua, Durango, Zacatecas, Coahuila, Tamaulipas, Puebla, Tlaxcala, Michoacán, and Oaxaca. The PCM's networks accomplished this by working through weakened formal structures previously created by the party; these included local PCM cells or local units of its peasant

---

37. I exclude Mexico City, as it is neither a state nor an agrarian place.

front, the CCI-Danzós. More informally, local Communists skirted state repression by creating fronts that appeared to be politically independent because the leaders obscured their communist identities. Other leaders simply immersed themselves in peasant struggles without advertising either current or former PCM affiliation or sympathies. These multiple reactive strategies therefore ensured that the peasant movements would be semi-autonomous. Aware of this, the PCM's national peasant leaders tried to link (and possibly control) them by traveling directly to where the action was and by organizing conferences. These extralocal communications undoubtedly facilitated the rapid expansion of the movement by creating a space in which militants shared their political experiences.

This argument does not imply that PCM networks led every land invasion in the country or were hegemonic among the peasantry. As noted, other left currents, such as the Maoist Línea Proletaria, were influential among peasants in Durango, Coahuila, Nuevo León, and later Chiapas (La Botz 1995, 33). According to Foweraker, from 1974 on, the Línea Proletaria became "the Union of Unions, one of the most successful peasant organizations in the [Chiapas] region" (1993, 88–89). Similarly, nonpartisan former students of the 1968 generation were successful in organizing peasants among the Native Americans (Yaqui and Mayos) in Sinaloa and Sonora (Collier 1994, 73).

Rather than imply that the PCM was hegemonic in the countryside, the following quantitative analysis will attempt to tease out where it was influential at the start of the cycle of protest, from 1970 to 1975. Specifically, I ask whether the above anecdotes are exhaustive of the role of PCM militants in the peasant protests or whether they are just the tip of the iceberg.

## The PCM's Peasant Bases of Support

I address the question of the extent of PCM influence with quantitative data permitting a cross-tabulation of the extent of peasant protest per state between 1970 and 1975 by whether or not the PCM had organized peasant bases in those states. As mentioned, data on peasant protest are drawn from a random sample of 221 cases in *Excelsior* newspaper reports that ran from January 1970 through December 1975 (see appendix B). I excluded cases of peasant protest reported by the communist media unless such reports appeared independently in my *Excelsior* sample. Since *Excelsior*'s reports did not systematically identify the municipality in which the protests occurred, I was forced to carry out a state-level analysis. While an ecological analysis with such large units is inconclusive, state-level comparisons can suggest patterns. For example, if the states with communist peasant bases were those with low levels of peasant protest, then it would be reasonable to infer that the Communists' reports documented isolated incidents. If, on the other hand, they were the states with high rates of peasant protest, it would be reasonable to infer that these reports represented only a fraction of actual protests.

I rely on several sources for information about Communist-organized peasant bases.[38] The anecdotes cited above provide evidence of the survival of some form of Communist-organized peasant structure in the following eleven states: Sonora, Sinaloa, Chihuahua, Durango, Zacatecas, Coahuila, Tamaulipas, Puebla, Tlaxcala, Michoacán, and Oaxaca. Both scholarly and official histories of the party corroborate that the rural areas of these states can be classified as communist strongholds. These sources further reveal that Communists organized large numbers of peasants in the states of Veracruz,[39] Morelos,[40] and Guerrero.[41] Thus, a total of fourteen states were coded "1" for having large Communist-organized peasant bases between 1967 and 1973.

Table 6 is a percentage distribution of states with high, average, and low levels of peasant protest between 1970 and 1975, as determined by whether Communists had organized peasant bases in these states between 1967 and 1973. Since these data comprise the population of Mexican states, the magnitude of difference between states is descriptive of the first half of the 1970s. The table clearly suggests that the states with the highest levels of peasant protest were eight times more likely to be those in which Communists had previously organized peasant bases (50 percent) than the states in which Communists had not (6 percent). Similarly, the states with the lowest levels of peasant protest were generally those without any previously organized communist peasant structures (47 percent) as opposed to the states with such structures (7 percent). The statistically significant Pearson chi-square value

38. Unfortunately, data on the size and the exact location of the PCM's rural membership are nonexistent, given the informality and even clandestine nature of its cadre's rural activism.
39. On peasants from the state of Veracruz, see Carr (1992).
40. The PCM maintained close ties to the guerrillero Rubén Jaramillo of Morelos and his followers (Martínez Verdugo 1985, 320).
41. Lucio Cabañas was a member of the PCM until 1970, and it supported him even after he founded the Poor People's Party (with Genaro Vázquez) in 1971. Although the PCM generally rejected the strategy of armed struggle, it backed Cabañas because, according to Martínez Verdugo, the Poor People's Party engaged in armed struggle in self-defense (Martínez Verdugo 1985).

Table 6  Distribution of thirty-one Mexican states with peasant protest, 1970 to 1975, by whether Communists had organized peasant bases from 1967 to 1975

|  | States with high levels of peasant protest | States with average levels of peasant protest | States with low levels of peasant protest | Number of states |
|---|---|---|---|---|
| States with communist peasant bases | 50% | 43% | 7% | 14 (100%) |
| States without communist peasant bases | 6% | 47% | 47% | 17 (100%) |
| Number of states | 8 | 14 | 9 | 31 |
| Pearson $\chi^2$ | 10.03* (df = 2) | | | |

NOTE: Communist organized peasant bases include local chapters of the CCI-Danzós, PCM rural cells, and communist peasant fronts.

*$p$ = .007 (two-tailed test)

of 10.03 with 2 degrees of freedom strongly suggests that Communists and their previously organized bases of supporters were systematically involved in the peasant movements. However, such early and systematic involvement does not tell us whether it was determined by—or, as I expect, the determinant of—peasant protests. To answer this question, I must specify a model that permits assessing the possible influence of communist networks net of other theoretically relevant causal factors.

*Specifying the Model*

Moral economy theory predicts that the landlessness, near landlessness, and rural unemployment of those displaced by the encroachment of capitalist markets on land helped incite the peasant revolts of the early 1970s (A. Bartra 1977; Canabal Cristiani 1984; Montes de Oca Luján 1977; Rubio 1987; Esteva 1983). It is possible, therefore, that party militants merely rode a wave of "defensive" peasant protests spawned by the expansion of land and labor markets, since those protests typically demanded land (the peasants' traditional means of subsistence).

Another possibility is that Communists and ex-Communists simply joined peasants who were already organized in preexisting community structures, such as communal villages (both ejidos and comunidades). Not only is the political and economic identity of ejidos and comunidades communal (whereby their rights and obligations vis-à-vis the state are corporate, not individual, and villagers must petition for credit as a corporate unit), but they were obviously also social units. As such, they can be expected to have exhibited a high degree of political solidarity.

A final possibility is that Luis Echeverría encouraged land invasions by rewarding them with land. As noted, despite his initial rejection of land reform, "Echeverría was eventually forced to cede large tracts of illegally concentrated land to thousands of peasants in the heart of some of Mexico's most fertile irrigated districts" (Fox and Gordillo 1989, 141). It is therefore feasible that his belated land reform policy, once underway, constituted a type of "political opportunity," suggesting both "elite allies" and selective incentives for protest.

The fully specified model thus examines the extent to which peasant revolts were influenced by communist peasant bases net of the economic crisis, the extent of prior communal organization, and Echeverría's land expropriations.[42]

*Data, Measurement, and Estimation*

The dependent variable in the ordinary least squares (OLS) regression is measured either as "all peasant protests" or as "protests for land." As we saw from the qualitative evidence, Communists and ex-Communists were concerned with state repression. Thus, while some may concede that Communists led the most militant protests, the less politicized land invasions might still be regarded as expressing "spontaneous agrarianism." I explore both possibilities.

The 1970 General Population Census defines the rural unemployed as those who were searching for employment in agriculture, ranching, forestry, fishing, or hunting at the time of the census but who had worked at some point during 1969 (Secretaría de Industria y Comercio 1972b, 972–80). While

42. The estimated linear regression is $P = a + b(U) + b(MinXCon) + b(C) + b(CPB) + b(HE) + e$, where P represents all peasant protest per state, U represents the number of unemployed agricultural workers, MinXCon represents the interaction of minifundistas vulnerable to subsistence crises with the extent of land concentrated by agrarian capitalists, C represents the indigenous organizational base in peasants' communal organization, CPB represents previously organized communist peasant bases, HE represents the number of hectares expropriated from private agrarian proprietors, and e is the error term.

government censuses routinely underestimate rural unemployment, this measure is the best available because it makes comparisons between states possible. With data from the Agricultural, Ranching, and Ejido Census (Secretaría de Industria y Comercio 1975), I computed an interaction term for the number of smallholders vulnerable to subsistence crises by the total amount of land in a state comprising capitalist units of production. Vulnerable minifundismo, or smallholding, is both a direct measure of near landlessness and a proxy measure of landlessness because minifundistas are those most likely to sell, rent, or simply abandon their land for more secure forms of livelihood. Following the Comisión Económica para América Latina (CEPAL), I defined vulnerable minifundistas as those whose parcels were less than or equal to four hectares of rain-fed land or its equivalent in 1970 (CEPAL 1982, 100–102). Capitalist units of production, in turn, were measured as those units of private property composed of at least one hundred "workable" hectares.[43]

Using data from the Agricultural, Ranching, and Ejido Census (Secretaría de Industria y Comercio 1975), I measured communal organization as the number of ejidos and comunidades per state. To control for a state's size and degree of agricultural production, I treated communal units of production as a percentage of the state's total units of production. Finally, I examined every *Diario Oficial* presidential decree announcing land expropriated from private proprietors (either individuals or families). I measured expropriations by the number of hectares taken because this was, in some states, far greater than either the frequency of expropriations or the number of individuals whose land was expropriated. I rescaled these data by multiplying the number of land invasions per year by ten and dividing the number of hectares expropriated per year by one thousand.

A significant problem with employing an OLS regression with a small sample is that the regression coefficients are sensitive to outliers. To identify outliers, I separately plotted the dependent variable against each of the independent variables. In all of the plots, the state of Tlaxcala was always aberrant. When I included this case in the regression analysis, the variable "states with communist peasant bases, 1967–73," not only appeared to have the strongest effects but was the only variable with statistical significance ($p = .05$, one-tailed test). I thus disadvantaged only my theory by omitting the state of Tlaxcala; the resulting analysis is of thirty unweighted cases.

---

43. This is land dedicated to crops and pasture, even if fallow during the census year.

## Explaining Net Difference

Table 7 presents the metric coefficients for an OLS regression of the net differences of *all* peasant protests on the independent variables. I carry out a five-step regression analysis. The base model, model 1, presents the effects of two variables, unemployment and the interaction of vulnerable minifundista production and land concentration by large capitalist proprietors. Model 2 presents the effects of the relative size of the communal sector in a state, model 3 presents the effects of previously organized communist peasant bases, and model 4 tests the hypothesis that Luis Echeverría's expropriations spurred peasant protests for land. Finally, model 5 shows the effects of the full model with protests for land (rather than *all* peasant protests) as the dependent variable.

Since my data comprise the population of Mexican states, the magnitude of the coefficients describes the effects of the independent variables on the peasant protests of the first half of the 1970s. Table 7 clearly shows that net of the strong effects of the peasants' subsistence crisis (measured as the degree of rural unemployment and the interaction effect of land concentration and

Table 7 Metric coefficients for OLS regression of net differences of all peasant protests on key independent variables, thirty Mexican states, 1970–75

| Independent variable | Model 1 | Model 2 | Model 3 | Model 4 | Model 5 |
|---|---|---|---|---|---|
| Unemployment | 3.77** | 3.89** | 3.48** | 3.47** | 2.57** |
| Interaction of minifundismo and land concentration | 2.18** | 2.18** | 2.07** | 2.07** | 1.36** |
| Prior communal organization | — | 0.09 | 0.10 | 0.11 | 0.04 |
| States with communist peasant bases, 1967–73 | — | — | 2.27* | 2.50 ($p = .07$) | 2.41* |
| Hectares expropriated | — | — | — | −0.28 | — |
| Intercept | −0.36 | −0.88 | −1.30 | −1.31 | −1.32 |
| $R^2$ | 0.69 | 0.70 | 0.73 | 0.73 | 0.67 |
| Adjusted $R^2$ | 0.67 | 0.66 | 0.68 | 0.67 | 0.62 |
| F change | — | 0.17 | 2.82* | 0.09 | 4.24** |

NOTE: The dependent variable in model 5 is protests for *land* rather than all peasant protests.

*$p < .05$; **$p < .01$ (one-tailed tests)

concomitant minifundismo), only the variable "states with communist peasant bases, 1967–73," had a large and statistically significant effect on protest. The small and statistically insignificant coefficient for the peasants' indigenous communal organizations (0.09) in model 2 was clearly not an improvement over model 1. This suggests that ejidos and comunidades are, by themselves, insufficient sources of solidarity for high-risk political activism. Further, model 4 shows that the land expropriations were not the political opportunity to peasant rebellion that they have been widely theorized to be. Indeed, fig. 4 illustrates the inverse relationship between the land expropriations and the peasant protests as suggested by the statistically insignificant negative coefficient (-0.28) associated with hectares expropriated in model 4.[44] Specifically, it indicates that the land invasions rose not with the government's expropriations of private proprietors but when the redistribution of land declined. It thus appears that peasants demobilized when they were promised land.

As models 3 and 5 clearly show, net of the effects of rural unemployment (which contributed about 3.5 protests for every ten thousand rural unemployed), as well as the interaction effect of minifundismo and latifundismo (which contributed about 2 protests for every unit increase in this interaction term), there were generally a little more than two additional protests in the states in which Communists had previously organized peasant bases of support than in the states where they had not. The significant F-change statistics associated with the variable "states with communist peasant bases, 1967–73," in both model 3 (F-change statistic = 2.82) and model 5 (F-change statistic = 4.24) provide better explanations for the variance than the base models do. These results strongly suggest that prior communist organization had a long-term influence on their supporters' mobilization potential; as such, land invasions were not just an expression of "spontaneous agrarianism." Further, the evidence implies that local PCM leaders and their supporters were not merely riding a wave of unrest but were an independent force impelling it.

Consistent with this picture is the fact that the PCM's membership grew an average of roughly 35 percent in the first four years of the 1970s (Condés Lara 1990, 75). In the Puebla/Tlaxcala region, which witnessed mass student and peasant mobilizations, the growth in the PCM's membership was

---

44. Land invasions and the government's expropriations began to positively correlate only in 1974, *after* the peasantry had already created a "national security problem" (*Excelsior*, 6/23/73). It appears, then, that land invasions led to the expropriations, rather than the other way around.

estimated at roughly 700 percent (PCM 1977, 77–78). Significantly, about half of the people who joined the party after 1972 had never before been PCM members (Martínez Nateras 1980, 40). They were, in other words, recruited from the movements in which PCM militants worked. Samuel Sánchez explained that in Michoacán, the "independent" leadership provided to peasants by the Comité de Defensa del Valle de Zamora drew noncommunist peasants into the Comité; in turn, the Comité fed peasants into the CCI's local chapters and ultimately into the PCM (*Oposición*, 7/10/74).

This is not to say that the PCM controlled all peasant movements or that it was responsible for every land invasion. Internal PCM documents illuminate the dynamics. In a self-critical report to the Central Committee that describes the involvement of PCM members in a clearly resurgent peasant movement, the PCM's national leader, Arnoldo Martínez Verdugo, bemoans the party's organizational inability to coordinate the local peasant protest in a strategic national campaign. The report is critical of the party's rural comrades and sympathizers for immersing themselves in peasant struggles independently of any political orientation (i.e., party line), coordination, or material resources from the national office:

> The Puebla and Tlaxcala march to Mexico City [discussed earlier], the land invasions in Puebla, Tlaxcala, and Sinaloa, the movements in Zamora and other regions of Michoacán, highlight the reactivation [of the peasant movement]. This is reflected in the reactivation of the CCI and other peasant organizations.
>
> The peasant movement's drive [*impulso*] is related to *our* elaboration of slogans that speak directly to the current agrarian problem and to the efficient effort of organizing and politically mobilizing peasants. The Party's organized work in the countryside is both retarded [*grave retraso*] and is without a clear [national] orientation about such problems as land invasions, which unfold either spontaneously or with the isolated help of the Party's rural organizations. (PCM 1973, 190; emphasis added)

Thus, the peasant protests of the first half of the 1970s were not controlled by the PCM, nor were they spontaneous. The evidence is clear that many of the PCM's local cadre and sympathizers led land invasions and that, in so doing, they helped give shape and momentum to a resurgent peasant movement.

## Conclusion

While Luis Echeverría's policies may have signaled a propeasant populist stance, his management of the unarmed land revolts was more repressive than has been previously understood. In the context of an expanding dirty war beyond the state of Guerrero, rural protest engendered at least as many political liabilities as political opportunities (at least until November 1975). Although the dirty war had succeeded in dismembering the 1968 student movement and the PCM, neither former students from the 1968 period nor former or existing PCM militants opted out of high-risk political action.

To the contrary, 1968 was a historical turning point because of the legitimacy crisis that multiplied political oppositions, some more radical than others. As I argued in the previous chapter, the political repression of 1968 radicalized many students by deepening their ideological commitment to social justice and high-risk political activism. Consequently, when the fires of student protest were extinguished in Mexico City, numerous youth participated not only in armed guerrillas (Shapira 1977; Ulloa Bornemann 2007) but also in the nonviolent peasant movements from the 1970s through the close of the 1980s (see Monsiváis 1987; Foweraker 1990, 9).[45] Whether they were originally influenced by the PCM or the nonpartisan pamphlet written by a socialist UNAM student in 1968, such former students often chose to immerse themselves in nonviolent peasant activism.

The evidence also highlighted the role of PCM cadre and ex-cadre. It showed that at the grassroots level, PCM members and sympathizers were consistently among the early risers in local peasant movements despite their lack of material resources and the risks of disappearing or being jailed or even killed. I argued that such local Communists worked closely with sympathetic networks of radical youth and peasants. Individual PCM cadre and ex-cadre protested despite repression not because they were mobilized by a national party but because they had genuinely internalized many of the party's political values. The PCM had cultivated among its members and sympathizers activist identities and an ideological antagonism to large landholding that even jail sentences could not destroy. Its political vision included the ideological commitment to land reform and to such politically disruptive direct action tactics as land invasions and marches.

45. On unions, see Pérez Arce (1990), Bennett (1993), and Collier (1994).

When state repression smashed the PCM at the national level, it succeeded in disconnecting its membership. But rank-and-file members and sympathizers retained their radical commitments and activist identities and functioned politically as dispersed conflict networks with broad peasant support. As with 1968 students, the state's ongoing repression deepened their activist identities and hardened their ideological stance against the Mexican state. In their ideological worldview, state repression was evidence that the government was unreformably "bourgeois," allied with latifundistas, and utterly corrupt.

The foregoing evidence supports Antonio Gramsci's and, more recently, Mayer Zald's contention that forms of consciousness, like movements themselves, do not emerge from nothingness. Rather, they are mobilized by social movement organizations—professionals at the manufacture of discontent. Social movement organizations, argues Zald, are central to the active processes of defining ideologies, framing grievances, and developing tactics (1996, 269). This is exactly what the PCM did, whether through its formal organizational structures (such as the CCI-Danzós and the Juventud Comunista Mexicana, JCM), through local peasant fronts, or simply informally through its grassroots participation in peasant struggles.

Even peasants who never adopted communist ideologies were influenced by the history of PCM organizing in the countryside. Communist frames about the existing social order, more than the ideal of communism, resonated with them. The government was clearly backlogged in the actual distribution of land promised in official land reform decrees, and complicated appeals processes seemed consistent with the communist frame that the Ministry of Agrarian Reform protected proven latifundistas. From the peasants' perspective, they had to prove that land was illegally concentrated to political authorities, who indeed seemed to be allied with the accused. In actual fact, the government was dependent on the international trade revenue generated by some agrarian capitalists.

Moreover, in the context of a widespread subsistence crisis, the PRI's CNC had clearly failed to adequately represent peasants (see N. Harvey 1990). The time was ripe for peasants to create their own *capacidad de gestión*. They did so via organizational instruments that were staunchly politically independent of the official corporatist associations (see N. Harvey 1990). As Neil Harvey notes about Chiapas, "Despite the often violent pressure exerted against independent opposition, resistance to co-optation has characterized each of the movements" in Chiapas and, I would add, in many places outside of Chiapas

(1990, 195). Paradoxically, these same organizations were frequently influenced, if not directly led, by members and ex-members of the PCM or other leftists. To the extent that leftist militants and ex-student radicals did not deviate from an *agrarista* agenda by trying to impose a workerist framework, peasants worked with them and, over time, their political collaboration undermined corporatism in the countryside.

In sum, the PCM's history of mobilizing rural protest significantly contributed to the political effervescence that not only brought peasants into contention with the state but, as we shall see in the next chapter, also forced agribusinessmen into political action and their own confrontation with the state.

# 4

Capitalists on the Road to Political Power in Mexico
*Class Struggle, Neopanismo, and the Birth of Democracy*

After 1968 we experienced a civic awakening and a desire to participate. The people are searching for leaders, and they obviously have begun to prefer the political vision advanced by the PAN. Indeed, we businessmen feel that we have found in the PAN a representative to defend our rights, but we do not control the party.... The crisis has created an entrepreneurial leadership.

—*José Luis Coindreau, Mexican businessman*

As noted in the previous chapter, the left's involvement in organizing peasants significantly contributed to the political effervescence that brought peasants into conflict with the state and agribusinessmen. Land invasions forced capitalists into defensive countermovements; at first, these just involved either attempting to forcibly remove the peasants from their land or relying on the state to remove them via local police or army units (see fig. 11 in appendix C). The thesis to be demonstrated in this chapter is that such interclass struggles ultimately transformed the agrarian capitalists' class and thereby contributed to Mexico's subsequent economic and political development. I argue that in order to defend themselves in the course of class conflict, businessmen created politically autonomous peak associations that functioned like radical social movement organizations. Their doing so undermined corporatism and created the organizational infrastructure with which to develop and disseminate neoliberalism, the ideology promoting the rights of private property, deregulation,

---

The epigraph is taken from Luna, Tirado, and Valdés (1987, 30).

free trade, open markets, and capitalism. While once an "alternative" ideology, neoliberalism eventually displaced the official nationalist discourse about the role of the state in developing a mixed economy.[1]

The politically autonomous peak associations that emerged in class struggles both reflected business interests and constructed them. Leaders of new peak associations violated long-held pacts between the public and private sectors in which the latter had tacitly agreed to refrain from organized political mobilization. Not only did businessmen engage in politics from the 1970s onward, but they also participated in disruptive social movements that challenged corporatism and presidentialism. They did this through the coordinating work of the Confederación Patronal de la República Mexicana (COPARMEX) and the Business Coordinating Council (CCE). In this way, then, their new peak associations sometimes functioned like social movement organizations by calling demonstrations and mobilizing resources for disruptive political protest.

Ultimately, the businessmen's mobilizations revitalized the Partido Acción Nacional (PAN). The goal of their movements, including that of the probusiness *panistas* (or *neopanistas*), was to strengthen civil society against a state they believed was potentially "totalitarian." In addition to undermining corporatism and rebuking presidentialism, radical businessmen helped democratize the country by turning the PAN into a competitive political party capable of defeating the once invincible PRI. Finally, the businessmen's increasing activism and even local electoral successes within the PAN gave them the power to help introduce neoliberal economic reforms in Mexico, a country with a nationalist history of economic protectionism and the state's direct involvement in production (i.e., a mixed economy) (see Gates 2009).

This analysis contributes to the scholarly literature on the political origins of neoliberalism in Mexico and, above all, the nascent democratization of its political system. It does so by helping to identify the concrete social forces, organizations, and institutions through which the once counterhegemonic right eventually won political power. Documenting the history and complex processes by which individual leaders and their networks built organizations and disseminated counterhegemonic ideologies adds to a growing number

---

1. Not all businessmen benefit from free trade. Several scholars point out that some small and medium-sized businesses, such as those organized by the Cámara Nacional de la Industria de la Transformación (CANACINTRA), oppose neoliberal policy (Thacker 1999, 72; Levy and Bruhn 2006, 86; Gates 2009).

of works casting doubt on the structural Marxian assumption that interests and voter allegiances are predetermined by the social structure. The evidence will illustrate that political leaders located in particular classes work hard to define and redefine their interests. They may do so, moreover, in the context of alternative, perhaps hegemonic, ideologies and discourses. It is my contention that specific class actors sharpen their analysis of their political interests during the course of social conflict with other forces. Consequently, political agendas are made (and remade) dialogically, in the context of conflict with a politically mobilized antagonist (Trevizo 2006).

## Postrevolutionary Nationalist Development in Twentieth-Century Mexico

Before explaining how social movements and their leaders helped influence economic policy and to democratize a semi-authoritarian state, I will describe the history of public-private relations that businessmen eventually restructured. The relationship between capitalists and the state during the postrevolutionary years was complicated by public officials' desire to spur capitalist development on the one hand and placate workers and peasants on the other. As noted earlier, the Revolution's Constitution of 1917 compromised between bourgeois and populist agendas because of the revolutionary role played by tens of thousands of peasants and even workers (see Knight 1986, 1:170, 619).[2] The Mexican state consequently adopted a subsidiary role in capitalist development while, at the same time, attempting to promote policy that would sufficiently appease peasants and workers.

President Lázaro Cárdenas further encoded a populist script into the national political agenda by excluding businessmen from representation in the dominant party. Not only did this exclusion ensure that populist policy that appealed to peasants and workers would be central to electoral politics, but it also defined business interests as particularistic. While businessmen historically countered that business interests served the nation via job creation, the view that business interests are private, rather than national, was consistent with Catholic ideas that tended to equate the pursuit of profit with greed. The cultural and political stigmatization of businessmen endured to

---

2. On Chihuahua, see Katz (1998, 814).

such a degree that "the persistence of inequalities in Mexico's development is blamed on *malos mexicanos* (bad Mexicans), usually members of the private sector" (Purcell and Purcell, cited in Camp 1989, 39). The "good" Mexican was defined by official nationalism as the mestizo, either peasant or worker, who worked hard to provide for the family.

A consequence of the compromise between capitalist development and populist agendas was that constitutional law retarded capitalist development in Mexico's countryside by not providing private property absolute rights (see chapter 1).[3] As noted in previous chapters, private proprietors proven to have concentrated land beyond the legal caps were subject to land expropriation. Their expropriated land was redistributed to those nearby peasant communities that could prove that they needed it.[4] Consequently, proprietors were legally limited in how they could expand agrarian production. Further, they produced with a relatively high degree of investment insecurity due to the ever-present possibility of land invasions. Peasants had an incentive to invade land because they were constitutionally entitled to it if they could prove that it was concentrated illegally. So even when markets in land expanded after 1940, land remained an unsafe investment. Despite the fact that the state also assumed the role of "principal promoter" of agrarian capitalism (de la Peña and Morales Ibarra 1989, 151; see also Grindle 1986), Mexico's countryside developed unevenly during the twentieth century.

Populist policy outside the countryside took the form of the import substitution industrialization (ISI) model of development (1940s–1982). ISI policies were nationalist. They sought to protect the nation's sovereignty by increasing industrial production within its borders, thus limiting the political leverage of core countries. Mexico's Ministry of Foreign Relations, for example, not only had to approve of foreign investment but actually limited foreign ownership to no more than 49 percent of a Mexican firm.[5] Some

---

3. With the exception of the significant increase in the number of irrigated lands built by the state, the means of agricultural production in 1940 had not developed beyond the level of the Porfiriato. As most roads remained unpaved, there was no national market (de la Peña and Morales Ibarra 1989). Consequently, agro-production was only 6 percent greater in 1940 than it had been in 1905.

4. The laws determining legal land caps changed over time but always varied according to land use (agriculture vs. pasture), land quality (arid, irrigated, temporal, mountainous, etc.), crop, and whether production was for domestic or export markets.

5. *Maquiladoras* were exceptional in that foreign companies were given 100 percent ownership. Maquila zones are export processing zones in which foreign companies set up plants that assemble parts before the firms export the finished product.

industries, such as oil[6] and banking, were excluded from foreign investment altogether. As noted, ISI policies also intended to ensure that industrial and consumer goods (with some exceptions) purchased in Mexico were made in Mexico. This was achieved by setting import quotas and tariffs, as well as by restricting licensing. Government planners believed that in substituting Mexican produced goods for imported ones they would promote national industrial growth, generate employment, and improve the standard of living for most nationals.

The government promoted national industrial development by building the infrastructure (roads, ports, airports, railroads, and electric power) necessary for markets, and by providing the credit and other inputs necessary for industrial production, tax exemptions, and the like. Between 1940 and 1970, the state's financial involvement in the economy amounted to roughly "41 percent of [all] capital formation" (Levy and Bruhn 2006, 152). During these thirty years, moreover, such policies worked. Mexico experienced an economic "miracle" in which its annual average rate of growth hovered at just above 6 percent. While Mexican industry did not grow at a rate capable of absorbing its ballooning labor force, populist policies and even temporary migration to the United States tempered the impact of persistently high unemployment and underemployment.

When signs of economic trouble began to emerge in the late 1960s (in the countryside) and early 1970s (urban centers), then-president Luis Echeverría (1970–76) further increased the state's role in the economy and even in production. The state had owned and operated about eighty enterprises prior to the 1970s, but its involvement in the direct production and redistribution of goods and services increased fourteen-fold over the course of that decade. Concretely, while the state had previously owned and operated the national oil company (Petróleos Mexicanos, PEMEX), railroads, and electricity, state ownership of firms jumped to 1,155 companies. Echeverría's presidency thus distinguished itself by its highly interventionist economic policy, which gave full substantive meaning to the ideals of a "mixed economy." The problem, however, was that foreign loans from commercial banks financed these investments (plus social spending) and, as a consequence, Echeverría's administration dramatically increased public foreign debt (from $4.2 billion in 1970 to $20 billion upon leaving office).

6. The state had owned and operated Petróleos Mexicanos (PEMEX) since 1938, when it expropriated British and U.S. oil companies.

In sum, from 1940 through the mid-1980s, the state proved to be a powerful "manager" of private capitalist accumulation in both the rural and urban centers. It was the principal promoter of agrarian capitalism despite the fact that the Constitution's concessions to peasants constrained production by limiting territorial expansion. Further, ISI policies tended to benefit private industry even if they limited firm competitiveness in the long term. This was so because while some populist policy (such as corporatist-negotiated wages) infringed on economic development, many governments after Cárdenas upheld a social pact between the public and private sector that favored businessmen.

## The Businessmen's Pact

Given their formal exclusion from the ruling party and stigmatized place in nationalist political discourse, most businessmen agreed to refrain from organized political activity.[7] In exchange, they relied on more direct, but always discrete, ways of influencing economic policy (Luna, Tirado, and Valdés 1987, 40; Camp 1989, 47; Shadlen 2000). From the 1930s on, businessmen were legally required to join trade-specific associations. For this reason, Mexico's president and other state officials had the capacity to articulate even the business interests of those semi-official corporatist associations technically excluded from the PRI (see fig. 2). The law had coercive power because government officials granted permits and licenses; they could also audit or force an inspection, limit wage increases, and declare strikes illegal. Further, the Ministry of Agrarian Reform was responsible for investigating violations of land tenancy laws, expropriating land from large private proprietors for such violations, and granting private landowners official guarantees against expropriation (called *certificados de inafectabilidad*). While some businessmen felt coerced into joining a trade association, most joined voluntarily because businessmen benefited from cooperative relations with the government (see Shadlen 2000, 86, 89).

In addition to being regularly, if discretely, consulted about policy, businessmen had grown accustomed to proposing economic policy directly to Mexico's presidents (Hansen 1971, 108; Levy and Bruhn 2006, 83). As noted,

---

7. COPARMEX proved to be an important exception.

post-Cárdenas governments spurred industrial and especially agrarian capitalism. Not only was state policy, especially after 1940, responsible for infrastructural development, credit, green revolution technologies, and the like (Rubio 1987, 44–45), but at least one president (López Mateos, 1958–64) repressed the railroad workers' strike and jailed many of its communist leaders on the grounds that he had to protect economic growth.

In short, the Mexican state's historic commitment to nationalist economic development sought to promote capitalism within the confines of placating the ruling party's most loyal voters—workers and peasants. The state forced businessmen to consent to a social pact in which they accepted a junior partner status in the joint project of capitalist development. According to Abruch Linder's colorful description, despite becoming "economic giants," businessmen remained "political dwarfs" (*enanos*) (1983, 25) until Luis Echeverría's left-leaning interpretation of ISI altered the terms of the businessmen's pact. When this occurred, businessmen mobilized in defensive, but highly disruptive, countermovements. They ultimately led their movement into the PAN, the political party that would eventually defeat the PRI. As I demonstrate below, the PAN emerged as a serious political force only because capitalists were forced into defensive countermovements during what businessmen refer to as the "twelve tragic years" (*docena trágica*) of the Echeverría and López Portillo administrations.

## Class Struggle and the Self-Organization of Capitalists

By 1975, the rising tide of local land invasions described in chapter 3 had become a national-level phenomenon (Trevizo 2002). As indicated in fig. 4, Echeverría expropriated large quantities of land only after peasant protest reached a crescendo in his last fourteen months in power. As I have concluded elsewhere, the state redistributed land from some of the most productive agrarian capitalists in direct proportion to the peasants' level of political disruption (Trevizo 2006). For example, in the month of November 1975, Echeverría expropriated thirty-five thousand hectares from wealthy agrarian capitalists in the states of Sinaloa and Sonora. A year later, just before leaving office, he redistributed two hundred fifty thousand hectares in Sonora. Not since Lázaro Cárdenas's presidency (1934–40) had such large quantities of arable land been expropriated from the wealthy for purposes of redistribution.

Those most affected by land invasions and expropriations responded belligerently. They challenged the state's right to intervene in the economy, as well as the state's corporatist model of interest representation. Sinaloa's agrarian capitalists, already independent from the state in the Confederation of Agricultural Associations of the State of Sinaloa (CAADES), led the way.[8] In December 1975, agrarian capitalists in Sinaloa and Sonora struck back by stopping all work on their lands. They also refused to sell their products to the government's food-buying agencies and even threatened to withdraw their money from the banks. They declared that they would not end their production strike until the government addressed "the insecurity of land tenancy due to the frequent invasions and expropriations" (*Excelsior*, 12/1/75, see also 12/2/75, 12/3/75; quoted in Trevizo 2003).

The agrarian capitalists' ideological work in this movement built on the neoliberal ideology of the radical right-wing businessmen's organization COPARMEX. Founded in 1929 to counter labor populist policy (Maxfield 1990, 55), COPARMEX was the oldest politically independent peak association. Key leaders with joint memberships in COPARMEX and CAADES began to contend that land expropriations violated the sanctity of private property. This argument was a new ideological frame, and it countered the government's and peasants' view that land expropriations were the legal outcome of breaking the law (by concentrating land beyond constitutional limits). Businessmen also argued that land expropriations were evidence of the kind of "statism" that evolves into either socialism or totalitarianism. In their view, only free markets—or capitalism—ensure individual liberty.

These ideas resonated with nonagrarian capitalists, especially those from the north. Sinaloa's merchants organized "rolling strikes" by temporarily closing the doors to their businesses on the grounds that they were defending "free enterprise." In their words, "We don't ask for anything more than respect for both private property and for the mixed economy, both of which have been severely attacked by the official sector [i.e., the state]" (*Excelsior*, 12/3/75; quoted in Trevizo 2003). Adalberto Rosas, a member of Sonora's employers' association in Ciudad Obregon, put it more boldly, arguing that the government was "taking a step toward communism. You realize that they

---

8. While agrarian capitalists live in all states of the country, agricultural exporters tend to live in the irrigated districts of the northwest, close to their principle market, the United States. Exporters of sugarcane and coffee (which ranked in the top five production values of all crops), however, lived in the south (Chiapas and Oaxaca) and along the Gulf (Veracruz).

[the government] will first do away with agrarian property and then with commerce" (*Excelsior,* 12/2/75; quoted in Trevizo 2003).

Manuel de Jesús Clouthier (1934–1989) was an important local agrarian capitalist, and as a member of COPARMEX, he had many connections to right-wing businessmen.[9] Clouthier, an expropriated agro-industrialist whose lands in Sinaloa had been invaded many times by peasants, was also a member of CAADES. In turn, CAADES led agrarian capitalists in the production strike that culminated in the founding of a politically autonomous peak association called the Unión Agrícola Nacional (UNAN). This proved to be a frontal challenge to the state's corporatist system of interest representation (Trevizo 2003). As such, the government's organizations charged that UNAN's founders were wealthy "reactionaries," and state functionaries purportedly tried to intimidate them (author interview, Lugo Chávez 1994). Clouthier resisted these pressures in part by helping UNAN's members find organizational refuge in COPARMEX, where they created a subsidiary, the Comisión Agropecuaria, that eventually evolved into the powerful Consejo Nacional Agropecuario (CNA) (author interviews: Lugo Chávez 1994; Gavito 1994; Zarazua Sandoval 1994).

Clouthier also contributed to a broader movement of capitalists seeking political independence from the state by helping to found the national-level Business Coordinating Council (CCE) in his home state in May 1975, just months before the agrarian capitalists' strike. The CCE was established for very similar reasons to UNAN: increasing class struggle and the fact that businessmen felt "attacked" (*golpeado*) by the state, which resulted in investment insecurity (Zarazua Sandoval 1994). The CCE's founding statement, for example, explicitly denounced class struggle as "antisocial" (quoted in Abruch Linder 1983, 25; see also Luna and Tirado 1992, 33). This accusation was made in the context of the kidnapping and murder of a businessman (Eugenio Garza Sada) by an urban guerrilla group (the 23rd of September Communist League, LC23S) just a year earlier, as well as the wave of land expropriations. As such, the CCE categorically supported the agrarian capitalists' strike and eventually, through Clouthier's leadership, incorporated their organization into the CCE's national umbrella structure (see fig. 5) (author interview, Lugo Chávez 1994).[10]

    9. Manuel Clouthier had been president of the Asociación de Agricultores del Río Culiacán, one of nine local associations making up CAADES. This organization helped lead agrarian capitalists from around the country into the politically independent organization Unión Agrícola Nacional (UNAN) (Trevizo 2003).
    10. The first president of the CCE, Juan Sánchez Navarro, was an industrialist whose family had held some of the largest latifundios in the country for over one hundred years (before, during,

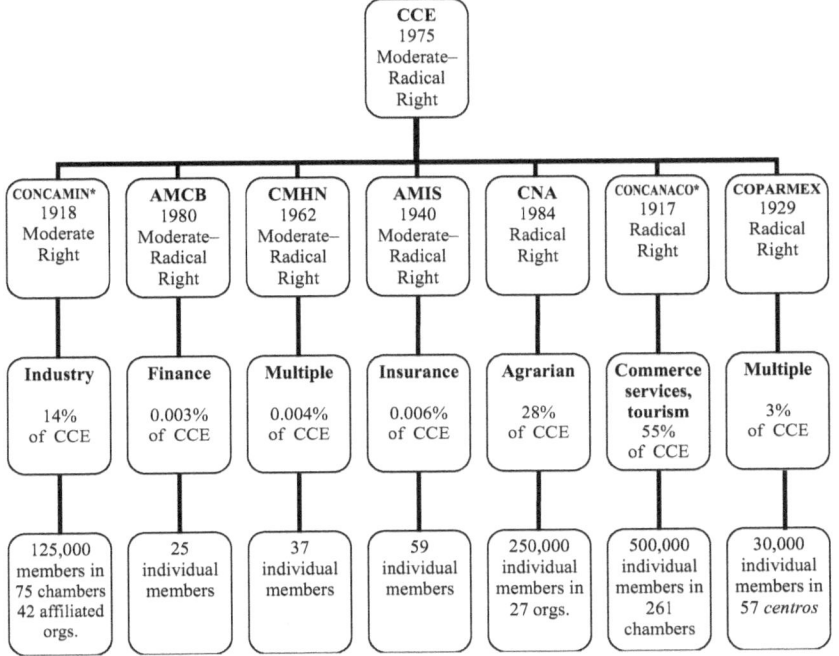

*Fig. 5* The organizational structure and political orientation of key segments of Mexico's capitalist class

SOURCE: Adapted from Luna and Tirado (1992, 34, table 1). Used with permission of the authors.

* These organizations have semiofficial status because Mexican law required membership of all but the smallest business firms in these chambers (Hansen 1971, 108).

CCE: Consejo Coordinador Empresarial (Business Coordinating Council; estimated indirect membership of 905,121 people)

CONCAMIN: Confederación de Cámaras Industriales

AMCB: Asociación Mexicana de Casas de Bolsa (formerly Asociación Mexicana de Intermediarios Bursátiles [AMIB])

CMHN: Consejo Mexicano de Hombres de Negocios

AMIS: Asociación Mexicana de Instituciones de Seguros

CNA: Consejo Nacional Agropecuario

CONCANACO: Confederación de Cámaras Nacionales de Comercio

COPARMEX: Confederación Patronal de la República Mexicana

---

and even after the Porfiriato) (Luna and Tirado 1992, 49–50). During the agrarian capitalists' strike, the CCE published at least two editorials, the more radical of which (signed by a select number of CCE state-wide federations) denounced the "arbitrary interpretation" of agrarian law that resulted in insecurity about land tenancy (read, private property). A more moderate position argued that private property in the countryside not only was a right guaranteed by constitutional law but was prosocial. It further held that only a climate of juridical security and tranquility makes for a productive agrarian sector (*Excelsior*, 12/6/75).

The CCE was essentially created to defend the business community against an increasingly interventionist state, which, in the judgment of neoliberal businessmen, seemed "in favor of establishing a totalitarian dictatorship in our country" (quoted in Abruch Linder 1983, 25). The CCE's founding statement questioned the ideals of the mixed economy by arguing that excessive state intervention in the economy was incompatible with democracy. Private property, in contrast, was described as a "natural" and inalienable right, one that the organization would defend along with other "fundamental liberties," including democracy. The CCE specifically argued that "the systematic tendency for the state to intervene as an employer constitutes a grave impediment to exercising the rights of individuals. As a guarantee that state intervention is subordinated to the demands of economic development and the common good, we need a free and effective political regime. . . . Centralized state planning of the economy is not compatible with a democratic regime" (CCE statement in May 1975, quoted in Gates 2009, 71n25).

The CCE quickly became powerful because it was founded as a national, politically independent peak association composed of other elite peak associations (see fig. 5). The CCE excluded most of the semi-official corporatist associations that gave the government unconditional political support (even when detrimental to their own financial interests) (see fig. 2).[11] By the early 1990s, the CCE represented seven distinct peak associations, and it indirectly represented nearly a million businessmen from all economic sectors, especially those owning the country's largest enterprises. According to Luna and Tirado (1992, 39), the CCE was the most representative and legitimate organization of the country's business peak associations. As such, the CCE's founding signaled the end to the era of state-business alliances and the organizational constitution of capitalists as a class for "themselves" (Luna 1992, 46–47).

By forming the CCE, capitalists undermined corporatism and created an organization that would effectively articulate and represent capital. This organization, and especially its radical leaders, proactively developed neoliberal ideas and politics. For example, in addition to funding research institutes (such as the Instituto Mexicano de Estudios Políticos, 1970), the CCE developed its own Social Studies Research Center (the Centro de Estudios Sociales)

---

11. The CCE excluded the Confederación Nacional de la Pequeña Propiedad (CNPP), the Confederación Nacional Ganadera (CNG), la Confederación Nacional de Cámaras del Pequeño Comercio (CNPC), the Cámara Nacional de la Industria de la Transformación (CANACINTRA), and the Cámara Nacional de Comercio de la Ciudad de México (CANACO-MEX).

in 1977. Its radical right subsidiary organizations followed suit: the Confederación de Cámaras Nacionales de Comercio (CONCANACO) developed the Coordinación de Ideología e Imagen in 1980, around the same time that COPARMEX's ex-presidents, at Manuel Clouthier's suggestion, began to train businessmen from all over the country in leadership skills (in a Programa de Liderazgo Empresarial). Between 1980 and 1982, COPARMEX taught two thousand businessmen to become civically engaged as an opposition leadership. In the words of one of its former presidents, COPARMEX was and is a "training school" (*escuela de formación*) that taught "extraordinary people" in the period even before the banks were nationalized (José Luis Coindreau García, quoted in Oppenheim 2004a, 13–14).

Interclass struggles, in short, forced capitalists into defensive countermovements that ultimately transformed their entire class. They sought political and organizational independence from the state, which, they argued, promoted class struggle and failed to represent them. Businessmen understood that state officials would always side with the PRI's voters, peasants, and workers, especially in the context of their mobilization. Thus, corporatism failed businessmen politically because, in their view, they were always forced into negotiating with a "united front" of public officials and the party's electorally supportive labor/peasant clients. In the words of one agrarian capitalist, official corporatist organizations were "affiliated with a political party which gave them the political line, one which frequently went against the very interests of their members [owners of private property]. This is corporatism. Because of corporatism, a group of producers headed by Manuel Clouthier took the initiative and decided to jump over these [corporatist organizations] to form their own organization, one which would be an authentic interlocutor, truthful, legitimate, and valid vis-à-vis the country's agrarian producers" (author interview, Lugo Chávez 1994).

Clouthier and other radical businessmen thus undermined corporatism, one of the central pillars of Mexico's version of authoritarianism. Their autonomous peak associations functioned like radical social movement organizations, both in developing neoliberalism as an alternative ideology and, as we will see below, in mobilizing businessmen in defense of their class. Through the politically independent organizations they created, these men articulated ideas about the sanctity of private property, free markets, and trade; they also argued that centralized state planning of the economy was incompatible with democracy. As this chapter will show, they used their organizations to mobilize businessmen and thereby confront the state with politically disruptive collective action. Over time, their neoliberal ideas would displace the official discourse about the role of the state and the mixed economy in national(ist) development.

## The México en Libertad Movement Attacks Presidentialism

While initially quite successful in rebuilding business confidence in the state, President José López Portillo (1976–82), Echeverría's unopposed successor, ultimately alienated capitalists from all economic sectors when he nationalized the banks. When López Portillo began his term, he attempted to fix the agricultural production problems by borrowing $325 million from the World Bank for his program Sistema Alimentario Mexicano (SAM). Then, after discovering new oil fields, López Portillo spent liberally on public works projects, social welfare, construction, and even food and consumer goods. In order to do this, he borrowed from foreign banks on the assumption that oil revenues would pay the rapidly growing international debt.[12] But instead of rising, oil prices declined sharply in the early 1980s. Meanwhile, Mexico's double-digit annual rate of inflation kept rising (to about 30 percent in 1981), while unemployment (at 25 percent) and underemployment remained high. In 1982, for example, fully half of the work force was underemployed.

In this context, leftists, including the Mexican Communist Party (PCM), led large demonstrations that apparently created the appearance of political instability (see the interviews with José Luis Coindreau and José María Basagoiti in Oppenheim 2004a and 2004b). Fig. 1 not only shows a second large wave of protest activity in this period but clearly indicates that workers and poor people were the primary actors in this movement. Their protests were not dispersed across the countryside, but rather, large numbers of workers and poor people protested in the urban centers, including Mexico City. In response, López Portillo raised the minimum wage by 30, 20, or 10 percent, depending on workers' base salary; he did so, moreover, in the context of peso devaluations. Consequently, Mexican businessmen withdrew money from their banks and invested it abroad. To prevent even greater capital flight (estimated at $22 billion), López Portillo nationalized fifty-nine of the country's banks on September 1, 1982, just months before leaving office.

---

12. The international debt nearly tripled from $20 billion in 1976 to $59 billion in 1982.

Given their leadership of both the CCE and COPARMEX, as well as their prior history of struggles against "statism," it was two agrarian capitalists, rather than bankers, who led the confrontation with the state over the nationalization of the banks (Loaeza 1987; Luna 1992, 84).[13] Manuel Clouthier, as president of the CCE, and José María Basagoiti, as president of its powerful subsidiary organization, COPARMEX, provided their organizations with some of the most decisive intellectual and political leadership of the business opposition.[14] In particular, they used these independent peak associations to organize a production strike and eventually to mobilize a movement called México en Libertad (Mexico in Freedom). According to Clouthier, the production strike sought to ensure that Mexico "would remain a free society" by preventing it from moving further toward a "totalitarian, communist, Marxist-Leninist state" (quoted in Abruch Linder 1983, 27). The CCE maintained that the banks' "expropriation is a definitive step toward the statification of the country's economy. Statification means inefficiency, bureaucratization, corruption, and is a totalitarian threat [*amenaza totalitaria*]. . . . The statification of the banks is a definitive attack on private enterprise and clearly signals that the country is now socialist [*una señala clara de la entrada del país al socialismo*]" (quoted in Abruch Linder 1983, 27).

Similarly, José María Basagoiti, COPARMEX's president, argued that the nationalization of banks was evidence that the country was moving toward socialism and that it was happening according to "Lenin's script: a surprise single blow" (quoted in Luna 1992, 71). Twelve years later, Alberto Núñez Esteva (a founding member of the CNA and eventual president of COPARMEX) agreed, arguing, "Mexico was moving to the left with the number of paraestatals [state firms], and the economy was controlled by the government. Mexico had moved toward the socialist left, and the bank nationalization consolidated this socialist position. This was a shock, and we were all profoundly worried and unhappy [*disgustados*]. . . . The Chamber of Deputies did not challenge the president on a decision that a president had no right to make. Such actions must be part of a legislative process. So that presidential action made fun of the Constitution. It was presidentialism" (1994). Radical

---

13. While not exclusively an agrarian capitalist, José María Basagoiti had tobacco interests, the key input for his companies Cigarros la Tabacalera Mexicana, S.A., and Mexican Tobaccos, S.A.

14. Clouthier served as president of COPARMEX from 1978 to 1980, and José María Basagoiti took over shortly thereafter (1982-84), around the time that Clouthier led the CCE (1981-83).

businessmen further held that the bank nationalization was the outcome of state policy that led to class struggle. The president of the politically more moderate Confederación de Cámaras Industriales (CONCAMIN) (see fig. 5) went so far as to state publicly that the government was attempting to make businessmen "an extinct class" (quoted in Luna 1992, 72).

To defend their class, Manuel Clouthier and José María Basagoiti mobilized local-level CCE and COPARMEX resources for México en Libertad meetings and rallies held in various cities. Their movement was both defensive and progressive. Significantly, its leadership began to argue that the separation of powers in Mexico was necessary in part "to avoid the class struggle" (quoted in Abruch Linder 1983, 28). As before, businessmen rejected corporatism but now also explicitly rebuked presidentialism. Presidentialism, they noted, came with such discretionary power that a single arbitrary presidential decision could destroy them financially. They demanded the state's democratization, seeking to limit the president's discretionary powers, and advocated for administrative "transparency" and less intervention in the economy (Luna, Tirado, and Valdés 1987, 18). Additionally, businessmen argued that the power of the Mexican state "atrophied" civil society, and they concluded that it was their social obligation to lead others in a civic awakening. Thus, radical businessmen led middle-class groups of students, housewives, and professionals in a broad movement of "civil society" against the "statist" state (Luna, Tirado, and Valdés 1987, 39). Their goal was to build "a stronger civil society, defined above all by its antigovernment character" (1987, 29).

On October 25, 1982, 2,500 businessmen meeting in León, Guanajuato, decided to retreat from disruptive tactics because a new president, Miguel de la Madrid, was about to assume power (Luna, Tirado, and Valdés 1987, 19). While some leaders continued to organize short monthly boycotts,[15] others, as we shall see below, invested in a longer-term strategy to revitalize the PAN. Crucially, many businessmen would remain supportive of disparate social movements by participating in demonstrations that demanded educational reform (read, pro-religious education),[16] protesting the socialist content of

---

15. The National Front in Defense of Liberty and Human Rights (Frente Nacional para la Defensa de las Libertades y Derechos Humanos) urged the boycott of gas, government stores (such as union shops or the Compañía Nacional de Subsistencias Populares, CONASUPO, and toll roads, and encouraged its followers to delay their tax payments (Luna, Tirado, and Valdés 1987, 38).

16. For example, business organizations participated in a 1984 rally in Mexico City to support educational "freedom."

government textbooks, or opposing the feminist movement's demands to decriminalize abortion. Businessmen thus formed important alliances with many middle-class groups in their general efforts to strengthen civil society against the state.

## The Businessmen's Neoliberal Agenda for Mexico

De la Madrid's government worked hard to improve relations with most sectors of the business community (except for COPARMEX). He not only expanded some political liberties but also introduced important neoliberal reforms. He reduced government subsidies, disemployed thousands of government employees, limited wage increases, and privatized fully 735 unprofitable state-owned firms (or 64 percent of the total). De la Madrid reduced trade protections so that Mexico could join the General Agreement on Tariffs and Trade (GATT) in 1986[17] and even went so far as to do what was once unthinkable to nationalist presidents: he opened up the economy to greater foreign investment. His successor, Carlos Salinas de Gortari (1988–94), went further. Salinas privatized such profitable state-owned enterprises as steel mills, telephones, banks, the last state-owned airline, hotels, sugar refineries, and fertilizer plants (Levy and Bruhn 2006, 167). He also distinguished himself as a neoliberal *priista* (PRI-ista) by signing the North American Free Trade Agreement (NAFTA), ending subsidies, and concluding Mexico's signature land reform program. He even had the Constitution reformed to legalize the privatization of *ejido* (communal) lands. The significance of Salinas's neoliberal reforms cannot be overstated; through presidential decrees, he concluded the nationalist protectionist policies most closely identified with the Mexican Revolution. In addition to ending the legal right to land among the landless and the inalienability of social property, Salinas opened up two-thirds of the country's productive activity to unqualified foreign investment (meaning that investors could own title to 100 percent of the stock or property of the firm) (Levy and Bruhn 2006, 170). Presidents Ernesto Zedillo (1994–2000), Vicente Fox (2000–2006), and Felipe Calderón (2006–) have not deviated from this neoliberal path paved by priista governments.

17. When the WTO was established in 1995, it replaced the GATT.

While these changes are frequently seen as the outcome of the economic crisis and external U.S. pressures (Levy and Bruhn 2006, 168–71),[18] the evidence below indicates that Mexican businessmen were also at the heart of some of the country's most important neoliberal reforms. Specifically, the evidence shows that businessmen used their independent peak associations as instruments to influence the economic policy of the last three PRI governments in the twentieth century (see Gates 2009). According to Héctor Lugo Chávez, Alberto Núñez Esteva (founding member of the CNA and eventual president of COPARMEX), and Carlos Zarazua Sandoval (former director general of the CNA), all of whom I interviewed in 1994, radical businessmen were directly involved in the NAFTA negotiations.[19] Indeed, Strom Thacker's research reveals that by the end of the negotiations, young government technocrats had met with neoliberal members of the business community about 2,600 times and did so to the general satisfaction of business leaders who trusted that the government had incorporated their views (1999, 68–70; see also Kaufman, Bazdresch, and Heredia 1994, 391; Gates 2009, 76–77).

The CCE's members from the agrarian sector (the CNA) also worked directly on NAFTA's agrarian provisions. Alberto Núñez Esteva (author interview, 1994) responded to my interview question about the role played by the government's corporatist associations in the NAFTA negotiations by saying, "I believe that they had a certain presence [*cierta presencia sí*], but they did not play the leadership role played by the [agrarian capitalists of the] CNA." Not surprisingly, export statistics indicate that agrarian capitalists in Mexico benefited early on from NAFTA. In 1996, just two years after it went into effect, the trade dividends from agricultural exports to the United States grew about 50 percent, nearly reaching parity with the dividends from oil exports.

---

18. Levy and Bruhn offer a compelling case that the technocrats' rise to power within the PRI was linked to the fiscal crisis of the Mexican state. Technocrats, officials reasoned, were needed to manage the economy so as to grow the state's coffers and lead it out of bankruptcy. Levy and Bruhn state, "The crisis and budget constraints created by Mexico's debt problems encouraged the rise of economic technocrats and enhanced their ability to push through risky economic reforms" (2006, 171). They show how international debt made Mexico more "vulnerable" to U.S. pressure for economic change. In their words, "Reliance on foreign investment significantly increased Mexico's vulnerability to what international investors thought of Mexican economic policy, of Mexican political stability, even of Mexican election returns" (2006, 171).

19. Thacker (1999) makes it clear that the CCE created the Coordinadora de Organismos Empresariales de Comercio Exterior (COECE), the organization that worked with the government in the NAFTA negotiations.

Ten years later, Mexico's most important exports continued to be manufactured goods, oil (and oil products), silver, fruits, vegetables, coffee, and cotton.[20]

Significantly, Héctor Lugo Chávez (author interview, 1994) reported that the CNA "was practically the initiator of the reforms to Article 27 of the Constitution in 1992." These reforms effectively undid key laws of the Mexican Revolution because they legalized the privatization of the ejido system (Carlos Zarazua Sandoval independently concurred with this analysis in a 1994 interview). Lugo Chávez explained,

> For nearly two decades, we proposed those changes and they [the reforms] were practically enacted just as we had proposed. The Consejo [CNA] was a fundamental ideological pillar for President Salinas's reforms.... The CCE published a book [called] *Propuestas de modernización al sector agropecuario*. The book is the reforms. It was here that the Consejo was a pioneer. All of the constitutional changes... Manuel Clouthier had all that information because his property had been invaded. He was one of the victims because his famous ranch, paralelo 38, was invaded. So the first projects taken on by the Consejo that had an impact on the federal government [were] the proposal to reform Article 27 of the Constitution, the proposal of a new agrarian law, the proposal for agrarian tribunals. All of this has happened, and this was thanks to the proposals of the Consejo.... We presented the proposals to de la Madrid and also to President Salinas. The president of the CCE, with all six members that constitute the CCE, went to see him and gave him the book; the same book that we had given [former president] de la Madrid was given to [former president] Salinas.[21]

Alberto Núñez Esteva was more circumspect and politically nuanced in speaking about the degree to which the CNA influenced then-president Carlos Salinas de Gortari's thinking about the constitutional reforms. In response to my open-ended question about whether the CNA had been successful in the last ten years, Núñez Esteva said,

20. These statistics on Mexico are drawn from the CIA World Factbook, available at https://www.cia.gov/library/publications/the-world-factbook/geos/mx.html (accessed September 20, 2010).

21. Chávez was the general director of the CNA during the three years that Víctor Gavito was president.

I personally think that while we have accomplished a lot, there is still much left to do.... I believe that our proposals to the government have been very important.... Reforming Article 27 of the Constitution has been our banner [bandera] from time immemorial. On behalf of the CNA, I personally presented that part of our proposals to President Salinas [at his residence] in Los Pinos. Our position was that Article 27 needed to be reformed before such reforms were on the national political agenda [cuando no se pensaba en México reformar el artículo 27].... At that meeting, President Salinas told us that [such reforms] were both inconsistent with his way of thinking [forma de pensar] and his strategy for the countryside.... I do not mean to indicate that we convinced him [President Salinas]. That would be incredibly pretentious and false. I am sure that he was already thinking about it [of reforming the Constitution], but that he could not pursue it because there was major opposition to such changes in the Chamber of Deputies. But then there was a change in the Chamber of Deputies after his thirdyear.... That is when he reformed Article 27 of the Constitution. But there is no doubt that our support and pressure on this question helped him a great deal to have confidence that this reform was possible.... The reform went hand in hand with economic liberalization.... So our influence was that we gave the president confidence to make the changes. Our ideas that there needed to be a reform [to Article 27 of the Constitution] converged.... There was much opposition to [reforming] Article 27 on the part of those who were privileged by its management [i.e., the Ministry of Agrarian Reform, the National Peasants' Confederation]. We countered that opposition. (Author interview, Núñez Esteva 1994)

Thus, while Alberto Núñez Esteva is careful to place the passage of these historic reforms in a complicated national political context, he also specifies how the CNA's historic commitment to reform Article 27 helped the president initiate this radical change, given that many political elites preferred the status quo. The importance of a neoliberal coalition composed of promarket businessmen and select government officials, as implied by Núñez Esteva's statement, cannot be overstated. As Strom Thacker argues, such political coalitions are necessary for the implementation and long-term viability of controversial policy. He observes that no matter how popular ideology is at the international level or among key national proponents, ideology alone is insufficient for the successful passage or even long-term sustainability of policy with significant internal opposition. For this reason, "policies require the mobilization of a coalition of political support in order to be successfully implemented and sustained" (1999, 57).

Further, Núñez Esteva's firsthand account of meeting President Salinas supports Thacker (1999) and Gates (2009), who argue that government leaders worked directly with CCE business associations in articulating neoliberal preferences. For her part, Leslie Gates contends that neoliberal "businessmen mobilized two major public assaults on government through business associations (in 1975 and 1982)" and, in so doing, were no longer the state's "silent partner" in the project of capitalist development (2009, 66). She credits the CCE for successfully pressing technocratic government officials into legalizing holding companies and allowing multipurpose banks and Mexican financial markets in 1976. In her view, because of the CCE's mobilization, the government agreed to a parallel financial sector after generously compensating bankers for nationalizing their banks in 1982. Gates also argues that the CCE can be credited with trade liberalization from 1987 on, as well as for the greater international capital flows beginning in 1989 (see Gates 2009, 66, table 1).

The bank nationalization, in short, constituted a categorical rupture of the old social pact between the state and businessmen. Once radicalized, businessmen began to do what was once unthinkable: they participated in organized political activity via indiscrete protest. Eventually, technocratic government officials invited their national peak association of independent and elite peak associations, the CCE, to the negotiation table. When this happened, businessmen helped marginalize more nationalistic government officials as well as protectionist corporatist business organizations (see Gates 2009, 76–77). As such, the CCE's political actions contributed to the dramatic 180 degree turn in economic policy, as witnessed in the rejection of ISI protectionist policies and the adoption of neoliberalism. This is an important point because, with few exceptions, the role of homegrown Mexican businessmen in pressing for neoliberal economic policies has been overlooked both by arguments about economic globalization and by arguments stressing the role of U.S.-trained technocrats purportedly operating as autonomous state agents (Babb 2001). I have argued that Mexican businessmen's independent push for economic liberalization constituted the kind of political support on which technocrats depended and which they used to push for neoliberal economic policy (Thacker 1999, 63; Gates 2009). Further, I propose that the confluence of international and national interests for neoliberalism may indeed help explain the paradox that Mexico adopted neoliberal economic policies earlier than many other Latin American countries despite the fact that it transitioned to democracy more slowly than most.

Finally, while the social movements of neoliberal businessmen were clearly and successfully defensive of capital, they were also progressive in their explicit calls for democracy. As demonstrated earlier, the México en Libertad movement frontally challenged presidentialism, the second pillar of Mexico's version of authoritarianism, and businessmen proved that they were capable of confronting state power. In addition to undermining corporatism and rebuking presidentialism, radical businessmen contributed to democratizing the country in the electoral arena. As we will see below, businessmen revitalized the PAN, the only right-wing political alternative to the ruling party (Hernández Rodríguez 1986; Luna, Tirado, and Valdés 1987, 29–32; Valdés Ugalde 1997; Chand 2001; Shirk 2005).

## Democratizing Mexico via the PAN: Capitalists on the Road to State Power

After the nationalization of the banks, radical businessmen led their social base into the PAN, turning the party into a real electoral force as well as a social movement organization. The PAN was founded in 1939, during a period of intense class struggle, as a reaction against President Lázaro Cárdenas's left-wing populist policies. At its founding, the party adopted an anticommunist stance and was critical of the state's involvement in the economy, the ejido system, and even the degree of presidential power in Mexico. The party shifted moderately to the left after Vatican II and was influenced by the Catholic left of the 1960s. During its Christian democratic phase (1950–72), the PAN concerned itself with such social justice issues as economic redistribution, human rights, women's workplace rights, profit sharing, universal social security, and local government accountability (Shirk 2005, 74). The PAN's Catholic leadership further maintained that elections should be treated as educational opportunities rather than as vehicles for winning political power. They held that their job was to educate civil society and to critique the political system, not to legitimate it by participating in elections. Thereafter, the PAN functioned more as a critical voice than as a truly competitive party.

The PAN began to return to its ideological origins in 1972, during the Luis Echeverría years, when José Angel Conchello displaced the Christian democratic leadership by winning the party's presidency. Conchello quickly began to foreground businessmen's right to private property at the expense of the social justice issues central to the party's Christian democratic phase. His general anticommunist, and specifically anti-Echeverría, stance increased the number and importance of businessmen in the PAN. This fact was noted by a key party leader, José González Morfín, who denounced the PAN for becoming "an instrument of *egoístas* servicing the businessmen from 'Grupo Monterrey'" shortly after resigning as president (quoted in Loaeza 1987, 96).

The 1982 crisis combined with the businessmen's financial/organizational resources and, above all, political acumen to place them at the head of the PAN. While the businessmen had begun gaining power within the party ten years earlier with Conchello's presidency, the 1982 nationalization of the banks tipped the power struggle between Christian democrats and secular businessmen (henceforth *neopanistas*) in favor of the latter. The neopanistas' rise to power is evidenced by the sharp increase in owners of small- to medium-sized firms in the party's membership, as well as in the important leadership positions businessmen occupied after 1982. From this point on, almost all of the PAN's presidential candidates, and a large number of governor and mayoral candidates, were businessmen (see Levy and Bruhn 2006, 85; Middlebrook 2004b, 18; V. Fox 1999, 60). Clouthier and others also recruited youth, housewives, patriarchs, and Catholics into the party (Luna 1992, 86).[22]

As noted by Arturo Warman, agrarian capitalists were decisive in rebuilding and redirecting the PAN. He explains, "Those who had been affected by land expropriations during the Echeverría years gave birth to *neopanismo*" (quoted in Loaeza 1990, 633). In other words, their prior history of class struggle had shaped many of the neopanistas' ideological positions about the failings of the mixed economy, corporatism, and presidentialism, as well as the need for fair elections. Drawing on this politically contentious history, leaders such as Clouthier and, to a lesser degree, José María Basagoiti, undid the old social pact that had barred businessmen from partisan political

---

22. On Clouthier, see Shirk (2005).

action.[23] In a congressional debate with López Portillo's successor, agrarian capitalist José María Basagoiti accepted the once serious charge that COPARMEX was engaging in politics, asserting that they were not "partisan politics" but rather "social politics, the politics of the common good" (quoted in Velasco Arzac 2004). For his part, Clouthier financed his own electoral campaigns, first as a gubernatorial candidate in his home state of Sinaloa in 1986 and then as a serious presidential contender in 1988.[24]

After joining the PAN in large numbers, other neopanistas joined Clouthier in both professionalizing the party (Shirk 2005) and giving it a decisive electoral direction (V. Fox 1999, 60). In the mid-1980s, for example, businessmen ran in municipal elections (Chihuahua, Durango, Baja California, Sinaloa, Puebla, and Coahuila) that frequently ended in massive protests (demonstrations and even hunger strikes) against electoral fraud (Luna, Tirado, and Valdés 1987, 36). According to Eisenstadt, who has analyzed such protests, the PAN's postelectoral conflicts would eventually force the authoritarians of the PRI regime to the informal bargaining table (Olvera 2004). Eisenstadt further notes that many of the PAN's 203 postelectoral conflicts between 1989 and 2000 yielded political spoils, including governorships, for the PAN (2003, 36–37).

As indicated in table 8, by 2000, the PAN had become the "catch-all" opposition party, mobilizing anti-PRI votes from the left as well as the right (Loaeza 1987). Notwithstanding the successful 1988 presidential candidacy of leftist Cuauhtémoc Cárdenas, in the 1990s the Partido de la Revolución Democrática (PRD) was still too new, too harassed by the PRI regime, and too internally fractured to capture left-of-center votes in the north. Additionally, public opinion shifted to the right as the ruling party lost legitimacy (Luna, Tirado, and Valdés 1987, 41; R. Bartra 2002; Camp 2004, 28). As table 8 shows, in the late 1980s, the PAN's municipal-level electoral victories were quickly followed by congressional victories (Middlebrook 2004b). By 1997, the PRI had lost its majority in the Chamber of Deputies and witnessed a

---

23. According to a list of four people identified by Luna, Tirado, and Valdés as "outstanding names" for their political role, two are agrarian capitalists—Manuel J. Clouthier and José María Basagoiti (the other leaders are Emilio Goicoechea and José Luis Coindreau) (1987, 35). Vicente Fox identifies other members of the so-called Bárbaros del Norte, including Ernesto Ruffo Appel, Pancho Barrio Terrazas, Fernando Canales Clariond, and Rodolfo Elizondo (1999, 57).

24. The 1988 campaign is significant because it was the first presidential race in Mexican history in which the ruling party candidate earned less than 40 percent of the vote and likely lost out to the leftist presidential candidate.

Table 8  PAN government officials elected to executive and legislative posts, 1985–2000

| Year | PAN senators | PAN federal deputies | PAN state legislators | PAN governors | PAN mayors | PAN city council members | % population governed by the PAN |
|---|---|---|---|---|---|---|---|
| 2000 | 46 | 207 | 299 | 9 | 329 | 4,046 | 41 |
| 1999 |    |     | 220 | 4 | 287 | 3,231 | 35 |
| 1998 |    |     | 287 | 4 | 287 | 3,231 | 33 |
| 1997 | 31 | 121 | 296 | 4 | 305 | 3,414 | 39 |
| 1996 |    |     | 267 | 4 | 249 | 2,527 | 24 |
| 1995 |    |     | 240 | 4 | 218 | 2,527 | 25 |
| 1994 | 25 | 119 | 176 | 3 | 128 | 1,864 | 16 |
| 1993 |    |     | 143 | 3 | 99  | 1,600 | NA |
| 1992 |    |     | 129 | 2 | 98  | 1,338 | 13 |
| 1991 | 1  | 89  | 116 | 1 | 49  | 1,209 | 10 |
| 1990 |    |     | 122 | 1 | 35  | 826   | 5  |
| 1989 |    |     | 115 | 1 | 29  | 705   | 4  |
| 1988 | 0  | 101 | 95  | 0 | 17  | 680   | .8 |
| 1987 |    |     | 60  | 0 | 17  | 669   | NA |
| 1985 | 0  | 32  | 51  | 0 | 26  | 200   | NA |

SOURCE: Adapted from Shirk (2005, 110, table 4.1). © 2005 by Lynne Rienner. Used with permission.

NOTE: NA = not available

dramatic rise in the number of PAN senators (from zero to thirty-one in ten years). Similarly, the number of PAN state legislators grew five-fold from 1987, and the number of PAN governors quadrupled from a decade prior. So, while not without some setbacks,[25] from the early 1990s through Vicente Fox Quesada's unprecedented presidential victory in 2000, the PAN was the only opposition party capable of defeating the PRI (Shirk 2005).

This changed in 2006 when the PAN's presidential candidate, Felipe Calderón, a conservative businessman who ran on a neoliberal platform, defeated the PRD's leftist candidate (who ran on a populist platform) by less than 1 percent of the vote. While this marginal victory is evidence of stiffer electoral competition between the left and right, it also shows that the electorate's support for the PAN was robust, if lower than in 2000. Significantly, the PAN's presidential candidate in 2006 outperformed the PRI's presidential candidate by a wide margin. This, in turn, suggests that the PAN's presidential

---

25. In 1998, the PAN lost some important gubernatorial races.

victories in 2000 and 2006 constituted a definitive blow to the PRI's monopoly on power. While it is theoretically possible that the former ruling party could win a presidential race in the twenty-first century, it could no longer rule in the imperial style to which it had been accustomed in the twentieth century (see Levy and Bruhn 2006, 6). Because party and state are no longer one, even the once invincible PRI would have to exercise a much greater sensitivity to public opinion, lest it be voted out of office. Thus, at least at the procedural level, the change of parties at the highest levels of power in the first twelve years of the twenty-first century constituted the birth of a democracy in Mexico.

It seems fair to conclude, then, that Mexico's radical right-wing businessmen, led by agrarian capitalists, have contributed to the democratization of Mexico. While Manuel Clouthier did not win the presidency in 1988, he paved the road for radical businessmen seeking state power. According to the first non-PRI president, Vicente Fox Quesada, it was, in fact, his "old friend" Clouthier who encouraged him to pursue politics as a public service and compete electorally (V. Fox 1999, 57). Fox was a businessman with deep personal and business ties to his family ranch in Guanajuato; once in power, he appointed many businessmen to government positions. According to Shirk, about 45 percent of Fox's top fifty-two appointees hailed from the private sector and had no previous public sector experience (2005, 192). Not surprisingly, Mexico continued down the path of neoliberalism.

In sum, businessmen, led by agrarian capitalists, acted as midwives to democracy by helping to turn Mexican elections into truly competitive political events (see Luna, Tirado, and Valdés 1987, 37). If the transition to democracy in this semi-authoritarian country was slow, it was in large part due to the evolution of an organizational infrastructure created to challenge the state over the course of the twentieth century, especially during the Echeverría and López Portillo years. Independent peak associations exercised and demanded greater political autonomy from the state. More important, in joining the PAN en masse, businessmen developed an electoral platform and ultimately infused the party with the financial, human, and intellectual resources—indeed, even the will—to compete in and win elections locally, then nationally (Shirk 2005; Loaeza 1990, 632).[26]

26. Levy and Bruhn point out that one group of businessmen, those organized in the National Association of Transformation Industries (ANIT) support the PRD while still others, like CANACINTRA, support the PRI (2006, 86).

## Conclusion

Radical right-wing businessmen helped both to introduce neoliberalism to Mexico and to democratize its political arena. First, in 1975, they undermined corporatism by creating politically autonomous peak associations that proved influential. As such, they transformed themselves from an economically and politically dependent class (or "client") with junior partner status into a class for themselves. In the wake of the banks' nationalization, they used their independent organizations as instruments to mobilize other capitalists in a frontal assault on presidentialism. Their movements demanded neoliberal policy reforms, a balance of powers, nonfraudulent elections, administrative transparency, rule of law, and efficiency.

CCE-affiliated businessmen succeeded in their goal of liberalizing the economy by working in tandem with technocratic government officials; they also pressed their agenda during an economic crisis that gave the International Monetary Fund (IMF) and the United States greater leverage in their case for Mexico's economic liberalization. I have argued that the confluence of international and national interests for neoliberalism explains why Mexico adopted neoliberal economic policies earlier than most Latin American countries despite a later transition to democracy.

The businessmen's demands for democracy yielded results more slowly than their push for neoliberalism in part because they challenged entrenched political interests not only at the apex of power but all the way down to the PRI's local-level political brokers. I have shown, moreover, that such a transition depended on creating the organizational infrastructure for it. For example, anti-authoritarian businessmen not only had to break away from corporatism to build their independent peak associations but also had to develop leaders and political strategies, rebuild an opposition party, and alter their ideological frames to compete in the electoral arena. Further, the PAN ultimately ended the dominance of the one-party state, first by winning multiple local-level elections, then fighting electoral fraud, and finally negotiating for political spoils. This slow local-to-national electoral strategy proved successful in 2000, and it indeed altered political opinion and activated and strengthened civil society.

The agrarian capitalist leadership of this procapitalist movement thus helped alter the path of Mexico's political and economic development. José María Basagoiti and especially Manuel Clouthier not only were major ideologues and political strategists but were also key to the PAN's success with the urban middle class (Abruch Linder 1983, 28; Luna, Tirado, and Valdés 1987, 39). They drew support from the middle class when they altered their discourse about "communism cum totalitarianism" and began to speak more concretely to the issue of democratization by organizing massive anti-fraud postelection rallies. In the face of PRI dominance and even political intimidation, neopanistas won hegemony among the middle classes and built strong voter allegiances, especially in the north of the country. In short, they created a cross-class alliance by reframing their grievances to focus on electoral fraud and democracy.

The success of these leaders suggests that social movement theory might benefit from focusing more on the role of leadership and ideology in mass mobilization. As noted, social movement theory has particularly ignored individuals because the drama of collective contention tends to obscure their roles, or because such a focus seems reductive. Clouthier and other leaders emerged from obscurity only because their organizations succeeded in mobilizing broad and contentious social movements and because Clouthier helped drive their movement into the electoral arena.

That said, this is not simply a story about great men with powerful organizations leading others on difficult journeys. These leaders never functioned in a social-political-economic vacuum. Rather, Clouthier and others developed their neoliberal policy preferences as well as their political strategies within the context of class struggle and, consequently, confrontations with state officials. From the perspective of businessmen, the law itself, most notably agrarian law, appeared to ignite and perpetuate class struggle. For example, not only were peasants constitutionally entitled to land available for redistribution, but they had to fight to prove that it was illegally concentrated beyond the legal caps set for private property in the countryside. Further, while the redistribution of the mid-1970s was insufficient to meet all peasant demands for land, it was large enough to alienate those affected by the land expropriations and to alarm other segments of capital as well. In the context of heightened and ongoing rural and urban class struggles, businessmen created the organizational tools and neoliberal ideology with which to defend capital, given that the state would fail to represent their interests if that meant alienating large segments of voters.

In other words, land invasions, land expropriations, urban guerrilla movements, and the bank nationalization radicalized Mexican businessmen. As such, it is fair to conclude that the businessmen's political agendas emerged dialogically, while fighting mobilized antagonists as well as the corporatist state, which was caught in the middle. Put differently, the course and outcomes of interclass struggles altered the path and direction of Mexico's economic and political development and continue to explain left vs. right movement-countermovement dynamics in Mexico's political arena. In the 1970s, interclass struggles sparked the countermovements of capitalists who, in defense of their class, pushed officials to begin substituting neoliberal economic policies for nationalist (i.e., import substitution) policies. Members of the CCE not only helped government officials with the terms of the NAFTA negotiations but also successfully advocated changes to the Constitution to make possible the privatization of Mexico's ejido system. Thus, class actors continued to struggle long after the Revolution was over in ways that further radicalized and mobilized businessmen. The heretofore untold story is that of capitalists on the road to political power, who contributed greatly to the unmaking of postrevolutionary nationalist economic policy and to the birth of a fragile democracy in Mexico.

# 5

## The Rural Sources of the PRD's Electoral Resiliency

The Partido de la Revolución Democrática's (PRD's) electoral resiliency in the twenty years since the party's debut contributed to Mexico's democratization in a number of ways. First, as Jaime Tamayo (1990) argues, the party's massive anti-electoral fraud protests contributed to the emergence of civic groups that would closely monitor elections. Second, the PRD's protests against political repression of their party militants raised the costs of repression (Bruhn 1997) in much the same way that antifraud protests had raised the political costs of electoral fraud. Third, Bruhn notes that the PRD's electoral competitiveness had a positive radical flank effect on the right-wing Partido Acción Nacional's (PAN's) electoral outcomes. She persuasively argues that the PRD's early success prompted the ruling party to cede power to the right-wing opposition party because their policies were more closely aligned (1997, 305). Fourth, Bruhn observes that the emergence of a left unity party "slowed Mexico's rush toward a de facto two-party system at the national level" (1997, 304).

As the origins and democratizing outcomes of the PRD have been systematically studied (Bruhn 1997), this chapter offers a different focus. It explains the rural sources contributing to the PRD's electoral resiliency. In contrast to the more erratic support of urban voters, some rural voters have consistently supported the PRD over time, despite state repression of party leaders. In contributing to the electoral resiliency of the PRD, rural voters also contributed to the evolution of a pluralistic political system and, by extension, Mexico's democratization.

As a fusion of numerous socialist parties and former left priistas, the PRD is a left political party that demands social justice for peasants, workers, the

*Fig. 6* The 2006 presidential election in Mexico, by the party winning the majority of votes per state
SOURCE: Adapted from the Instituto Federal Electoral's (IFE's) map of the 2006 presidential election results. For the yellow and blue state illustration, see http://www.ife.org.mx/documentos/Estadisticas2006/presidente/m_pdte_1.html. Map courtesy of Erin Greb.

poor, and indigenous peoples. While an important segment of the PRD's supporters are those who have been marginalized by neoliberalism, economic marginalization does not fully explain why some rural people, but not others, consistently support the PRD. Research shows that notwithstanding the 2000 presidential election,[1] voting in Mexico is strongly ideological (that is, based on party platform),[2] and while socioeconomic status, occupation, education, and skin color influence voting, region is a stronger predictor (Moreno and Yanner 2000; Moreno 2003; Klesner 2004, 2005, and 2007, 29–30; Ramírez Mercado 2006; Moreno 2007; Lawson 2007, 46). Fig. 6 clearly illustrates the regional cleavages in the voting behavior of Mexicans in the 2006 presidential election.

    1. The 2000 election is a significant exception that witnessed quite a bit of vote switching. In that election, voters decided first whether to hurt or support the regime and only secondly whether to vote on the basis of the candidate's program (Domínguez and McCann 1996). On the 2000 presidential race, see Klesner (2005, 122).
    2. The debate about whether ideological voting is becoming stronger or whether young Mexican voters are undergoing a process of dealignment is beyond the scope of my analysis (see Klesner 2005).

Since the PAN has historically drawn much of its support from the more affluent urban areas in the north (Klesner 2005), and since the south is more rural than the north, part of what drives this regional dynamic could be the urban-rural divide. This is especially plausible given that on the basis of municipal-level data of electoral outcomes in five federal deputy elections from 1991 to 2003, Joseph Klesner concludes that the PRD "has become a party of nonindustrial areas" and, in the last couple elections, "finished somewhat better in more rural areas" (2005, 111; see also Klesner 2004, 104, table 5.5; Eisenstadt 2003, 39). Based on exit poll data, he further shows that whereas individuals who voted for the PRD in the 2000 presidential election were only somewhat more likely than the average voter to hail from the countryside, "loyalists" are "more likely to live in rural areas and to be poorer than PAN loyalists" (Klesner 2005, 124). Klesner notes that in contrast to PRI loyalists, PRD loyalists are "better educated, somewhat younger, and more often male" rural dwellers (2005, 124; see also 113). Regarding the 2006 presidential election, Moreno similarly observes that individuals "employed in the informal or the agricultural sectors were slightly more likely to vote for [the leftist candidate] López Obrador than for the PAN candidate, although the difference is not substantial" when compared to the importance of ideology (2007, 18).

This chapter argues that those electorates in the rural south that tend to consistently support the left do so in part because of the legacy of left-led social movements in the countryside, which nurtured social bases of rural support. A logistic regression analysis that controls for the urban population, along with some marginalization variables, suggests that the states in which the left had previously organized peasants were also the states in which electorates offered electoral support for left presidential candidates over time. At the same time, these historic rural strongholds of prior left activism are negatively correlated with electoral support for the right-wing opposition, the PAN, over time.

## The Peasantry's Political Predispositions

This chapter contributes to the literature insofar as the existing scholarship has overlooked the impact of the peasantry's left political predispositions on democratization. Movement scholars, for example, have emphasized the role of *urban* "popular"[3] movements in Mexico's democratization processes but, with some exceptions, have underemphasized the peasantry's contributions (Haber 2007). Kathleen Bruhn, for example, argues that the pattern of agricultural support for the PRD is surprising, as the "association with [the] agricultural population represents a departure for the Mexican left, which was always strongly urban" (1997, 295, see also 112, 211; Klesner 2007, 29). While Bruhn notes that the PRD was able to retain more rural voters than urban voters in the volatile first ten years after its founding, she cannot fully explain why this is so (1997, 295; see also Carr 1989). Given data limitations, Joseph Klesner is also unable to fully explicate why votes for the PRD are negatively related to the variables "percent urban" and "percent employed in manufacturing" (2004, 104, table 5.5). He concludes that the "PRD draws much of its support from the politically engaged poor" (2004, 103) and that the modal PRD supporter was a relatively secular, "older male, [who was] moderately well educated but poor" (2004, 107).

One reason why scholars have neglected many rural people's consistent electoral support for the PRD is that the official party (the PRI) historically legitimated itself via the peasant vote. As noted earlier, the PRI was able to legitimately monopolize power for seven decades, in part by exchanging concrete benefits for votes. Further, while peasants banked on PRI patronage, their electoral support for the PRI was also ideological. The PRI had a substantial history of agrarian reform and had, as late as the mid-1970s, redistributed some of the largest amounts of good-quality land to peasants while, at the same time, increasing state support for agrarian production. So even after the government's peasant association lost control of the peasantry to independent movements in the 1970s, peasants continued to vote for a semi-authoritarian ruling party in the absence of electoral options. Additionally, the PRI emphasized the state's (re)distributive role, as well as nationalist duty in direct economic production, throughout López Portillo's administration (1976–82). Despite its many failings, both in the reach of its programs and in professional execution, Mexico developed an incomplete—indeed, corrupt—welfare state whose safety net was cast in agrarianist and workerist

---

3. Some scholars argue that "popular" movements are distinct from social movements in part because the former are said to be "distrustful of the organized left" (Foweraker 1990, 6). This analysis shows that, at least among peasants, the left and the autonomous peasant movement were mutually influential. As I suspect that the distinction between popular movements and political parties is too dichotomous, I employ the concept of the social movement.

terms. In consequence, the PRI maintained electoral support in rural areas longer than in urban ones.

But as the PRI lost control of resources and the capacity for patronage, and as it adopted neoliberal policies that displaced peasants from their lands, rural dwellers in the center and south of the country eventually withdrew electoral support from the ruling party (Mackinlay 2004; Klesner 2005, 128–29). JoAnn Martin documents this change in Tepoztlán, a village in Morelos. In 1988, she writes, peasants were bussed to a rally where they feigned support for the PRI's presidential candidate so as to "garner the personal benefits of associating with those in power" (2005, 174). Because they were not enthusiastic about Carlos Salinas de Gortari, the contingent of villagers at the rally had to rehearse their chanting and rally behavior in order to more convincingly pretend that they were backing the PRI. Privately, however, Tepoztlán villagers voted five to one for the left opposition candidate, Cuauhtémoc Cárdenas (Martin 2005, 172–78).

In the twenty years since its debut, some rural dwellers in the central and southern regions of the country have consistently supported the left opposition PRD rather than the older and better established right-wing opposition party, the PAN. This long-term electoral support is noteworthy given that urban voters switched their support from the left-wing PRD to the right-wing PAN after 1988. In 2000, for example, urban PRD voters were far more likely to defect from the PRD than were rural voters (Klesner 2005, 125). Finally, in the 2006 presidential election, rural Mexicans were slightly more likely to vote for the PRD's candidate, Andrés Manuel López Obrador (Moreno 2007, 18).

As there have been extreme right-wing fascist movements among some rural dwellers (most notably in Jalisco; see Romero 1986), the peasants' propensity for left-wing political predispositions calls for explanation. For her part, Kathleen Bruhn offers in passing that "the sheer scarcity of viable options for . . . voters in rural areas helps explain why the PRD apparently kept more rural voters than urban voters" in the decade since the PRD's emergence (1997, 298; see also 252). This book develops this point by showing that, in fact, left groups with socialist and communist ideals built strong bases of political support in the countryside for many years *prior* to the emergence of the PRD. While chapter 3 demonstrates the involvement of the left in peasant movements since the mid-1930s and especially in the early 1970s, this chapter focuses on the left's involvement in peasant protests from 1977 through the early 1980s.

Based on quantitative data and the secondary sources, I argue that peasants and rural workers are predisposed to support the left partly because radical Marxist groups, especially the Mexican Communist Party (PCM), made greater headway in the countryside than any opposition (i.e., non-PRI) group or party on the right. As we saw in chapter 3, the role of leftists was obscured in the first half of the 1970s because they operated clandestinely to avoid repression. A similar dynamic was at work in the second half of the 1970s, though some of the most important national organizations that led peasants in political protests were clearly identified with one of several far-left groups (Rubio 1987, 187).

## The Data and Results

As explained in appendix C, I created a data set of 727 cases of rural protest events based on Blanca Rubio's handwritten spreadsheets, which counted the number of peasant protests in Mexico between 1979 and 1984.[4] Rubio's primary source was Información Sistemática, a newspaper clippings archive.[5] Recoding her spreadsheets proved invaluable because I was able to code for political grievances at each event, as well as the type of organization involved. In addition to her spreadsheets, Rubio gave me summary statistics on the number of peasant protests per state between 1977 and 1983 and the number of instances in which rural activists denounced government repression between 1977 and 1983 (*denuncias contra la represión*). Rubio coded this latter variable herself; it included rallies, marches, and *plantónes* (the occupation of an office) to protest state repression in the countryside. I used government census data for population statistics. Finally, on the basis of internal PCM documents (archived at Stanford's Hoover Institution) as well as the secondary sources, I coded the variable "states with communist peasant bases, 1967–73," per state.

---

4. The data on which Rubio's 1987 publication are based represent 2,372 cases of collective events. My sample is much smaller because her spreadsheets did not include the years 1977 and 1978. Further, I coded strictly for protest events. When in doubt about whether an event in her spreadsheets was a noninstitutional form of protest, I excluded the case from the analysis.

5. Appendix B offers a discussion about the utility of newspaper sources in which I agree with Earl et al.'s conclusion that "newspaper data does not deviate markedly from accepted standards of quality" (2004, 77).

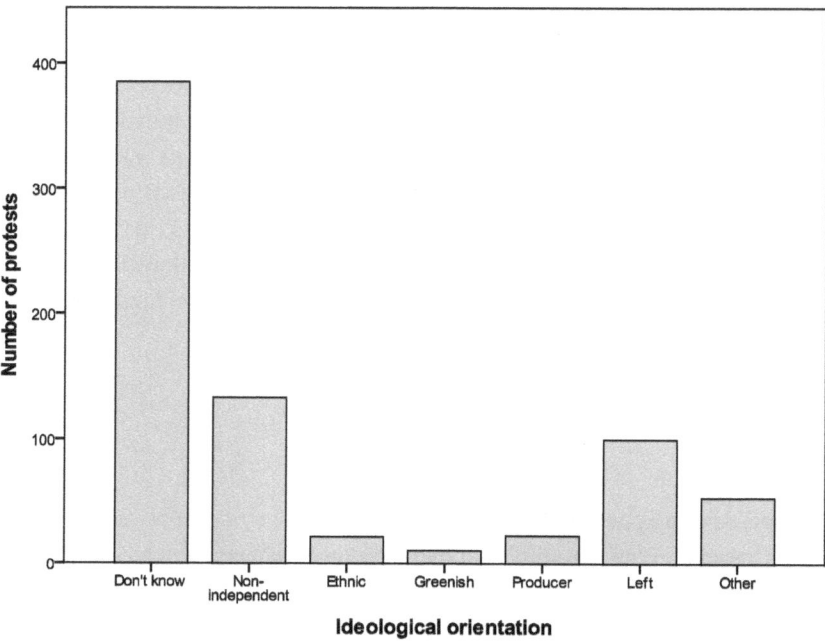

*Fig. 7* The ideological orientation of the peasant organizations engaged in 727 cases of peasant protest, 1979–84
SOURCE: Created from Blanca Rubio's raw data, based on newspaper articles in Información Sistemática.
NOTE: Ethnic peasant organizations include Comuneros Organizados de Milpa Alta (COMA), Frente Campesino Independiente de Oaxaca (FCI), Organización Independiente de Pueblos Unidos de las Huastecas (OIPUH), Organización Campesina Emiliano Zapata (OCEZ), Unión de Pueblos de Morelos (UPM), and Unión de Comuneros Emiliano Zapata, Michoacán (UCEZ). Greenish peasant organizations include the Pacto Ribereño.

Fig. 7 identifies the ideological orientation of the peasant organizations engaged in protest movements between 1979 and 1984, based on the names of the peasant organizations that led the protests. The largest category in fig. 7 is "don't know," because it includes those cases in which the newspaper sources failed to identify the organization leading the protest (coded "-1"). This does not necessarily mean that the 385 cases of protests for which we are missing organizational data were "spontaneous" or without organizational infrastructure or leadership. Rather, because the organizational field in the countryside was densely populated (Lúa, Paré, and Sarmiento 1988; Carton de Grammont and Mackinlay 2009),[6] it is reasonable to suppose that many of the peasant organizations in the "don't know" category are left groups. As I demonstrated in chapter 3, many leftists operated clandestinely in the countryside to avoid repression. It is equally reasonable to suppose that this "don't know" category also includes ethnic and greenish peasant groups (defined below), which were not known to journalists. However, the "don't know" category likely excludes pro-regime organizations. Such organizations are categorized as nonindependent in fig. 7 because they were official organizations directly affiliated with the ruling party (such as the National Peasants' Confederation, CNC), were satellite parties (such as the Socialist Workers' Party, PST), or were in some clear way pro-regime.[7] Such organizations were well known to journalists and are thus unlikely to significantly contribute to the "don't know" category.

I define ethnic organizations as those that identified themselves as indigenous *and* were not strongly linked to a left party. I use the term "greenish" to denote peasant organizations that demand money for land damaged by oil spills or for land appropriated by the government's oil company, Petróleos Mexicanos (PEMEX) (see Flores Lúa et al 1988, 109). Producer organizations are those that organized at least two local producer groups, usually ejidos (but sometimes also indigenous groups or private cooperatives), for an agro-industrial project (Fox and Gordillo 1989, 142; N. Harvey 1998). I treated the Coalición de Ejidos Colectivos de los Valles del Yaqui y Mayo (Coalition of Collective Ejidos from the Yaqui and Mayo Valleys, CECVYM) and the Unión Regional de Ejidos y Comunidades de la Huasteca Hidalguense (Regional Union of Ejidos and Communities from the Huasteca, Hidalguense, URECHH) as strictly producer organizations, even though they were originally founded, respectively, by the Línea Proletaria and the old Popular Action Movement (MAP), both of which were Maoist (Rubio 1987, 173; see also fn. 3). Despite their radical origins, the CECVYM and URECHH became

---

6. On Chiapas, see N. Harvey (1998).
7. Other pro-regime peasant groups, coded as nonindependent in fig. 7, include the Consejo Nacional de Pueblos Indígenas (CNPI), the Consejo Nacional Cardenista (CONACAR), the Antorcha Campesina (AC), the Alianza Campesina del Noroeste, all of the groups that signed the Pacto Ocampo (the CNC, Consejo Agrarista Mexicano [CAM], etc.), and the Unión Nacional de Trabajadores Agrícolas (UNTA). It is important to note that this coding is conservative. As Carton de Grammont and Mackinlay (2009) suggest, many organizations worked closely with the CNC in order to benefit from the state's resources. That said, these organizations are categorically different from those that proactively fought political co-optation to defend their autonomy in the hopes of building a "revolutionary" peasant movement.

economically dependent on the government, yet maintained their political independence (Rubio 1987, 164–65, 180–81; see also Carton de Grammont and Mackinlay 2009). The "other" category to the far right of fig. 7 comprises local and amorphous peasant organizations; each of these organizations accounted for less than 1 percent of all protest events, and their ideological orientations are unknown. The "other" category essentially aggregates all of the outlier organizations.

Finally, the organizations coded as "left" in fig. 7 were those that were led directly by a left party or by a left party front. It includes groups led by the PCM or Partido Socialista Unificado de México (PSUM), as well as those organizations with strong ties to the PCM or PSUM, such as the Central Independiente de Obreros Agrícolas y Campesinos (CIOAC) and Coalición de Obreros, Campesinos y Estudiantes del Istmo (COCEI) (see Lúa, Paré, and Sarmiento 1988; Bruhn 1997, 113; N. Harvey 1998). I also coded the Coordinadora Nacional Plan de Ayala (CNPA) as left because many of its founding organizations were led by far-left groups and, after it purged all nonindependent organizations, far-left groups—including individual leaders associated with the Trotskyist party, the Partido Revolucionario de los Trabajadores (PRT)—remained in the national leadership (Rubio 1987; Robles and Moguel 1990; N. Harvey 1998).[8] Like the CIOAC and COCEI, this national front was composed of multiple organizations, many of which represented large numbers of indigenous peasants and all of which consciously resisted political co-optation (Rubio 1987; Paré 1990, 85). All of the groups coded as left not only were proactively independent of the government but also shared general political ideals while differing on long-term strategies, especially regarding the peasantry's role in a socialist or communist transformation.

As mentioned, the "don't know" category includes those left organizations that operated clandestinely. But even if we remove it from fig. 7, the remaining bars suggest that the left was quite active in Mexico's peasant movements between 1979 and 1984. Independently of these data, Graciela Flores Lúa, Luisa Paré, and Sergio Sarmiento likewise argue that the left was very involved with peasant movements from the 1970s through the mid-1980s (1988, 233–35; see also Craig 1990).

8. The CIAOC and the Coordinadora Campesina Revolucionaria were among the CNPA's ten founding organizations (Robles and Moguel 1990). Neil Harvey (1998) reports that members of the PRT were also in the national leadership. Robles and Moguel (1990) note that the communist-affiliated COCEI helped host the fourth national meeting (El Cuarto Encuentro Nacional) called by the CNPA.

To more carefully explore the degree of left involvement in peasant protests, I estimated an ordinary least squares (OLS) regression using "states with communist peasant bases, 1967–73," as my independent variable. As noted, I coded this variable myself by reading internal PCM documents and the secondary sources.[9] The dependent variable, "all peasant protests between 1977 and 1983," not only reflects protests during a later period but was also coded by Rubio based on newspaper articles in Información Sistemática. Because journalists did not always identify the *municipio* in which the event(s) occurred, the data are organized by state. The unit of analysis in various regressions is thus the state. Consequently, I exclude Mexico City because it is neither a state nor a rural center.

While an ecological analysis with such large units is inconclusive, state-level comparisons suggest credible patterns, especially when important control variables are introduced to discipline the analysis. The control variables in this analysis include the degree of rural unemployment per state and the percentage of indigenous people in the rural population. As we saw in chapter 3, rural unemployment was positively associated with earlier peasant movements because it reflects economic marginalization in the countryside. This variable is based on the 1970 General Population Census, which defines the rural unemployed as those who were searching for employment in agriculture, ranching, forestry, fishing, or hunting at the time of the census but who had worked at some point during 1969 (Secretaría de Industria y Comercio 1972, 972–80). As noted previously, while the census likely underestimated the degree of rural unemployment, this measure is the best available.

The percentage of indigenous people in the countryside is an important control variable because Native Americans were quite active in the peasant movements of the late 1970s and beyond. A frequency distribution of the number of protests against government repression reveals that the repression was harshest in the indigenous regions. For example, whereas no antirepression protests occurred in seven states between 1977 and 1983, there were ninety-four such protests in the state of Oaxaca, seventy-seven in Chiapas, sixty-one in Veracruz, and fifty-seven in Puebla during the same period. In some of these states, antirepression protests even exceeded protests that

---

9. The following fourteen states were coded "1" for having large Communist-organized peasant bases between 1967 and 1973: Sonora, Sinaloa, Chihuahua, Durango, Zacatecas, Coahuila, Tamaulipas, Michoacán, Morelos, Puebla, Tlaxcala, Veracruz, Guerrero, and Oaxaca.

demanded land (Rubio 1987, 148). Furthermore, according to the 2000 Mexican census, these four states are home to the largest populations of indigenous people in rural areas.[10] This measure also controls for economic marginalization, given that indigenous people account for 33 percent of all of those people officially classified as living in extreme poverty.

These two control variables, then, allow us to see whether prior communist rural strongholds correlate with later peasant protest, net of economic and social marginalization. Table 9 reports the metric and standardized beta coefficients for an OLS regression. It shows that net of important control variables, the states with communist rural strongholds between 1967 and 1973 were positively related to subsequent peasant protests between 1977 and 1983, and that this relationship is not due to chance ($p = .06$, two-tailed test). That prior organizing by the PCM and its fronts had a large (17.31) effect on peasant struggles nearly a decade later is not surprising given the party's enduring history of organizing peasants, as documented in chapter 3. Although the standardized coefficients for rural unemployment (0.59) and the percentage of indigenous people in the rural population (0.33) were more critical, the PCM's prior organizing in the countryside was still very important to subsequent peasant protest movements, all else being equal. As the F-ratio is significant, we have good evidence that introducing the independent variable "states with communist peasant bases, 1967–73," improved our ability to predict all subsequent peasant protests between 1977 and 1983.

It is important to note, moreover, that this last independent variable ignores Maoist strongholds. The secondary sources show that Maoists participated in many unarmed (as well as armed) peasant movements (Carton de Grammont and Mackinlay 2009), including movements in some areas where the old PCM was weaker. Finally, having arrived later in the countryside, the Trotskyist PRT seems to have played a comparatively minor role[11] nationally with peasant activists, even though some of its leaders proved influential in the nationally significant CNPA during the mid-1980s (N. Harvey 1998, 138). By 1983, the CNPA represented eighteen regional-level organizations and was

---

10. A better measure would have been the number of indigenous people in the countryside in 1970 or even 1980. Unfortunately, those data were not available (in the "universe") in the IPUMS-International digitized census data from Mexico (Minnesota Population Center 2007).

11. Although its impact was smaller than that of other leftists, the PRT's claim that it suffered extreme state repression is plausible. The PRT claims that about five hundred of its members disappeared at the hands of the state (Rubio 1987, 150).

Table 9 Metric coefficients for OLS regression of net differences of all peasant protests on key independent variables, thirty Mexican states, 1977–83

| Independent variable | Model 1 | | Model 2 | |
| --- | --- | --- | --- | --- |
| | Metric coefficients— unstandardized B | Standardized coefficients | Metric coefficients— unstandardized B | Standardized coefficients |
| Rural unemployment, 1969 | 0.003*** | 0.67 | 0.002*** | 0.59 |
| % indigenous rural population, 2000 | 0.83*** | 0.35 | 0.79*** | 0.33 |
| States with communist peasant bases, 1967–73 | — | — | 17.31* | 0.26 |
| Intercept | −9.01 | | −10.75 | |
| $R^2$ | 0.53 | | 0.58 | |
| Adjusted $R^2$ | 0.49 | | 0.54 | |
| F change | — | | 12.66*** | |

SOURCE: The "rural unemployment" variable is from Mexico's 1970 General Population Census (Secretaría de Industria y Comercio 1972b). The "percent indigenous of rural population" variable is based on the 2000 Mexican census, as harmonized by IPUMS-International (Minnesota Population Center 2007). The variable "states with communist peasant bases" was coded by the author based on the archival record and the secondary sources.

*$p < .10$; **$p < .05$; ***$p < .01$ (two-tailed tests)

important among indigenous groups.[12] A better measure of left involvement might reveal an even stronger relationship than what is shown here and allow for exploring how much the degree to which indigenous people were repressed was due to the dirty war against Communists. But although it is clear that multiple left organizations were involved in peasant movements in the late 1970s and early 1980s, the data coded by Rubio suggest that the majority of left groups leading peasant protests in unarmed struggles were either directly or indirectly affiliated with the PCM.

12. After purging progovernment members and organizations, the CNPA not only focused on constitutional land reform but supported indigenous claims for ancestral lands. It also focused on community control of natural resources, the state's support for agricultural production, marketing and consumption, the unionization of rural workers, and even the defense of indigenous

## The Left in Rural Mexico in the Late 1970s

As I argued in chapter 3, despite the state's dirty war against leftists in the 1970s and early 1980s, dispersed and fragmented networks of Maoists and especially sympathizers of the PCM provided the leadership for many of the peasant protests during the period. The involvement of radical Marxist groups in nonguerrilla protest movements reflected the principled antiparliamentarian stance maintained by numerous leftists through the first half of the 1980s. Like many right-wing *panistas,* leftists did not want to legitimate a corrupt political system by participating in unfair elections (Tamayo 1990). As documented in chapter 3, left groups placed a high priority on working with grassroots movements, and many did so in a clandestine or semi-clandestine way to skirt state repression.

While cadre and ex-cadre from left parties were involved in peasant movements, they did not control peasants in a "top-down" way. From the 1970s onward, the PCM and other leftists improved their relations with peasants by learning to respect extant rural movements on their own terms. This respectful attitude departed from prior left practices in which party cadre competed for hegemony over peasant organizations or simply tried recruiting key individuals to their party. According to Lúa, Paré, and Sarmiento, in the 1970s and 1980s, leftists and peasant activists developed "horizontal relationships between social movement organizations and political parties based on a mutual respect and a recognition of the potential for agreements, joint action, and even differences [*divergencias*]" (1988, 234). Regarding left activists in the Laguna region, Ann Craig similarly observes that party cadre

> tapped into movements that were emerging, sometimes amorphous and frequently informal. They [left activists from outside the region] contributed to the intensity and extent of popular mobilization and to divisions between popular organizations. They did try to influence agendas, to formalize organization, to build alliances through individual leaders or formal agreements between organizations. They extended movements beyond local, community boundaries and in this

---

culture (Paré 1990, 85). As Paré emphasizes, the demands of indigenous peasants differ from those of mestizo peasants in that the former see their struggle for land as part of their larger effort to survive physically and culturally. In other words, by retaining land they also seek to preserve their customs, language, and culture (1990, 85).

way increased the visibility and effectiveness of popular organizations' negotiating capacity. The alliances that endured the longest were those that resulted from a dialogue between outside institutions or leaders and the grassroots base—a dialogue that resulted in a compromise agenda and strategy. The result was not only a greater accountability of leaders . . . but a process of political learning and network building. (1990, 67)

This political learning to which Craig refers worked in both directions and was, therefore, dialogical. The left disseminated radical ideas that resonated with independent peasant groups in the context of a dirty war. While the left and most peasants agreed that the state should play an important role in both supporting economic production and redistributing national resources (land), leftists helped sharpen the critique of presidentialism, corporatism, U.S. imperialism, political repression, and unfair or corrupt elections (see Carr 1989, 370). For their part, as we see below, leftists learned to work in politically decentralized and more democratic coalitions.

On the radicalization of the peasantry, Lúa, Paré, and Sarmiento explain that "the vast majority of the independent peasant organizations were forced to reflect upon their political independence, talk explicitly about the various political [i.e., Marxist] currents within their peasant organization, and discuss issues of democracy and power" (1988, 234). The public slogans of the national-level CNPA reflect the radicalization among the peasants whom it led. As noted, far-left groups helped found the CNPA and, in the 1980s, won hegemony of the national organization after purging all nonindependent groups. Although it demanded land for the landless, the CNPA was explicit in its goals to "abolish private property" and to develop collective property in the countryside (Robles and Moguel 1990, 427). Concretely, the demand for land for the landless was seen as a first step toward abolishing large, privately held property (i.e., the *latifundio*), which the CNPA believed was necessary to undercut the economic power of the bourgeoisie (Rubio 1987, 176).

Though the radicalization of peasants was neither as ideologically coherent nor as utopian as that of their leaders, the government's incessant repression was consistent with the left's position that radical change was in order. Their radicalization is partly evident in the way in which the CNPA framed its mission. According to Luisa Paré, it originally used the slogan "'today we fight for land, tomorrow for power.'" As political repression increased during

José López Portillo's administration, the CNPA "changed its slogan to 'today we fight for land and for power'" (1990, 86; Robles and Moguel 1990, 427).

Rubio argues that the diversification and radicalization of peasant demands reflects a dialectical dynamic in which the deepening agricultural crisis nationally (1987, 64–65) led both to greater peasant protest and, consequently, to a more violent response from the state. She maintains that to counter mounting pressure from unarmed peasant movements, López Portillo's administration made land invasions illegal and intensified rural violence (1987, 27–28). Not only were there ten thousand peasants behind bars at the end of his administration (1987, 144), but nearly one hundred villages were attacked, and some of these attacks ended in massacres.[13] Rubio concludes that the struggle for land turned into a struggle against the state's authoritarianism (1987, 153).

At the most aggregate of levels, the data are consistent with her conclusion. Whereas the majority (161 out of 221, or 72 percent) of peasant protests between 1970 and 1975 focused on the demand for land redistribution (see table 13 in appendix B), by the early 1980s peasants were increasingly confronting state officials with political, not just economic, grievances (Rubio 1987, 64–65). Fig. 8 charts the political issues peasants raised in 355 protest events by year between 1979 and 1984. The figure only looks at those protests—about half of the 727 in the data set that I recoded—in which peasants articulated a political grievance in addition to the demand for land. Specifically, the data indicate that between 1980 and 1983 peasants were more likely to protest government repression than they were previously; many demanded justice if a fellow activist had disappeared or been killed. Rubio notes that whereas peasants protested government repression 24 times in 1977, they did so 142 times in 1983. Furthermore, whereas antirepression protests accounted for 11 percent of all peasant protests in 1977, they constituted 27 percent of all peasant protests in 1983 (Rubio 1987, 69).

Fig. 9 charts the peasants' mobilization tactics in 720 cases of peasant protest in Rubio's data set between 1979 and 1984. An analysis of changing tactics over time provides more texture to the mobilization-repression dialectical dynamic suggested by Rubio. This figure shows that between 1981 and 1983 peasants both diversified their protest repertoire and adopted

13. Rubio lists the following villages as having experienced massacres during López Portillo's administration: Golonchan, Tlacolula, Venustiano Carranza, Pantepec, Juchitán, and San Juan Copala (1987, 28).

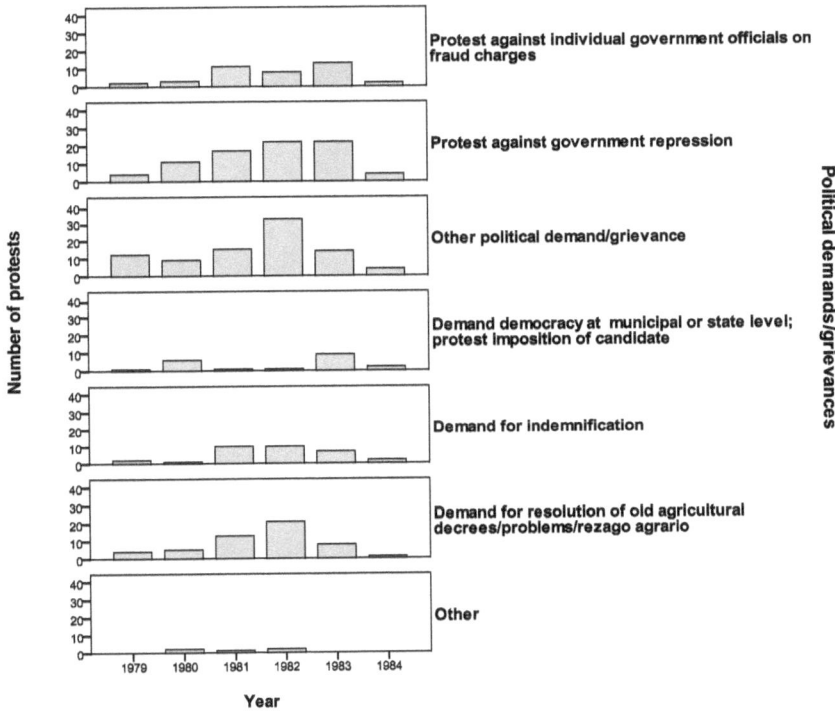

*Fig. 8* The political issues in 355 cases of peasant protest, 1979–84
SOURCE: Created from Rubio's raw data, based on newspaper articles in Información Sistemática.
NOTE: The last panel, titled "Other," refers to those protests that accounted for less than 5 percent of the total (they included calls for ejido self-management vs. deforestation, and the like).

increasingly antistate and high-risk tactics. Specifically, fig. 9 indicates that peasants were more likely in the early 1980s than previously to organize rallies, out-of-town marches to a government office, and *plantónes* (which block access to an office), or even to occupy ("sit in" on) government offices. Like land invasions, sit-ins and plantónes are high-risk tactics, as they are far more likely than demonstrations or strikes to engage social control forces. They are also likely to end in *desalojos* (physical expulsion), since they essentially challenge government officials to forcibly remove the activists (see fig. 11 in appendix C). That said, out-of-town marches, demonstrations, and plantónes require more organization and coordination than local land invasions. The only nongovernmental organizations capable of regional- and national-level coordination during this period were led by leftists, including the CNPA.

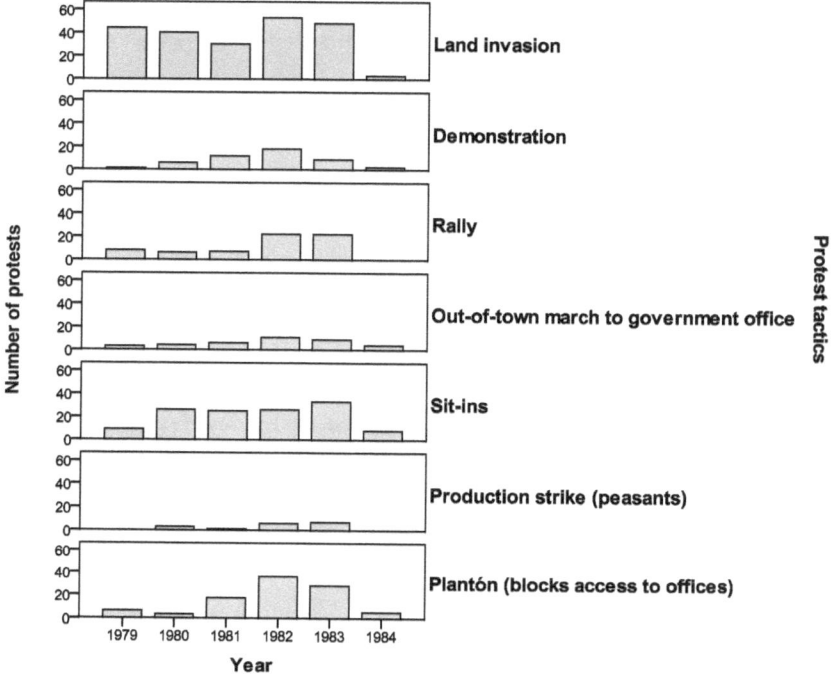

*Fig. 9* Protest tactic by year in 720 cases of peasant protests, 1979–84
SOURCE: Created from Rubio's raw data, based on newspaper articles in Información Sistemática.
NOTE: Protest events in Mexico City excluded from this analysis.

According to Rubio's (1987) own estimates, the CNPA and the CIOAC, which was also led by leftists, mobilized one-third of all extralocal and extraregional peasant protests between 1979 and 1983.[14]

Thus, while deepening economic grievances might motivate more people to protest—indeed, even against rising state repression—it does not necessarily explain why peasants adopted the kinds of radical tactics indicated in fig. 9. I submit that their tactics were increasingly radical because left parties and organizations were becoming ever more involved in peasant movements. Their involvement changed the course and methods of peasants' struggles.

Finally, while Rubio's national-level data do not extend beyond 1983, the left argues that rural activists were murdered for political reasons even

14. Rubio reports that they organized forty-four *encuentros campesinos,* regional- or national-level conferences attended by rural activists after 1979 (1987, 168).

throughout Miguel de la Madrid's and Carlos Salinas de Gortari's administrations. While much of the rural violence in the neoliberal period (post-1983) seems to have been carried out by private gunmen rather than by government officials, Amnesty International "alleges that some local authorities have been directly involved in political killings" in at least some cases (Foweraker and Landman 1997, 95). Estimates on the number of peasants killed for political reasons between 1982 and 1987 range from 705 to 814 (see Paré 1990, 88; N. Harvey 1990, 192).[15] The victims of these killings tended to belong to such independent peasant organizations as the Organización Campesina Emiliano Zapata (OCEZ) and the CIOAC (N. Harvey 1990, 192). As noted earlier, the latter had strong historic ties to the PCM.[16]

Fig. 8 indicates that in addition to protesting political repression, peasants explicitly demanded democracy by protesting the abuse of local power, the imposition of officials at the local level, or electoral fraud after a local election. According to Rubio, protests that demanded that local mayors be removed from power occasionally turned violent. She reports cases in which protesters set the municipal palace on fire (Chiapas) or used dynamite elsewhere (Yucatán). Neil Harvey states that by the end of 1987, protests against corrupt mayors had occurred in the majority of Chiapas's municipalities (1998, 160). Peasants also mobilized against local government representatives, such as official peasant or ejido leaders (i.e., representatives of the government's CNC, or the *comisariados ejidales* supported by the government). In still other cases, they marched to the capital to demand that government officials working for the Ministry of Agrarian Reform be dismissed from their posts. These officials were responsible for investigating land disputes and deciding which villages, if any, were granted land. In 1982, the left-led CNPA organized a national march involving three hundred peasants that resulted in their occupation of government offices (Rubio 1987, 156).

15. Whereas President José López Portillo declared amnesty for 950 peasants incarcerated for their political activity in 1970, ten years later, President Salinas de Gortari freed 1,300 people, mostly peasants, who had been incarcerated for political reasons yet "charged with common crimes" (Paré 1990, 88). Further research must be conducted to clarify whether the peasants released during Salinas's administration were, in fact, jailed while he was in office.

16. In a later publication, Neil Harvey notes that politically motivated killings had been especially high in the state of Chiapas since 1982 and worsened both during and after the Ejército Zapatista de Liberación Nacional's (EZLN's) armed rebellion (1998, 171–72, 218). Foweraker and Landman suspect that Mexico's human rights record continued to deteriorate even in the urban centers through the 1990s as the regime sought to contain a growing opposition that mobilized both electorally and through disruptive political protest (1997, 111; on the repression of the PRD, see Bruhn 1997).

While demanding the dismissal of various officials, peasants supported alternative candidates at the local level. As we know from chapter 2, the 1977 electoral reforms of the Ley Federal de Organizaciones Políticas y Procesos Electorales (LFOPPE) motivated left groups to compete electorally. The evidence clearly shows that when they did, they also mobilized peasants around local-level elections (Rubio 1987, 157). Rubio adds that indigenous groups in particular used elections to vote for their organic leaders (1987, 157). Some such groups, like the COCEI in Oaxaca, had close ties to the PCM.

As indicated in fig. 8, local-level calls for democracy appear to have been greater in 1983, during de la Madrid's first year in office, than they were earlier. According to Rubio, while demands relating to electoral fraud were fewer in number than other political demands (constituting roughly 13 percent of all peasant protests), the issue grew steadily, with demands registering a 4.7 percent annual increase between 1977 and 1983. While such local protests were not initially numerically impressive, they were politically significant because they drew in larger swaths of the rural population (Rubio 1987, 154–55). This, Rubio concludes, illustrated the declining legitimacy of the PRI regime in the countryside (1987, 155). Indeed, such contentious postelectoral mobilizations continued throughout de la Madrid's presidency and, as we know, became a key mechanism through which the PRI regime was ultimately defeated (Eisenstadt 2003).

Together, figs. 8 and 9 suggest that between 1979 and 1983, peasants were increasingly alienated from and critical of the Mexican state, as evidenced by the radicalization of their tactics, which increasingly targeted state offices, and the commensurate politicization of their demands over time. Peasant protests in the early 1980s differed from those in the early 1970s in that they went beyond the demand for land to include a more widespread and sustained critique of repression, as well as calls for electoral democracy. While the pattern is similar to other cases in which economic struggles turned into political struggles in authoritarian contexts, I conclude, with Joe Foweraker, that the process does not happen automatically (1989, 186). Rather, political processes intervene. In this case, the evidence strongly suggests that as the left multiplied in Mexico's countryside, peasant movements radicalized. I submit that the radicalization of the peasantry, including that of indigenous groups, is explained by the fact that left parties reached out to them in their villages. In other words, peasants were radicalizing before 1985 and certainly well before the watershed presidential election of 1988—in which a left candidate nearly won power—because of the long history of left organizing in Mexico's countryside. As urban social movements were also increasingly critical of the PRI's austerity programs and of the state's failure to deal with the shantytowns that emerged in the devastating aftermath of the 1985 earthquake in Mexico City, the historical evidence indicates that civil society was ideologically and organizationally ready for the emergence of a left opposition party well before the 1988 presidential election.

## A Left Unity Party: The Emergence of the PRD

Prior to the late 1970s and 1980s, the history of Mexico's left can be characterized as "sectarian, authoritarian, opportunistic and politically myopic" (Tamayo 1990, 135). The left's sectarianism and authoritarianism sometimes even led to left-on-left violence, including murder. According to Crespo, after the PCM gained the legal standing to compete in elections, it tempered its radical ideological views and general political strategy, as suggested by the fact that it dropped the hammer and sickle symbols (2004, 68). Indeed, the party's decision to enter the electoral arena may ultimately explain why, in the late 1970s and 1980s, the left learned to work in "fronts and coalitions of the center-left" (Tamayo 1990, 135).[17] In the countryside, for example, leaders of the PCM-affiliated CIOAC and Unión General de Obreros y Campesinos de México-Roja (UGOCM-Roja) worked closely with the CNPA, whose national leadership included some Trotskyists. Though she did not identify the ideological orientation of various peasant organizations, Rubio reports greater coordination among these groups between 1977 and 1983 (1987, 169).

The left's growing ability to work in coalitions from the late 1970s onward pushed many activists to exercise political tolerance. Just as peasants had learned from left activists, activists learned from peasants by developing horizontal, rather than vertical, links to grassroots peasant movements. This experience was at least one factor that ultimately facilitated the party mergers

---

17. The left's transformation was neither complete (as in all groups) nor unilinear. Some factions of Trotskyists, for example, never joined the left coalition on the grounds that they could not work with such bourgeois candidates as the renegade priistas. Further, even those leftists who eventually joined the PRD remained factionalized along old party lines. According to Bruhn (1997), personal loyalties undergirded political identities until about 1994 and would continue to link leaders to old bases of social support long afterward.

of the 1980s, which culminated in the emergence of the Partido de la Revolución Democrática (PRD). Specifically, large segments of the left began to tolerate political ideologies that differed from their own and learned to appreciate decentralized (i.e., non-Leninist) leadership styles and internal discussion; they even experimented with democratic practices. The LFOPPE reforms contributed to these shifts in that they provided leftists with concrete incentives to work together in electoral coalitions.

In 1981, the old PCM was dissolved so as to join forces with four other groups in an organization called the Partido Socialista Unificado de México (PSUM). By 1985, additional groups on the left had formed an electoral coalition with the PSUM to better engage in regional electoral campaigns. In a document signed by the National Revolutionary Coordinating Committee, the major left parties agreed to electoral coalitions at the regional level on the grounds that "encouraging, consolidating, and legitimizing democratic popular regional movements are of great interest to progressive forces" (quoted in Tamayo 1990, 127). In 1987, the members of the PSUM reorganized and joined forces with additional groups to form the Partido Mexicano Socialista (PMS). These party mergers were likely responsible for the electoral turn taken by many social movement organizations that had likewise previously held an antiparliamentarian stance.

Civil society, in short, was organizationally prepared for a left unity political party long before Cuauhtémoc Cárdenas led the popular front (Frente Democrático Nacional, FDN) that evolved into the PRD. It was ready, I submit, because of prior left activism in the countryside and, undoubtedly, in the urban centers. Thus, when nationalist elites broke with the ruling party due to ideological differences with the increasingly dominant neoliberal technocrats, there was already a large pool of well-organized potential allies outside of the PRI.[18] By 1987, these nationalist elites (dubbed *políticos*) had found no way of reversing the neoliberal path adopted by the official party—a path that leftist priistas believed threatened the historic alliance of the state to workers, peasants, and popular classes—so they broke ranks to create the FDN. The FDN then ran Cuauhtémoc Cárdenas as a presidential candidate (on the Partido Auténtico de la Revolución Mexicana's [PARM's]

---

18. Given the economic crisis of the early 1980s, U.S.-educated technocrats rose quickly to the top of the ruling party's hierarchy despite lacking significant prior political experience. Unfamiliar with the party tradition of compromising with opposing political factions, party technocrats alienated long-standing *político* nationalists.

ticket)[19] against the PRI's candidate, Carlos Salinas de Gortari. This decision proved successful in that many people believe that Cuauhtémoc Cárdenas actually won the 1988 election but was accorded about 31 percent of the vote through fraud.[20]

Though Cuauhtémoc Cárdenas's charisma and symbolic importance as the son of a national hero partly explain his electoral success in 1988, his pre- and postelection rallies turned out extant social movement organizations of alienated workers and peasants, along with networks of radical students and intellectuals. These social movements proved quite receptive to the formation of a left-of-center party. According to a Corriente Democrática founder, organizers were pleasantly surprised that civil society was "ready to participate" with a new party (quoted in Bruhn 1997, 113). As Tamayo points out, the 1988 elections proved simply to be a new arena for already existing social struggles (1990, 132–35). This was especially true among peasants, whose history of working with the left made supporting *neocardenistas* a logical step (Lúa, Paré, and Sarmiento 1988, 234). Bruhn explains, "The Cárdenas vote was not a pure punishment vote but represented support for action on specific issues raised by the FDN, and salient to Mexican voters in 1988, including debt, decline in living standards, and the corrupt authoritarianism of the PRI. At the same time, the *cardenista* rhetoric and name evoked traditional commitment of the Mexican Revolution to social equity in a particularly timely way. Cárdenas was ideally suited to capturing protest that focused precisely on the PRI's lack of attention to popular needs" (1997, 128).

The FDN's leadership worked with the leaders of various splinter parties and social movement organizations to channel their electoral support into a left unity party. The PRD registered as a party in May 1989. However, despite Cárdenas's and the FDN's best efforts, the PRD ultimately failed to retain the social movement organizations in their new political party (Bruhn 1997, 213). While the newly created PRD claimed that it would represent democracy, the Constitution, and the Revolution, party leaders floundered in their

---

19. The PARM was a parastatal organization with a long history of kowtowing to the PRI. The left widely judged it to be a "tool" of the ruling party. See Bruhn (1997, 110–11) for detailed information about the political intrigue surrounding Cárdenas's acceptance of the PARM's nomination in 1988.

20. Even the right-wing PAN allied itself with the left-wing FDN in mass demonstrations defending the Cárdenas vote in 1988. It based its claims of electoral fraud on a six-day delay in reporting the electoral results. Additionally, there was evidence of burned ballots and ballots dumped in rivers or in alleys, suspicious rates of voter absenteeism in Cárdenas's strongholds, and computations that did not add up (Bruhn 1997).

attempts to achieve more concrete political direction. Further, a combination of internal problems and external pressure from state officials, including the relentless repression of PRD activists, stymied party consolidation efforts (Bruhn 1997, 136–270).[21] As internal factionalism and external repression raised the economic and political costs of aligning too closely with the left opposition, social movement organizations left the party. So too did individual voters. While Cárdenas lost nearly two-thirds of his voting base, urban voters, more so than rural voters, switched support to the other opposition party, the right-wing PAN (Bruhn 1997, 250, 291, 295).

This history, then, calls for an explanation of the loyal strongholds of rural PRD supporters. In the section that follows, I specifically ask whether there is a relationship between prior left organizing in the countryside and long-term electoral support for the PRD.

## The PRD's Voter Strongholds, 1988–2006

To investigate long-term electoral support for the PRD, I estimated two separate multivariate logistic regressions predicting votes for either the PRD's or the PAN's presidential candidate. For the dependent variable—consistent voting for an opposition party—I used the presidential electoral results by state between 1988 and 2006, as reported by Manuel Ramírez Mercado (2006). According to Buendía, it is in presidential elections that voters are more likely to break with the incumbent because candidates in such campaigns emphasize changes that they hope to introduce (2004, 123). Thus, consistent voting for one party's candidates over time strongly suggests an ideological affinity to that party's platform.

I coded states as having consistent PRD supporters if, in at least three of the four presidential races since the FDN/PRD's debut in 1988, a left candidate won a minimum of 20 percent of the vote. This standard is based on the fact that in the 2006 election, in which a left candidate nearly won power (losing the presidency by less than 1 percent of the vote), about 20 percent of

---

21. The degree of state repression of PRD activists during Salinas's presidency cannot be overstated. The PRD reports that its activists were threatened, subjected to extortion, expelled from towns, kidnapped, and even murdered. While the National Human Rights Commission corroborated only two politically motivated slayings, the PRD alleges that during Salinas's six-year term, 250 of its activists were killed for political reasons. Nearly half of these deaths (112), it claims, were linked to elections (Eisenstadt 2003, 36).

Mexico's voters identified themselves as being ideologically left of center (Moreno 2007, 17).[22] Furthermore, a victory in three out of four presidential races is evidence of consistent electoral support for a party. This standard excludes those states in which voters opted for a left opposition candidate for temporary situational reasons; such reasons might include specific campaign tactics or personal pocketbook assessments (Buendía 2004).[23] For consistency, I coded states as having electoral strongholds of ideologically right-wing supporters if at least 20 percent of votes in those states were cast in favor of the PAN candidate in three of four presidential elections since 1988.

I treat the number of instances in which rural activists denounced government repression between 1977 and 1983 (Rubio's *denuncias contra la represión*) as a key independent variable. Specifically, I argue that it is a proxy for the left's involvement in peasant protests during these years. As noted, military forces, local police, and even paramilitary groups targeted leftists for repression during the years of the dirty war (1968–82). To illustrate, in the state of Hidalgo, where political repression was especially brutal (over five hundred peasants were killed in just four years), the military justified erecting barriers around the perimeter of eighteen rural municipalities in 1980 on the grounds that its mission was to capture arms and Communists (Rubio 1987, 150). Since fighting Communists was a clear objective of political repression, antirepression protests are a good proxy for left involvement. Indeed, while Rubio estimates that about half of all antirepression protests were led by the CNPA (40 percent) and the CIOAC (7 percent)—two nationally influential left-led organizations that also organized many indigenous groups (Rubio 1987, 177–80)—I suspect that the figure is much larger. We know, for example, that journalists did not document the names of all organizations involved in protest. Further, while she did not make this inference herself, five of the eight organizations that Rubio lists as having led indigenous women and others to protest repression are clearly identified with a far-left group. Women were organized in such protests on the assumption that the state was likely to temper its response accordingly. Finally, as Rubio's *denuncias* variable is

---

22. A greater number, fully 34 percent, said that they were right of center. About 18 percent said that they were squarely in the center, and 28 percent marked "no placement" in *Reforma*'s national exit poll (Moreno 2007, 17).

23. The voting patterns in the state of Sinaloa are one such example. About 30 percent of Sinaloa's votes went to the PRD's presidential candidate in 2006, but PRD candidates received far less than 20 percent in 1988, 1994, and 2000. On average, Sinaloa's voters do not appear to consistently support the PRD, and thus I coded the state "0."

continuous, it is superior to the dichotomous variable "states with communist peasant bases, 1967–73."

Because Rubio's antirepression protest data are organized by state, I use the state as the unit of analysis. While there are municipal-level data on the electoral results over time, we have no comparable municipal-level data on the left's involvement with peasants. Consequently, it is impossible to directly test the mechanism that I have suggested. In the absence of ideal data, the quantitative analysis that follows only suggests a pattern of long-term PRD supporters.

As fig. 6 illustrates, voting in Mexico is highly regional and, as this phenomenon is frequently measured on a state-level basis (Ramírez Mercado 2006), the country's electorate can be described as living in either a blue (PAN) or a yellow (PRD) state. While the blue vs. yellow state phenomenon was most pronounced in the 2006 presidential race, it is not new. In twenty-five of thirty-two states, a minimum of 20 percent of voters have consistently opted for one opposition party or the other in the presidential races since 1988. In just four federal entities—Baja California Sur, Mexico City (the Distrito Federal), Tlaxcala, and Zacatecas—have voters consistently given at least 20 percent of the votes to both the PRD *and* the PAN in the last three of four presidential races. Only in three states—Campeche, Hidalgo, and Nayarit—have voters appeared indifferent to the PAN and the PRD by failing to meet the threshold of 20 percent of the votes for either party in three of four presidential elections since 1988.

These findings lend strong support to Klesner's argument that Mexico's opposition parties are propped up by specific regional social bases. He attributes the development of such social bases to the opposition party strategy of winning elections locally and regionally in the 1980s. He argues that by the 1990s, what had developed "looked like two parallel two-party systems, PAN-PRI competition in the north and center-west and PRD-PRI competition in the south" (2005, 135). I hypothesize that the latter interparty dynamic was initiated a decade earlier than Klesner suggests. In other words, while I agree with Klesner's important conclusion about the strength and importance of bipartisan regional competition (PAN-PRI vs. PRD-PRI), I suspect that the history of left-led protest movements in the 1970s and early 1980s helped pave the road for subsequent political alignment with the left party, the PRD, in the south. Neil Harvey's research in the southern state of Chiapas during the 1980s reveals this dynamic, albeit solely for Chiapas. He specifically argues that a politically independent peasant group, the CIOAC, which was closely linked to the old PCM, mobilized its members to support Cuauhtémoc Cárdenas in the 1988 presidential elections (1990, 194–95). Outside of Chiapas, I have found evidence directly linking CIOAC and/or some incarnation of the old PCM (PSUM/PMS) to three or more peasant struggles between 1979 and 1984 in such southern states as Oaxaca, Puebla, and Veracruz, as well as in such northern states as Durango and San Luis Potosí. Put differently, the ratio of intensive far-left involvement in the rural south as compared to the rural north is about 2:1.

To explore whether a relationship existed between prior left organizing and long-term electoral support for left candidates, table 10 presents a simple cross-tabulation of electoral support for left presidential candidates by the number of times rural activists denounced state repression between 1977 and 1983. As noted previously, antirepression protests serve as a proxy for the left's involvement in the countryside, because the state systematically repressed leftists during the dirty war. Thus, the table shows the percentage of states in which a minimum of 20 percent of the vote was cast in favor of

Table 10 Distribution of thirty-one Mexican states showing support for FDN/PRD presidential candidates, 1988 to 2006, by degree of rural protest against government repression from 1977 to 1983

| Independent variable | % states with consistent support for the FDN/PRD, 1988–2006 | % states with less consistent support for the FDN/PRD, 1988–2006 | Number of states |
|---|---|---|---|
| 25–94 anti-repression protests | 63 | 38 | 8 (101%) |
| 8–23 anti-repression protests | 13 | 88 | 8 (101%) |
| 1–6 anti-repression protests | 13 | 88 | 8 (101%) |
| No anti-repression protests | 29 | 71 | 7 (100%) |
| Pearson $\chi^2$ | 6.47* (df = 3) | | |

NOTE: The independent variable—the number of anti-repression protests—is allowed to vary by the (rough) quartiles of its distribution. Additionally, total percentages may not add up to 100 percent due to rounding error.

*$p < .10$; **$p < .05$ (two-tailed tests)

the FDN/PRD presidential candidate between 1988 and 2006, and the degree to which rural activists protested political repression between 1977 and 1983 (the final dirty war years).

As expected, table 10 suggests a positive and statistically significant correlation between the number of antirepression protests and long-term electoral support for the PRD. The states with the highest number of protests were twice as likely (63 percent) as those with zero protests (29 percent) to have electorates give at least 20 percent of the vote to the FDN/PRD's presidential candidates from 1988 on. Similarly, in states that registered zero antirepression protests, electorates tended to be significantly less supportive of the left party over time. It follows that in states with no protests during those dirty war years, there were not large numbers of left activists in the countryside.

Table 11 gives the percentage distribution of states in which electorates showed long-term support for the right-wing opposition party, the PAN, in presidential elections from 1988 to 2006, and the degree to which rural activists protested political repression between 1977 and 1983. As expected, table 11 suggests the inverse pattern identified in table 10, supporting Klesner's point that the "PRD's strengths are the converse of the PAN's" (2005, 115). The data in table 11, however, suggest that this converse pattern emerged earlier than the 1980s. Specifically, states registering zero antirepression protests were far more likely to have electorates that consistently voted for the PAN in the nearly two decades that followed. Since communist rural activists were targeted during those dirty war years, it follows that local states in which activists did not denounce government repression did not have many communist rural strongholds. Such states also tended to be those with electorates that have consistently supported the PAN in presidential races since 1988.

To more carefully explore my hypothesis that prior left organizing in the countryside influenced subsequent left opposition voting in presidential campaigns, I introduce economic and social marginalization control variables.[24] Taking into account the Native American population in the countryside controls for both economic and racial marginalization. I do this by calculating

---

24. To do so, I estimate the following logistic regression equation:
$\ln(P/1-P) = a + b_1(ARP) + b_2(INDG) + b_3(EDRL) + b_4(UNEMPL) + b_5(URBPOP17) + e$, where $\ln(P/1-P)$ is the log odds of a minimum of 20 percent of a state's electorate consistently voting for an opposition party's candidate in three of four presidential races between 1988 and 2006. In all logistic regressions, the independent variable ARP represents the number of protests against the repression of rural activists between 1977 and 1983; it is a proxy variable for the degree of left organizing in the countryside.

Table 11 Distribution of thirty-one Mexican states showing support for PAN presidential candidates, 1988 to 2006, by degree of rural protest against government repression from 1977 to 1983

| Independent variable | % states with consistent support for the PAN, 1988–2006 | % states with less consistent support for the PAN, 1988–2006 | Number of states |
|---|---|---|---|
| 25–94 anti-repression protests | 25 | 75 | 8 (100%) |
| 8–23 anti-repression protests | 100 | 0 | 8 (100%) |
| 1–6 anti-repression protests | 75 | 25 | 8 (100%) |
| No anti-repression protests | 86 | 14 | 7 (100%) |
| Pearson $\chi^2$ | 12.279** (df = 3) | | |

NOTE: The independent variable—the number of anti-repression protests—is allowed to vary by the (rough) quartiles of its distribution.

*$p < .10$; **$p < .05$ (two-tailed tests)

the percentage of the rural population that is indigenous, according to the 2000 census. Further, as Klesner previously found that votes for the PRD are negatively related to the variable "percent urban" but positively related to being poor yet relatively well educated (2004, 107), I also control for the urban population, the degree of unemployment, and rural education. I specifically control for the size of the urban population old enough to vote (the voting age is eighteen) by including, as one of my variables, the total number of people in a given state who are older than seventeen years of age and were classified by the 2000 census as living in an urban center. The number of unemployed per state, also reported in the 2000 census, is an additional economic marginalization control variable. Finally, I control for rural education by including a variable representing the percentage of the *rural* population whose educational attainment, as reported by the 2000 census, is higher than high school (i.e., "normal schools through university").

In a second logistic regression, the dependent variable is electoral support for the PAN over time. Because I have tested for left-wing strongholds rather than merely for states with antiregime electorates, my proxy variable for a history of left-wing rural activism should be negatively related to consistent electoral support for the PAN in the countryside, all else being equal. The third and final regression examines the effect of prior left rural organizing on electoral support for the PRD at a subnational level. The dependent variable in model 3 is a dichotomous variable coding for whether or not the PRD had ever won the state's governorship, as of 2007. As the old ruling party, the PRI, was far more reluctant to relinquish governorships to the PRD, as compared to the PAN, PRD gubernatorial victories only have a recent history.[25] Such governorships were won in some of the PRD's strongholds; they comprise just over half of the states in which the PRD received consistent support from a minimum of 20 percent of electorates in the presidential races between 1988 and 2006.[26]

Even after the introduction of control variables, table 12 indicates that the positive and statistically significant relationship between prior left organizing in the countryside and long-term electoral support for the left party in presidential races remains. Net of other factors, every additional antirepression protest in a state during the dirty war increased the odds that at least 20 percent of the state's electorate would support the left party in subsequent decades. In states where there were ten such protests, the odds increased by more than three ($\exp[10^*.12=1.2]=3.32$) that a left presidential candidate would receive a minimum of 20 percent of the electorate's votes in three of four elections from 1988 on.[27] The second model in table 12 estimates a logistic regression predicting long-term loyal support for the right-wing party, the PAN. The negative coefficients are as expected. Specifically, every additional antirepression protest in a given state during the dirty war decreased the odds by a factor of 0.87 that at least 20 percent of that state's electorate would vote for the PAN's presidential candidate over time.

The only other variable that was statistically significant in both regressions predicting long-term electoral support in presidential elections was the

25. According to Todd Eisenstadt, in some instances, the PRI regime gave the PAN governorships even after PRI candidates had officially won the gubernatorial race (2003, 29).

26. The states in which the PRD won governorships include Baja California Sur, Chiapas, Guerrero, Michoacán, Tlaxcala, and Zacatecas. In contrast, a minimum of 20 percent of the electorates from the states of Oaxaca, Tabasco, and Veracruz consistently voted for a left presidential candidate over time but have, as yet, failed to elect a PRD governor. However, the 2000 gubernatorial race in Tabasco was very close, and the PRD party claimed victory.

27. To control for the theoretical possibility that the full-scale militarization of the state of Guerrero during the dirty war drove the dynamic evident in the first regression, I excluded Guerrero in a second regression not presented in table 11. When Guerrero was excluded, the odds were actually six times greater ($\exp[10^*.18=1.8]=6.05$) that in states with prior left organizing at least 20 percent of the electorate would consistently vote for the left party in the presidential races from 1988 to 2006.

Table 12 Logit coefficients for regression of propensity to support political parties in presidential elections (1988–2006) and PRD governorships, by the number of protests against government repression from 1977 to 1983, in thirty-one Mexican states (excluding Federal District)

| Independent variable | Loyal FDN/PRD electoral support, 1988–2006[a] | | Loyal PAN electoral support, 1988–2006 | | PRD governorships as of 2007 | |
| --- | --- | --- | --- | --- | --- | --- |
| | B | Odds multiplier | B | Odds multiplier | B | Odds multiplier |
| Number of anti-repression protests per state | 0.12** | 1.13 | −0.14* | 0.87 | 0.17*** | 1.18 |
| % indigenous rural population | −0.21* | 0.81 | −0.10* | 0.91 | −0.34*** | 0.71 |
| % rural population with post-secondary education | 0.17 | 1.18 | 0.26 | 1.30 | 0.31 | 1.37 |
| Unemployed in state | 0.00 | 1.00 | −0.00* | 1.00 | 0.00 | 1.00 |
| Urban population ≥ 17 years of age | 0.00 | 1.00 | 0.00* | 1.00 | 0.00 | 1.00 |
| Constant | −0.81 | 0.45 | −0.34 | 0.72 | −1.00 | 0.37 |
| −2 log likelihood | 19.514 | | 12.893 | | 18.380 | |
| Model chi-square | 17.84*** | | 24.46*** | | 12.09*** | |
| Nagelkerke $R^2$ | 0.63 | | 0.78 | | 0.52 | |

SOURCE: The first independent variable is per Blanca Rubio's data on anti-repression protests, based on newspaper articles in Información Sistemática. Data for the remaining independent variables are based on the 2000 Mexican census, as harmonized by IPUMS-International (Minnesota Population Center 2007) (all weighted cases).

[a] I also ran this regression by excluding the state of Guerrero. Doing so produced slightly better results (beta was 0.18** and the odds multiplier was 1.20).

*$p < .10$; **$p < .05$; ***$p < .01$ (one-tailed tests)

estimated degree of the rural indigenous population. The relationships are negative in all regressions. The higher the percentage of the rural indigenous population in the countryside, the less likely it was that the electorate would consistently vote for the PRD or the PAN, all else being equal. While it is unsurprising that indigenous peoples do not vote for the right-of-center party, the PAN, it is surprising that they do not consistently vote for left presidential candidates. As noted earlier, the left was very active in organizing indigenous groups in rural protest. However, the data suggest that while Native Americans mobilized with the left to protest politically, they have not necessarily followed the left in electoral campaigns.

The finding that rural Indian peoples appear to be nonpartisan at the electoral level is consistent with the works of other scholars. According to Hernández Castillo, "The link between indigenous peoples and partisan politics has always been a weak one" because Native Americans have felt exploited by the PRI, disrespected by the PAN, or simply ignored after elections by the PRD (2006, 117). Similarly, Guillermo Bonfil argues that Mexico's Native Americans vote strategically rather than ideologically. In his observations, their voting reflects such short-term considerations as "finishing a road, building a school or a drinking water system; small benefits that help resolve ancestral problems which shape their daily lives" (quoted in J. Fox 1994a, 170n47). Further, some groups, such as the neo-Zapatistas of the Ejército Zapatista de Liberación Nacional (EZLN), go so far as to reject electoral democracy altogether.[28] While additional research is necessary to carefully tease out these issues,[29] the point here is that the degree of ethnic marginalization in the countryside has correlated negatively with electoral support for both the PRD and the PAN in the presidential elections since 1988.

Since high levels of antirepression protest during the dirty war is a proxy for left involvement and, indeed, leadership, the logit coefficients in table 12 suggest that the left nurtured social bases of support among some rural dwellers, as evidenced in their tendency to vote for left presidential candidates over time. In a final exploration of this possibility, I examine whether consistent left voters were widespread enough to have elected left governors

28. Despite supporting the PRD's gubernatorial candidate in Chiapas in 1994, the EZLN has rejected the electoral route as a means of promoting change. During the 2000 presidential election, Subcomandante Marcos issued a communiqué stating that the EZLN would neither sabotage the elections in the Zapatista-controlled areas nor "call for voting for any of the candidates or their parties" (General Command of the EZLN 2000). This was an important message given a NACLA report indicating that civilian supporters of the EZLN had engaged in acts of sabotage during the 1997 midterm elections to protest state violence in Chiapas (Stephen 1997). During that election, about 30 percent "of the polling stations were either destroyed or not installed" because of such actions (Stephen 1997, 10).

The EZLN's abstentionist stance took on a more critical tone in the period leading up to the 2006 presidential election when Subcomandante Marcos criticized the PRD's presidential candidate (Andrés Manuel López Obrador) and compared the left party, the PRD, to the other capitalist parties (General Command of the EZLN 2005). In this declaration, the EZLN called for "another campaign" (*otra campaña*), in which indigenous peoples and their grassroots organizations would convene to formulate a left program that would hopefully lead to a "new national constitution" (Hernández Castillo 2006, 115).

The distancing of the EZLN and the PRD is partly explained by the fact that in 2001, PRD senators voted for a constitutional reform that initially excluded the EZLN's principal demand for autonomy. Further, in 2004, PRD municipal officials violently repressed a peaceful demonstration by EZLN supporters who demanded potable water (see Hernández Castillo 2006, 119).

29. For an introduction, see Hernández Castillo (2006).

in their states. Whereas the presidential vote over time tracks the depth of loyal voting (in three of four races) among at least 20 percent of the electorate, my dichotomous measure of PRD governorships (coded as no = 0; yes = 1) speaks to the breadth of left party support. Left gubernatorial victories suggest that large swaths of the electorate in a given state lean to the left. Of course, a better measure would include gubernatorial victories in multiple races (over time), but such data are unavailable. As noted, left opposition gubernatorial victories are a recent phenomenon in Mexico.

The final column in table 12 is consistent with the first model in that it indicates a positive and statistically significant relationship between prior protests against repression of rural activists and whether electorates in those states eventually elected a left governor. The statistically significant beta coefficient of 0.17 means that had there been ten protests against state repression previously, electorates in such states were over five times more likely to subsequently elect a left governor than were electorates in states without a history of left activism ($\exp[10^*.17=1.7]=5.47$).

These regressions suggest that some rural voters consistently supported the PRD partly because the history of left-led protest in Mexico's "provinces" nurtured social bases of support. These bases of left-leaning rural people would be predisposed to support leftist presidential candidates over time and would also be more likely to elect a left governor than those electorates residing in states without such a history. More research, however, must be conducted to determine whether consistent electoral support speaks to clientelism or to specific support for the PRD's agrarianist political ideology. It is theoretically possible that it implies clientelism, because the PRD has integrated former left priistas and their clients (Klesner 2005, 132) along with the left's former social bases of support. Nonetheless, I suspect that consistent electoral support does not significantly reflect clientelism because, while vote-buying efforts continue (and may even have increased with electoral competitiveness), the PRD is unlikely to have more patronage resources than the PRI or the PAN, nationally or locally. More important, since the 1990s, voting has been "overwhelmingly secret" (Schedler 2000, 14),[30] and secret ballots tend

---

30. The government issued voting identification cards with photographs and required opposition parties to serve as electoral observers at all polling stations. Further, the politically independent Instituto Federal Electoral (IFE) designed new voting booths for all 112,500 polling stations in the country to ensure secret voting. Finally, a national coalition of tens of thousands of citizens in the Alianza Cívica monitor elections and are even allowed to staff polling places, along with other independent observers (Holzner 2006, 88).

to increase the odds that people will vote according to their consciences. In other words, secret voting likely tempers the effects of entrenched authoritarianism or clientelism at the local level, at least in the voting booth.

While the pattern of left voting over time suggests a political alignment of prior left social bases and subsequent left voting, qualitative research into political attitudes is clearly still necessary. Such research should carefully tease out the extent to which rural activists of the past perpetuated populist agrarianist ideas via family and friends. Although the PRI's old agrarianist organizations (the CNC) and programs (such as land reform) were sources for such political socialization, it is unlikely that they were the only ones, given the depth and breadth of the history of left opposition politics identified in this chapter and in chapter 3.

## Conclusion

Mexico's left proved to be a surprisingly viable contender in the presidential elections of 1988 and 2006. The PRD's electoral resiliency has contributed to democratization in a number of ways, not least of which is that it has helped make the country's political system pluralistic. The PRD has blocked the road to a two-party system at the national level, and viable three-way presidential races have ensured that policy options do not regress toward the center. In offering genuine political alternatives to neoliberalism, the PRD has played a leading role in turning elections into ideological races between the left and the right.

But the ideological nature of presidential elections is not just an effect of the PRD's resiliency. Rather, the data presented here strongly suggest that its resiliency reflects a legacy of left activism, including that in the countryside. This legacy is undoubtedly more complicated than what I have outlined here. It is also paradoxical. While the evidence shows that leftists reached out to peasants and indigenous peoples, especially in center and southern states, indigenous groups seem to have maintained a nonpartisan electoral stance despite their earlier alignment with left groups in political protests. Leftists, peasants, and indigenous peoples paid a high price, whether in jail or with their lives, for their social movement activity during the dirty war.

Although the left seems to have failed with many indigenous groups, at least in the electoral arena, it clearly succeeded in cultivating bases of rural electoral support. Such bases appear to have propped up the PRD over time despite ongoing state repression of party cadre, and this has led to municipal and gubernatorial victories in some instances. Put another way, the PRD's electoral resiliency, especially given its young organizational history and the fact that it had to endure state repression, is explained by the fact that Mexico has an important left heritage. The legacy of vaguely socialist peasant revolutionaries, as well as the subsequent nationalist discourse of the PRI, which claimed to have institutionalized the Revolution, is a part of that heritage. As I have shown in this chapter, the left, especially the PCM and its networks, is also key to understanding Mexico's political heritage.

The PCM had an especially long history of antiregime activism in the twentieth century, and of organizing poor people in the countryside. The right-wing party (the PAN) played a similar oppositional role but tended to draw most (not all) of its electoral support from large cities, especially those in the north (Eisenstadt 2003, 37, 39; Klesner 2005, 113).[31] Another indicator of the PAN's relative insignificance in the countryside comes from Todd Eisenstadt's study of contentious postelectoral mobilizations between 1989 and 2000. He shows that even though the PAN placed a high priority on postelectoral contention through 1995, it did not challenge the PRI's claim to local electoral victories in the rural areas (2003, 39).

The foregoing discussion suggests that the work of the PRD's socialist predecessors in Mexico's countryside helps explain why some peasants have consistently voted for a young and organizationally weak left opposition party in the face of regime harassment and even the international hegemony of neoliberalism. The argument advanced here is that the history of left activism partly explains the left vs. right voting patterns that scholars have identified in the 2006 presidential election. As noted in the introduction, while scholars have found that socioeconomic status, occupation, education, and skin color influence voting, region is the strongest predictor (Klesner 2005 and 2007, 29–30; Ramírez Mercado 2006; Moreno 2007; Lawson 2007, 46). I argue that one reason why region is such a strong predictor of consistent left voting is the legacy of left activism in the countryside.

31. A notable exception is rural Guanajuato.

# Conclusion

*The Post-1968 Struggle for Democracy in Rural Mexico*

Thirty years of political struggles, including those in the countryside, contributed to the evolution of democratic electoral institutions and interparty dynamics that ended the longest hold on political power by any one party in the twentieth century. For the first time in Mexico's history, its political system has begun to meet many of the formal criteria of democracy identified in the introduction and reiterated below.

I have demonstrated not only that the 1968 student movement highlighted the repressive tendencies of Mexico's version of authoritarianism, but also that the repression radicalized a generation that took up the banner of 1968 in subsequent social movements. In the short run, the student massacre created a legitimacy crisis for the state. In the medium term, ex-student radicals immersed themselves in political struggles and, as the state expanded the dirty war in response, other social groups and classes radicalized. In this context, many organized independently of the state, making possible what Pérez Arce has called a "popular insurgency." He argues that from 1968 onward political protest "reached every sector in the country" (1990, 119–20). While fig. 1 bears this out, it also shows that peasants generated the largest wave of protest during the mid-1970s. The evidence makes it clear that ex-student radicals with both formal and informal ties to the Mexican Communist Party (PCM) were, in fact, immersed in the nonviolent peasant protests of this period.

Governing officials sought to manage massive political unrest by liberalizing the voting and civil rights for some, but engaging in greater repression and the violation of the human rights of others. As explained in chapter 2, it was in the context of this massive protest cycle that José López Portillo democratized electoral law by passing the Ley Federal de Organizaciones Políticas y Procesos Electorales (LFOPPE) in 1977. Through it, the government offered social movements incentives to function less radically by competing electorally. Leftist groups responded by mobilizing their social bases into political parties. The LFOPPE reforms are thus widely regarded as a decisive step toward making Mexico's political system more pluralistic. In addition, the LFOPPE law created the Instituto Federal Electoral's (IFE's) institutional precursor, the Comisión Federal Electoral, which infused electoral politics with a new discourse about democracy by seeming to promise electoral oversight.

After 1988, the major opposition parties on the left and on the right mobilized postelectoral protests and successfully brought national and international attention to the issue of independent electoral oversight. Their efforts contributed to the development of the Alianza Cívica (Civic Alliance), a nonpartisan national coalition composed of tens of thousands of prodemocracy advocates who monitor elections and government with the aim of making officials accountable (Olvera 2004, 427–32). According to Avritzer, the Alianza Cívica "changed the political landscape of the country by restoring a moral component to the process of electoral competition" (2002, 4). While it is irrefutable that civic electoral monitoring along with partisan postelectoral protests further evolved electoral institutions, my point is that the LFOPPE provisions began this process in the context of highly disruptive post-1968 protests—that is, the wave of protests during the mid-1970s. The paradox, then, is that more democratic political institutions evolved in response to the political crises created by some of the most "populist authoritarian" moments in Mexico's twentieth-century history.

As trust in the effectiveness of voting for opposition parties increased, so did electoral competition (see Camp 2004). By 1997, the PRI had lost the majority in Congress, and on the eve of the historic 2000 presidential election, opposition mayors governed half of the people in Mexico (Domínguez 2004, 336). In 2000, the Partido Acción Nacional's (PAN's) presidential candidate defeated that of the PRI, not only because of the televised exposure to Vicente Fox Quesada's effective campaigning but also because of a growing trust in the integrity of the electoral process, especially among those who did not identify with the ruling party (Lawson and Klesner 2004, 78, 83–84). The local, congressional, and finally presidential victories of the political opposition persuaded Mexicans that the PRI could be defeated and that alternative parties could govern.

But while the struggle for democracy became the leitmotif of all antiregime forces (Carr 1989, 373), electoral democracy was the political outcome, "not the starting point," of disruptive social movements (Foweraker 1990, 55; see also Foweraker and Landman 1997). In addition to the general influence of post-1968 political disruption, movement-countermovement dynamics that originated in the countryside deserve specific credit for the gradual development of political pluralism. What began as demands for land evolved into broader, increasingly politicized social movements as peasants and then businessmen became alienated from the PRI state, which failed to adequately represent them in the course of their interclass conflict.

Given the legal-political contradictions of agrarian law, peasants and businessmen created voluntary associations through which to defend their material interests. Their very emergence contributed to Mexico's democratization to the extent that they undermined the government's corporatist associations and confronted presidentialism. In breaking free from the state's corporatist system of interest representation, peasants and businessmen developed the organizational resources with which to discern and effectively articulate policy preferences independently of the state. This latter development was a major step toward strengthening civil society. It had been weakened by corporatism, which offered citizens only two political roles: they either passively accepted the decisions made by political elites in negotiation with corporatist leaders, or they took risks by opting to join a political opposition.

In articulating their own political perspectives, peasants and businessmen found themselves defending their political autonomy against government officials who attempted to co-opt or intimidate them. Many peasants were violently repressed in the process. Thus, while both peasants and businessmen initially focused on economic issues, their ideologies radicalized in the course of confronting corporatism and presidentialism. Collectively, leftists and peasants who survived state violence, as well as right-wing businessmen whose property rights were violated, were at the forefront of ultimately successful struggles for democracy. Indeed, after the bank nationalization in 1982, such dynamics turned rightist agrarian businessmen into party leaders in the crude competition for political power.

That narrow economic interclass struggles evolved into broader, more politicized movement-countermovement dynamics was not an occurrence unique to Mexico. Joe Foweraker argues that democratization struggles rarely start out focusing on democracy. In nondemocracies, ordinary people engage in interclass conflict, the contingent outcomes of which may or may not move civil society in the direction of democracy (Foweraker 1989). In Mexico, they did, and ultimately interclass struggles converged in the electoral arena. The political parties in which businessmen and peasants mobilized are viable precisely because they reflect well-organized social bases.

Chapter 4 further showed that businessmen not only revitalized the PAN but also learned to appeal to the middle class by focusing on electoral democracy rather than on the threat of a communist totalitarian state. Chapter 5 contended that the history of left-led social movements in the countryside nurtured rural bases of support, which helps explain the Partido de la Revolución Democrática's (PRD's) resiliency in the countryside over time. I argued that peasants and rural workers are ideologically predisposed to support the PRD partly because radical Marxist groups, especially the PCM, made great headway in the countryside. I also showed that the historic strongholds of left activism are negatively correlated with electoral support for the right-wing opposition, the PAN. This suggests that such left strongholds are not composed merely of opposition voters (since they have not supported the PAN over time) but rather are specifically motivated by left ideas incorporated into electoral platforms. In other words, the history of left-led organizing in the countryside helps account for why voting is so highly regional in Mexico.

The social movement origins of these parties are seen not only in ongoing postelectoral protests but also in the degree to which left vs. right ideological choices continue to resonate with voters. This was most evident in the 2006 presidential race, in which the candidates turned the elections into a referendum on the country's neoliberal path of the last twenty-five years. In this highly ideological race, slightly over half of Mexico's electorate identified as being either on the right or on the left (see Moreno 2007, 16; Boudreaux 2006).[1]

In summary, the course and outcomes of movement-countermovement dynamics helped alter the path and direction of Mexico's economic and especially political development. The growing trust in the validity of voting

---

1. Presidential elections between 1988 and 2000 involved a "two-step" process in which voters first decided to support or oppose the PRI; the second step was voting right-wing or left-wing on the basis of their ideological predispositions (Domínguez and McCann 1995; on the 1988 elections, see Carr 1989; Bruhn 1997, 128). The PAN's victory in 2000 made it so that the 2006 presidential race was primarily a choice between the left and the right.

has given Mexicans more substantive membership in the political community. Voting in presidential elections is no longer a measure of successful PRI patronage, corporatist mobilization, or voter intimidation. Instead, it increasingly represents individual choice about policy. As such, presidential voting is now a solid mechanism by which political elites may consult citizens about policy options. While the right to suffrage is not exercised universally, these changes in voting behavior go a long way toward making political citizenship more equal and more autonomous than ever before. Beyond the national level, the meaning of citizenship has also deepened in midsized municipalities where citizens mobilize to demand goods and services from the local leaders they elect (Grindle 2007). In other words, Mexico's citizens are now freer than before to discern and express their political views and elect their rulers. As Domínguez noted, this gives "concrete meaning to 'the consent of the governed'" (2004, 341).

## Consolidating Democracy: The Challenges and Promising Directions

As noted in the introduction, Seymour Martin Lipset argued that democracy required more than the consultative and constitutionally bound relationship between the state and civil society. He emphasized that democracy also has economic, social, and cultural prerequisites, such as a growing and increasingly egalitarian economy and a supportive political culture. While the empirical chapters traced the movement-countermovement forces that contributed to electoral democracy, what follows is a brief discussion of some of the challenges to, and promising directions for, democratic consolidation.

In terms of challenges, it is clear that while Mexico has been removing many of the shackles that previously fettered its economic development, the benefits of economic growth have thus far been grossly unequal. In order to protect its newborn democracy, the economy must not only grow but also benefit citizens more widely than it has in the past (see Middlebrook 2004b, 40–41; Reis 1996, 131). According to the Instituto Nacional de Estadística y Geografía (INEGI), about half of all Mexicans live in poverty. The recent deepening of poverty has increased violent crime and the drug trade, both of which threaten democracy by increasing insecurity about public safety, corrupting some local-level elections, undermining civil trust, and even militarizing law enforcement (Magaloni and Zepeda 2004; Velasco 2005). Public insecurity and the militarization of law enforcement potentially threaten the recent gains in civic self-organization. Further, the breadth and depth of the poverty of a citizenry that shares a society with some of the wealthiest people in the world creates the objective conditions that have historically contributed to armed movements in Mexico.

To avoid such political polarization, the economy must create the jobs that grow the middle class. In other words, Mexico's democracy is fragile both because it is newborn and because of the continued history of gross income inequality between a few rich and many poor, with few in between. As Middlebrook points out, gross income inequality leaves large segments of the population "vulnerable to political coercion, clientelist domination, and violence of different kinds, thus precluding the development of individual and associational autonomy so crucial to the functioning of a democratic polity" (2004b, 41–42).

But while income inequality continues to be entrenched, the political culture has been changing in promising directions (see Camp 2004). Beyond the role of the PAN and PRD in altering voter behavior, the Catholic Church encouraged voting by denouncing as sinful the PRI's history of promoting the "fear vote" (Camp 2004, 35). Perhaps even more important is the fact that the mass media has become more independent of the government since the 1980s and 1990s (Lawson 2004). As such, it has helped strengthen civil society and contributes to the creation of critical publics and fairer electoral competition.

The sharp rise in nongovernmental and social movement organizations in the last twenty years has also strengthened civil society. Such organizations focus on the environment, human rights, women's rights, indigenous peoples' rights, health and welfare services, economic justice, and rural development (Olvera 2004, 427–32). Some participate in politically disruptive protests to demand alternative policies. Recent challenges include the unarmed rural debtors' movement El Barzón; numerous consumer protests, such as those against the private telephone monopoly (1993–, 1996–98) and the Federal Electrical Commission (1988–89); and the teachers' movement in Oaxaca. Despite significant political setbacks in Chiapas, the Ejército Zapatista de Liberación Nacional's (EZLN's) armed uprising strengthened the indigenous peoples' movement while influencing public opinion about indigenous peoples' cultural and political rights (N. Harvey 1998; Womack 1999). Clearly, civil society not only has reorganized but also continues to challenge authoritarian state practices.

As I argued in chapter 2, Mexico's human rights organizations especially stand out for bringing national and international attention to the massive and ongoing human rights violations in that country. Family members of disappeared political dissidents emotionally and relentlessly denounced the PRI state's dirty war and, over the long term, contributed to the (1990) emergence and subsequent evolution of the Mexican state's National Commission on Human Rights (CNDH). As Olvera observes, such human rights groups, along with a variety of other informal human rights networks, not only maintained the spotlight on the regime's authoritarianism but also "heralded democratic values as something unprecedented in Mexican political culture, and transcended local and economic goals" (2004, 435).

Now that the state is formally charged with protecting human rights, it has created a normative framework for governance against which its actions can be judged and held accountable. While the CNDH needs to be more aggressive to actually protect people from, rather than merely document, police abuse, especially at the local and state level (such as in Guerrero, Chiapas, and Oaxaca), it has played a progressive role. As the CNDH's programs and initiatives develop under the pressure of national and international scrutiny, it is likely to contribute to the legal codification of norms that will better protect citizens from arbitrary action by government officials. So while its short history has yielded limited successes in the battle for human rights, the CNDH's very emergence represents significant, if incomplete, progress because Mexico is now positioned to take greater steps toward protecting its people from government abuse. My main point is that the post-1968 rise of human rights organizations over time contributed to a new normative and institutional framework for governance that has the potential to create more democratic policing practices and deepen democracy. As either the direct or indirect victims of state repression, former students, radicals, and family members of those who disappeared were at the forefront of the human rights struggle in Mexico. It thus seems fair to conclude that the CNDH and its normative framework are progressive long-term outcomes of the 1968 student movement. Because post-1968 human rights activists have been among the nation's loudest proponents of the public's right to know, they may also deserve a little credit for the recent passage of "transparency" laws recognizing the citizenry's legal right to government information.[2] While changing a deep-seated culture of secrecy in government affairs will be a slow process, in the long run, the new transparency laws could potentially deepen democracy by offering tools with which to make government more transparent and accountable (Fox et al. 2007).

To conclude, various politically disruptive social movements from 1968 onward demanded greater civil liberties, human rights, land reform, government accountability and administrative transparency, a balance of powers, neoliberal economic reforms, and free and fair elections, among other things. While, at first glance, such movements seem to have failed either by eliciting no positive responses from the government or by being met with state repression, some movements succeeded in the long run. Students who survived 1968 launched a protest cycle that helped undermine state corporatism by reorganizing civil society. With this reorganization came an increase in political struggles that further undermined corporatism, frontally challenged presidentialism, and ultimately reformed electoral laws. These movements eventually channeled their social bases into a new or an old political party, successfully competed in the electoral arena, and altered voter behavior. Social movements both unwittingly achieved parliamentary democracy and contributed to a more democratic political culture that values voting, allows for multiple political parties, and demands that the state treat its political opposition humanely.

My research complements the recent scholarship on Mexico's transition to democracy not only by looking at domestic processes but by specifically focusing on grassroots movement-countermovement dynamics in bringing about neoliberal economic reforms and especially democratization. As noted in the introduction, the "globalization" or "transnational waves" scholarship stresses the role of international pressure in the adoption of neoliberalism and democratization. While not refuting the influence of international pressure, I argue that national agendas also played a significant role and may help account for the relatively early adoption and long-term viability of neoliberalism in Mexico. Although other scholars likewise focus on domestic processes, their works either emphasize the role of national political elites in electoral

2. Once the PRI was removed from power, Congress unanimously passed a transparency law (the Federal Law for Transparency and Access to Information, LFTAIPG) and a new federal agency was created to help with citizens' requests for information. As Fox and Haight observe, the "years of civil society mobilization, reinforced by the IFAI's [the new federal agency's] public media campaigns, appear to have made a difference" in altering the perception among large sectors of society that they indeed have a right to government information (2007, 57).

reforms or focus on voter behavior or urban social movements since the mid-1980s. My work, in contrast, begins earlier, in 1968, and looks more broadly at political change from the bottom up, while recognizing that global catalysts did indeed influence students, peasants, and government officials. Finally, while their organizational independence and eventual support for opposition political parties was not unique to the experience of peasants and agribusinessmen, their role in Mexico's civic awakening and consequent transition to democracy has been underemphasized.

## Movement-Countermovement Dynamics and Outcomes in Repressive Political Contexts

This research holds some general implications about movements and countermovements as well as about their role in the making of political parties and democracy. Regarding social movements, my work is clearly aligned with earlier insights about the consequential power of properly framed, yet highly disruptive, social movements. It adds to this scholarship by developing an empirical focus on the role of political leadership in these processes; this contributes to the social movement literature insofar as this body of work does not pay enough attention to the role of leadership and ideology in mass mobilization. The work of leaders is frequently obscured by the drama and power of disruptive collective action. But, as my analysis showed, behind the drama of collective performances are the behind-the-scenes actions of obstinate leaders who develop the political ideologies that mobilize their networks. I demonstrated that such leaders as Ramón Danzós Palomino on the left and Manuel Clouthier on the right patiently created the organizational infrastructure through which to elaborate and disseminate their political ideologies. These leaders organized regional conferences, leadership schools, new peak associations, and organizational fronts. Clouthier and friends funded research centers, some of which not only functioned as think tanks but also cultivated leadership skills. These leaders were intent on training others in the art of being the "opposition"; they developed and disseminated their political ideologies and cultivated the activist identities of the people whom they trained. In short, they manufactured political discontent and created organizations to further disseminate their ideas and mobilize others (see Gramsci 1971; Zald 1996). Their movements eventually contributed to the consolidation and/or viability of opposition parties. Thus, if the transition to democracy in this semi-authoritarian country was slow, it inched forward in part because leaders had to create or rework much of the organizational infrastructure with which to challenge the state. They did so, moreover, during the repressive Echeverría and López Portillo years.

Furthermore, I traced when, why, and to what effect movement leaders experimented with their ideological frames. I demonstrated that while middle-class students succeeded in appealing to other students, they failed to do so with political elites and lost the support of the nation's nonyouth by framing their prodemocracy movement as a revolutionary one. Leftist leaders in the 1970s and 1980s, in contrast, hid their communist political agendas and made their claims about land redistribution more palatable to the middle class and political elites by framing them in terms of constitutional rights. This experimentation with frames led even politically antagonistic social movements to eventually use comparable frames in their claims making. For example, in 1988, both the left and the right converged in a temporary alliance to denounce electoral fraud. Businessmen were especially successful in gaining the support of the middle class when they reframed their grievances about the potentially "totalitarian" state as concerns about the lack of electoral democracy. Concretely, they called for a balance of powers, nonfraudulent elections, administrative transparency, rule of law, and efficiency. In 2000, the democracy master frame was successfully reframed as an election call for "regime change." This new campaign frame was influential among independent voters and made it possible for an opposition party to finally remove the PRI from power (Domínguez 2004). Political leadership, in short, is crucial to the emergence and success of frames and, thus, social movement trajectories and outcomes.

That said, this research also has implications for understanding social movements as aggregate phenomena. By focusing on movement-countermovement relations over time, I examined the outcomes of dynamic processes that have heretofore been understudied. A first general observation about the processes analyzed is that social movements are not just in a dyadic relationship with the state. They function in a multi-organizational environment within civil society that includes supporters, political opponents, and, of course, bystander audiences, including the media. Though the state's responses are indeed crucial to determining movement outcomes, the interplay of movements can lead to outcomes that go well beyond immediate state policy concessions.

I further demonstrated that there are short-, medium-, and long-term, as well as intended and unintended, consequences of movement-countermovement mobilizations. This suggests that when countermovements mobilize, the concessions that they win or lose as the opposition, and even what organizational forms they adopt, shape the course and outcomes of initial movement challengers (Meyer and Staggenborg 1996, 1654). For example, agribusinessmen not only followed peasants in making claims via a disruptive strike but also eventually created a politically independent organization that would prove consequential in terms of altering the Constitution to end land reform. Peasant and agribusiness movements ended up in the electoral arena, and their frames eventually converged around the struggle for democracy.

In integrating insights from the framing, movement outcomes, and countermovements literatures, my work addresses the relationship between protest movements and long-term institutional change. While consistent with the classic arguments pointing to the power of properly framed yet highly disruptive social movements, this work also shows that social movements may, in the long run and in unexpected ways, bring about democracy. It adds empirical support to the claim that domestic political disruption can bring about large-scale institutional reforms, including by democratizing civil society and the state (Foweraker 1990; Munck 1990; Giugni, McAdam, and Tilly 1998; McAdam, Tarrow, and Tilly 2001; Schock 2005).

Social movements contribute to democratization because, first, politically disruptive claims engage others, possibly even a countermovement, in articulating policy preferences. Second, interest articulation from the bottom up may prompt public officials to participate in two- or three-way negotiations about policy. Finally, social movements carry the threat of actually holding public officials accountable via continued, and perhaps greater, political disruption. Consequently, movements sometimes succeed in eliciting immediate policy concessions. As demonstrated in the preceding chapters, social movements may also result in major institutional reforms in the medium and long term.

If social movements in Mexico democratized a semi-authoritarian political system and even altered some aspects of the political culture, then the most general lesson that can be learned from this book is that social movements can move mountains even in repressive political contexts. The state was effectively challenged on the lack of civil liberties, corporatism, the hypercentralization of power in presidentialism, and the dirty war that more than one president authorized. Clearly, state repression did not demobilize all activists forever. While it succeeded in deactivating nonradicals who participated in the 1968 movement as youth, rather than as ideologically committed leftists, political repression also deepened the antistate ideologies and activist identities of those leftists who had gone through formal ideological training in a communist organization. The left, in other words, had an ideological apparatus with which to interpret state repression. PCM members, for example, concluded that the Mexican state's dirty war was clear evidence that the state was now completely bourgeois and, in consequence, a "new revolution" was in order. This new analysis departed from their previous view, which had called for a united front with the "progressive nationalist bourgeoisie." This new analysis was not radical enough for some youth who had either directly participated in the student movement of 1968 or identified with the activists.

Thus, instead of deactivating them, state repression radicalized and then dispersed activists across different geographical locations and/or across opposition movements. Operating as loose conflict networks in distinct fields of political action, deeply committed activists launched a protest cycle that began in the 1970s, not the 1980s. They protested in all sectors of society and unwittingly forced public officials into liberalizing electoral law. If state repression deactivates the less committed but strengthens the activist identities of the deeply committed, it follows that the impact of state repression is contingent. I have argued that political repression is contingent because it interacts with such movement characteristics as ideology, commitment on the part of activists, and movement frames. Not only do salient frames have the potential to increase the number of movement activists and the odds of support from others (including elites), but they may also decrease the odds of repression by gaining sympathy from state elites.

It thus follows that political opportunities are more dynamic and dialogically emergent than has been previously theorized. This suggests that while an authoritarian state's closed characteristics and penchant for repression are important variables, their impact is indeed contingent. The concentration of state power, the degree of democracy, political competition, associational parties, and the state's propensity to repression interact with movement characteristics to determine outcomes. The extent to which movement leaders successfully negotiate the particular political and cultural contexts of their societies determines the level and quality of political change.

# *Appendix A*

## The Research Design: Methods and Data Sources

I conducted field research in Mexico City in the fall of 1992 and again in the fall of 1994, during extremely charged political debates about Mexico's future. The struggle over the country's economic and political direction resulted in tragic, yet illuminating, events. For example, my 1994 trip occurred just nine months after the start of armed Zapatista insurrection in Mexico's poorest state (Chiapas) and six months after the politically motivated assassination of the PRI's presidential candidate (Luis Donaldo Colosio); I left just before the devastating peso devaluation. As I was in Mexico City when José Ruiz Massieu, the PRI's general secretary, was assassinated, I learned of the rumors of a potential military coup. The deep political differences within the PRI and, indeed, between citizens made my questions about political conflict relevant to all parties interviewed. As a consequence, my interview subjects offered rich, sometimes passionate, responses.

While in the field, I also observed left meetings, an election rally at the National Autonomous University (UNAM), and a massive demonstration (on October 12, 1992) about the state of Mexico's indigenous peoples five hundred years after the so-called discovery of America. While in the United States, I analyzed presidential speeches and land reform decrees, declassified U.S. intelligence, and, as discussed below, read hundreds of newspaper stories on peasant protest. I also conducted archival research out of Stanford's Hoover Institution, where I examined the internal documents produced by the Mexican Communist Party (PCM). I focused on the PCM because when I recoded Blanca Rubio's data (described below), it became clear to me that of all of the left groups operating in Mexico's countryside, the majority of unarmed protests that journalists identified by organization were either directly or indirectly linked to the PCM (see chapter 5). That politically independent newspaper sources indicated that the PCM had the largest base of support among *unarmed* peasants could be explained by the fact that, as compared to Maoists, Castroists, and Trotskyists, the PCM had a much longer history of operating in the countryside. Through my archival research at the Hoover Institution, I sought to shed better light on that history.

While archival research, interviews, and observations offer contextually rich, detailed information on why people do what they do, they may lead the analyst to exaggerate the role of particular interview subjects or informants. Whenever possible, I tried to avoid this potential methodological pitfall by triangulating some, though clearly not all, truth claims. For example, my work on the PCM is based on archival research that I conducted in 2000 by reading internal PCM documents. The fact that some of the claims made in these documents were corroborated by sources that were independent of, and in some cases antagonistic to, the party bolstered my confidence in my findings about the extent of PCM activism in the peasant revolts.

My analysis of businessmen is based on interviews conducted in Mexico City in the fall of 1994. I also traveled to Guanajuato, Guanajuato, and to the state of Mexico. I triangulated accounts by comparing what businessmen working in different cities actually said. I found additional independent evidence of the role played by secondary figures in the various retrospectives celebrating the Confederación Patronal de la República Mexicana's (COPARMEX's) seventy-five years in existence. These retrospectives comprised a series of interviews with COPARMEX's ex-presidents.

However, while triangulation helps corroborate truth claims, it is not possible in all analyses. By necessity, my account of the student movement draws heavily on published student testimonials and recently declassified CIA documents. Official Mexican documents on the events in Tlatelolco in 1968 have not been opened to the public. Consequently, chapter 2 also relies heavily on the secondary sources, including the possible mistakes therein.

Like my qualitative analyses, my quantitative work relies on multiple data sources. Data on peasant protests between 1970 and 1975 comprise an original probability sample of 221 cases gleaned from the daily newspaper *Excelsior* (see appendix B for an explanation of the random sampling technique). No previous account written on peasant protest in Mexico during this period utilizes such systematic and national-level data. In Armando Bartra's (1985) classic work, for example, he presented no systematic examination of when and where the protests occurred, how many actually took place, or who was involved. Appendix B addresses potential concerns about selection bias in newspaper coverage. I conclude that the data set is reasonably reliable and valid given that *Excelsior* was the only politically independent national-level newspaper at the time, and given the random selection of the days read and the hard news reported. Further, as Earl et al. argue on the basis of a comprehensive review of the literature on the utility of newspaper sources, "newspaper data does not deviate markedly from accepted standards of quality" (2004, 77).

The data on peasant protests from 1979 to 1984 were organized from Blanca Rubio's handwritten entry of 727 cases of such events (see appendix C). Other statistical evidence is based on government censuses, reports, and the secondary sources.

# Appendix B

## A Random Sample of 221 Cases of Peasant Protest, 1970–1975

I created an original random sample of peasant protests by examining every third day of the newspaper *Excelsior* (Mexico City) from January 1, 1970, through December 5, 1975. This method yielded 221 cases of such protest. These were coded by grievance, tactic, target, and, where possible, the size of the protest as well as the government's response. The data were organized on a per-state basis because the reporters did not always include the county (*municipio*) in which the demonstration, rally, or land invasion occurred. Table 13 provides basic summary statistics.

While other scholars (such as Rubio 1987; Aguado López, Torres Franco, and Scherer Ibarra 1983) provide systematic data on peasant protests during the post-Echeverría era (1977–82), my work is the only published account offering systematic data on the peasant protests from 1970 to 1975. This is not to suggest that the data are ideal. Because they are based on newspaper sources and the sample selection bias therein, the data underestimate the extent of contentious political action in the countryside. Sample selection bias in newspaper coverage is a function of the editors' political perspective, mundane editorial concerns such as space, deadlines, journalistic norms, and the characteristics of the issues and events (Earl et al. 2004; Oliver and Maney 2000).

However, despite many examples to the contrary, it is possible for a newspaper's editor to see "news value" in antigovernment protest. Julio Scherer García was such an editor for *Excelsior* (and eventually for the left-leaning *Proceso*). In the first half of the 1970s, not only was *Excelsior* Mexico's only politically independent newspaper, but it also tried to cover political discontent nationally. Though few of the articles I coded were front-page stories (probably to avoid intimidation by government officials), there were plenty of accounts of peasant protest in a section entitled "Los estados." This type of coverage departed from the journalistic norms of that period since political opposition, government repression, government corruption, and electoral fraud were generally taboo journalistic topics. While not officially censored, Mexican reporters tended to engage in self-censorship for fear of economic reprisals or even government harassment (Lawson 2004). Indeed, *Excelsior*'s

Table 13  Frequency of peasant demands in 221 protests in Mexico, 1970–75

| Demand or grievance | % of total protests | Number of protests (all states) |
|---|---|---|
| Land | 65.00 | 161 |
| Water rights | 0.81 | 2 |
| Credit | 1.21 | 3 |
| Wages or unions | 1.62 | 4 |
| Other economic issue[a] | 6.07 | 15 |
| Anti-state protests[b] | 25.00 | 62 |
| Total protests[c] | 99.00 | 247 |

SOURCE: Data from a one-third sample of *Excelsior* reports, January 1970–December 1975.

[a] Such as payment for crops, indemnification for land, or anti-tax protests.
[b] Of the 62 protests that also articulated a political grievance, 27 percent focused on government corruption, 18 percent focused on the failure of the government to distribute land promised in previous land reform resolutions, and 15 percent protested government repression. The remainder were "other" political grievances.
[c] Total number of protests equals 247 rather than 221 because in 26 protests peasants raised both economic and political demands.

Julio Scherer García's departure from journalistic norms came at a price. President Luis Echeverría organized a violent occupation of the newspaper's offices on July 8, 1976. According to Alan Riding (1976), "The ousting of Mr. Scherer and [two hundred of] his liberal associates is equivalent to the silencing of independent opinion in Mexico since *Excelsior* offered the only forum for serious analysis of the country's problems and for criticism of the Government's performance." This example of counterhegemonic journalism illustrates why we should contextualize the political bias of newspapers rather than dismiss them as a source of data (Earl et al. 2004; Oliver and Maney 2000).

In the developing world, sample selection bias may also result from limited financial resources and communications networks. Consequently, even national newspapers may not have access to all locations and events. In Mexico, however, the very centralized structure of corporatist political representation connected both peasants and agrarian capitalists at the municipal level to authorities in Mexico City, where their national confederations were headquartered. It is reasonable to assume that journalists learned about local peasant protests from some of the many sources reporting such events to the corporatist leaders of the National Peasants' Confederation (CNC) or to either of the two confederations organizing agrarian capitalists (the Confederación Nacional de la Pequeña Propiedad [CNPP] and the Confederación Nacional Ganadera [CNG]).

Between 1970 and 1975, *Excelsior* reported on protest events in nearly every state in Mexico.[1] It follows that a random sample of newspaper reports covering protests should be reasonably representative of the actual levels of underlying social movement activity. Finally, because *Excelsior* is the only primary source of information on peasant protests nationally, triangulation of media sources is impossible. But given the newspaper's political independence, counterhegemonic biases, the institutional links between local and national politics, the random selection of days, and hard news reporting, the data set is reasonably reliable and valid (Earl et al. 2004, 77).

---

1. See the maps in Trevizo (2002), which can be viewed at http://caliber.ucpress.net/doi/abs/10.1525/sop.2002.45.3.285.

## Appendix C

### 727 Cases of Peasant Protests, 1979–1984

Using Blanca Rubio's handwritten spreadsheets counting the number of peasant protests in Mexico between 1979 and 1984, I created an electronic data set representing all newspaper reports of peasant protest events during this period. According to Rubio, newspapers focus on big events; in terms of protest, big events are the most significant because they speak to high levels of organizational and human resources. Rubio's primary source was the newspaper clippings archive Información Sistemática. She triangulated her sources by examining which peasant organizations were represented in a loose coalition of politically independent peasant groups called the Coordinadora Nacional Plan de Ayala (CNPA). The CNPA called its first national peasant congress in 1979 (see A. Bartra 1985, 147). Rubio found that the organizations represented by the CNPA were those that the press reported as leading a high number of peasant protests. Because journalists did not always identify the name of the organization leading peasants in protest, or the *municipio* in which the event(s) occurred, the data are organized by state. Finally, to locate the ideological orientation of the organizations identified in Rubio's data set, I relied on the secondary sources.

Figs. 10 and 11 identify peasant protests by tactic, target, and the role of social control forces over time. They are supplementary to figs. 8 and 9 in chapter 5.

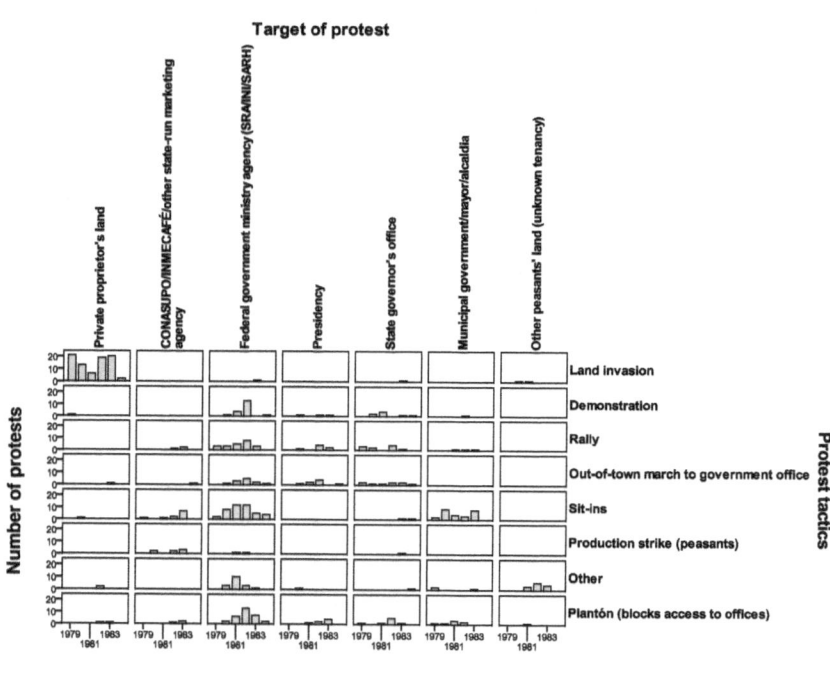

*Fig. 10* Demands by tactic and target in 720 cases of peasant protest, 1979–84
SOURCE: Rubio's data set, based on newspaper articles in Información Sistemática.
NOTE: Protest events in Mexico City excluded from this analysis.

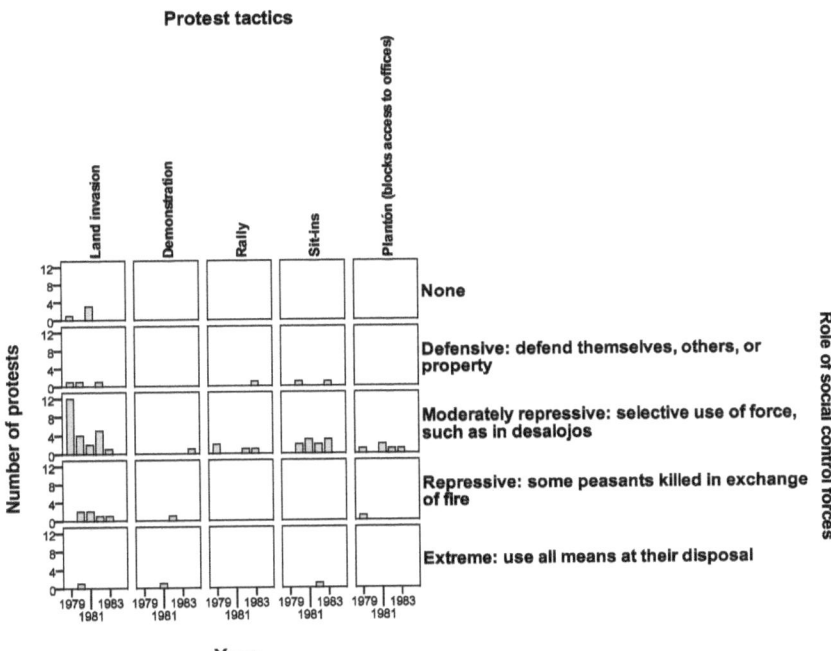

*Fig. 11* Protest tactic by the role of social control forces in 720 cases of peasant protest, 1979–84

SOURCE: Rubio's data set, based on newspaper articles in Información Sistemática.
NOTE: Protest events in Mexico City excluded from this analysis.

## Appendix D

### The Nomenclature of the Direct Rural Producers

Table 4 defines "peasant-workers" as those producers whose parcels are so small (four hectares or less of rain-fed land) that they are considered sub-subsistence producers. As such, they sell their labor power on at least a seasonal basis to survive. Peasants who work seasonally tend to do so on large, nearby, private estates during the harvest period. Others migrate to Sonora and Sinaloa, or to the United States for seasonal work (Martínez, Foncerrada, and Bautista 1980, 34). Still others may temporarily work in urban and tourist industries if their villages are near cities or resorts. As table 4 shows, both ejido sector peasant-workers (922,294) and private sector peasant-workers (500,602) constituted such part-time or seasonal workers in 1970. Using a different measure, the 1970 Agricultural Census estimated that over two million rural people were temporary or seasonal workers (*trabajadores eventuales o temporales*). (If a person worked less than half a year but a minimum of one-third of a year, then he/she was counted as a temporary or seasonal worker.) Both the Comisión Económica para América Latina's (CEPAL's) estimates and the census estimates are conservative given that the years between 1967 and 1970 were particularly depressed.

In contrast to peasant-workers, landless agricultural workers (henceforth agricultural workers) survive by selling their labor power on a full-time basis. Typically born in the countryside, agricultural workers were generally once peasants but lost their parcels to creditors or buyers, or simply abandoned them because they consistently produced below their subsistence requirements. In the 1960s and 1970s, full-time agricultural workers tended to be migratory workers, harvesting cotton in the Laguna region, sugarcane in the Gulf states, or tobacco and coffee in the southeast (Gutelman 1971, 199). Migratory workers thus tend to be concentrated where capitalist agriculture is most fully developed. In 1960, fully 76 percent of Baja California's agricultural labor force, 67 percent of Sonora's, and 59 percent of Coahuila's were migratory workers (Gutelman 1971, 199).

Based on the 1970 Agricultural Census, I conservatively estimate that there were about 433,788 full-time agricultural workers employed in 1969. The Agricultural Census cautions that the "employed" category is incomparable to the 1970 General Population Census's "economically active population" category, which constitutes those who worked for at least fifteen hours per week at some point during 1969. It does not specify how many weeks one would have had to work to be considered part of the economically active population. Unfortunately, the government's statistics do not permit a more precise analysis. The Agricultural Census, which distinguishes between temporarily and permanently employed workers, does not provide information on the "economically active population" or urban workers. The 1970 General Population Census, on the other hand, does not distinguish between temporary and permanent workers. According to this census, all agricultural workers (part-time, temporary, and full-time) constituted about 30 percent of all workers listed as economically active (Secretaría de Industria y Comercio 1972b, 133, table 42).

# *References*

## Author Interviews

Calderón Salazar, Jorge Alfonso. 1992. Mexico City, October 8. Congressman for the PRD.
Cortez, Rosario [pseud.]. 2000. E-mail communication, August 31. Female peasant leader and former member of the PCM.
Gavito, Víctor. 1994. Mexico, October 6. Founding member of the CNA and eventual vice president of COPARMEX.
Lugo Chávez, Héctor Samuel. 1994. Guanajuato, Guanajuato, October 12. Undersecretary of agriculture, livestock, forestry, and fisheries for the Ministry of Economic Development.
Muñoz Ledo, Porfirio. 1992. Mexico City, October 1. PRD founder and senator.
Núñez Esteva, Alberto. 1994. Mexico City, October 21. Founding member of the CNA and eventual president of COPARMEX. Vice president of AGROBIOA, S.A., of C.V. Sector Alimentos.
Valdés Abascal, Rafael. 1992. Mexico City, October 19. Legal advisor to the planning undersecretary of the Ministry of Agriculture.
Zarazua Sandoval, Carlos. 1994. Mexico City, September 27. Director general of CNA.

## Government Documents

Comisión Nacional de Derechos Humanos (CNDH). 2001. *Informe de actividades.* Mexico.
———. 2006. *Informe de actividades.* Mexico.
*Diario Oficial.* 1971–75. Government gazette, Mexico.
Díaz Ordaz, Gustavo. 1968. *Cuarto informe que rinde al H. Congreso de la Unión el C. Presidente de la República Gustavo Díaz Ordaz del 10 septiembre 1968.* Mexico City: Secretaría de Gobernación.
National Security Archive, George Washington University. U.S. government intelligence documents. http://www.gwu.edu/~nsarchiv/NSAEBB/NSAEBB10/nsaebb 10.htm (accessed June 8, 2010).
Procuraduría General de la República. 2006. *Informe histórico a la Sociedad Mexicana.* Mexico. http://www.gwu.edu/~nsarchiv//NSAEBB/NSAEBB180/index.htm (accessed June 8, 2010).
Secretaría de Agricultura y Recursos Hidráulicos, Dirección General de Extensión Agrícola. 1977. *Programa de Inversiones Publicas para el Desarrollo Rural, 1977.* Mexico.
Secretaría de Industria y Comercio, Dirección General de Estadística. 1972a. *Anuario estadístico del comercio exterior de los Estados Unidos Mexicanos, 1971.* Mexico.

———. 1972b. *IX censo general de población, 1970: Resumen general*. Mexico.
———. 1974. *Anuario estadístico del comercio exterior de los Estados Unidos Mexicanos, 1973*. Mexico.
———. 1975. *V censos agrícola—ganadero y ejidal, 1970: Resumen general*. Mexico.
Secretaría de Programación y Presupuesto. 1975. *Anuario estadístico del comercio exterior de los Estados Unidos Mexicanos, 1975*. Mexico.

## Other Primary Sources

Boudreaux, Richard. 2006. "The Deciding Factor May Be the Undecided." *Los Angeles Times*, June 24.
Cámara Nacional de Comercio de la Ciudad de México. n.d. *Organismos privados en México*. Mexico City: CANACO.
Confederación Patronal de la República Mexicana. 2004. "Enfoques: Jorge Ocejo." *Coparmex-Entorno*, no. 194 (October). http://www.coparmex.org.mx/contenidos/publicaciones/entorno/2004/oct04/4.htm (accessed August 26, 2010).
Consejo Nacional Agropecuario. 1990. *Propuestas del sector empresarial para la reactivación productiva del campo mexicano*. Mexico: CNA.
*El Día*. 1968. Daily newspaper, Mexico City.
¡Eureka! 1989. *Eureka: Historia gráfica, doce años de lucha por la libertad. México 1977–1989*. Mexico City: Multiediciones California.
*Excelsior*. 1970–75. Daily newspaper, Mexico City.
General Command of the Zapatista Army of National Liberation (EZLN), Clandestine Revolutionary Indigenous Committee. 2000. "EZLN Communiqué Regarding Elections." http://flag.blackened.net/revolt/mexico/ezln/2000/ccri_elections_june.html (accessed September 16, 2010).
———. 2005. "Sixth Declaration of the Selva Lacandona." https://webspace.utexas.edu/hcleaver/www/SixthDeclaration.html (accessed September 21, 2010).
Johnson, Reed. 2008. "Putting a Spotlight on the Massacre of 1968." *Los Angeles Times*, February 16.
Martínez Nateras, Arturo. 1975. *El Partido Comunista en la sociedad mexicana actual: Informe del Comité Central a la segunda Conferencia Nacional de Organización*. Mexico: Ediciones de Cultura Popular.
———. 1980. *Punto y seguido: Crisis en el PCM?* Mexico: Arturo Martínez Nateras.
Martínez Verdugo, Arnoldo. 1985. *Historia del comunismo en México*. Mexico: Editorial Grijalbo.
Minnesota Population Center. 2007. *Integrated Public Use Microdata Series International, Version 3.0*. Minneapolis: University of Minnesota.
*Oposición*. 1970–74. Bimonthly magazine, Mexico.
Oppenheim, Charles. 2004a. "José Luis Coindreau: La Coparmex es una escuela de formación de empresarios." *Coparmex-Entorno*, no. 16 (June): 12–16. http://www.coparmex.org.mx/contenidos/publicaciones/entorno/2004/jun04/4.pdf (accessed September 9, 2010).
———. 2004b. "José María Basagoiti (1982–1984): Los años que vivimos en peligro." *Coparmex-Entorno*, May. http://www.coparmex.org.mx/contenidos/publicaciones/entorno/2004/may04/9.htm (accessed September 9, 2010).

Partido Comunista Mexicano (PCM). 1973. *Partido Comunista Mexicano, 1967–1972.* Mexico: Ediciones de Cultura Popular.

———. 1974. *Partido Comunista Mexicano: Resoluciones y saludos.* Mexico: Talleres Gráficos de México. (Orig. pub. 1973).

———. 1977. *Informe y resoluciones del Primer Congreso Regional: Puebla y Tlaxcala.* Puebla: Ediciones del Comité Regional del PCM en Puebla y Tlaxcala.

Partido Comunista Mexicano (PCM), Comité Regional en La Comarca Lagunera. 1971. *El campesinado lagunero ante la política reaccionaria de la burguesía.* Torreón: El Comité.

Reyes Salcido, Edgardo. 2004. "Las cinco etapas de la Coparmex." *Coparmex-Entorno*, no. 195 (November): 14–15. http://www.coparmex.org.mx/contenidos/publicaciones/entorno/2004/nov04/5.pdf (accessed September 9, 2010).

U.S. Department of State, Bureau of Democracy, Human Rights, and Labor. 2004. "Mexico." Country report on human rights practices. http://www.state.gov/g/drl/rls/hrrpt/2004/41767.htm (accessed September 9, 2010).

Velasco Arzac, Guillermo. 2004. "Coparmex en la historia de México." *Coparmex-Entorno*, no. 193 (September). http://www.coparmex.org.mx/contenidos/publicaciones/entorno/2004/sep04/4.htm (accessed September 9, 2010).

*La Voz de México.* 1968–69. Weekly magazine, Mexico.

## Secondary Sources

Abruch Linder, Miguel. 1983. "La cruzada empresarial." *Nexos* 65 (April): 25–29.

Ackerman, Peter, and Christopher Kruegler. 1994. *Strategic Nonviolent Conflict: The Dynamics of People Power in the Twentieth Century.* Westport, Conn.: Praeger.

Aguado López, Eduardo, José L. Torres Franco, and Gabriela Scherer Ibarra. 1983. "La lucha por la tierra en México (1976–1982)." *Revista Mexicana de Ciencias Políticas y Sociales* 28, nos. 113–14 (July–December): 43–66.

Alcañiz, Isabella, and Melissa Scheier. 2008. "New Social Movements with Old Party Politics: The MTL Piqueteros and the Communist Party in Argentina." In Stahler-Sholk, Vanden, and Kuecker 2008, 271–85.

Almeida, Paul D. 2003. "Opportunity Organizations and Threat-Induced Contention: Protest Waves in Authoritarian Settings." *American Journal of Sociology* 109, no. 2 (September): 345–400.

Almeida, Paul D., and Hank Johnston. 2006. "Neoliberal Globalization and Popular Movements in Latin America." In Johnston and Almeida 2006, 3–18.

Almeida, Paul D., and Linda Brewster Stearns. 1998. "Political Opportunities and Local Grassroots Environmental Movements: The Case of Minamata." *Social Problems* 45, no. 1: 37–60.

Alvarez, Sonia. E., Evelina Dagnino, and Arturo Escobar, eds. 1998. *Cultures of Politics, Politics of Cultures: Re-Visioning Latin American Social Movements.* Boulder, Colo.: Westview Press.

Alvarez, Sonia E., and Arturo Escobar. 1992. "Conclusion: Theoretical and Political Horizons of Change in Contemporary Latin American Social Movements." In Escobar and Alvarez 1992, 317–29.

Amenta, Edwin, and Neal Caren. 2004. "The Legislative, Organizational, and Beneficiary Consequences of State-Oriented Challengers." In Snow, Soule, and Kriesi 2004, 461–88.
Amenta, Edwin, Bruce G. Carruthers, and Yvonne Zylan. 1992. "A Hero for the Aged? The Townsend Movement, the Political Mediation Model, and U.S. Old-Age Policy, 1934–1950." *American Journal of Sociology* 98:308–39.
Amenta, Edwin, and M. P. Young. 1999. "Democratic States and Social Movements: Theoretical Arguments and Hypotheses." *Social Problems* 46, no. 2: 153–68.
Amnesty International. 1998. *Mexico: "Disappearances": A Black Hole in the Protection of Human Rights.* http://www.amnesty.org/en/library/info/AMR41/005/1998 (accessed October 11, 2010).
Andrews, Kenneth T. 2001. "Social Movements and Policy Implementation: The Mississippi Civil Rights Movement and the War on Poverty, 1965–1971." *American Sociological Review* 66:71–95.
———. 2002. "Movement-Countermovement Dynamics and the Emergence of New Institutions: The Case of 'White Flight' Schools in Mississippi." *Social Forces* 80, no. 3: 911–36.
Arditi, Benjamin, and José Carlos Rodríguez. 1987. *La sociedad a pesar del estado: Movimientos sociales y recuperación democrática en el Paraguay.* Asunción, Paraguay: El Lector.
Arizpe, Lourdes. 1985. "The State and Uneven Agrarian Development in Mexico." In *Politics in Mexico,* edited by George Philip, 206–20. London: Croom Helm.
Arriola, Carlos. 1987. "De la pérdida de confianza en el buen gobierno, 1970–1982." In *La vida política mexicana en la crisis,* edited by Soledad Loaeza y Rafael Segovia, 41–60. Mexico City: El Colegio de México, A.C.
Avritzer, Leonardo. 2002. *Democracy and the Public Space in Latin America.* Princeton: Princeton University Press.
Babb, Sarah. 2001. *Managing Mexico: Economists from Nationalism to Neoliberalism.* Princeton: Princeton University Press.
Babb, Sarah, and Marion Fourcade-Gourinchas. 2002. "The Rebirth of the Liberal Creed: Paths to Neoliberalism in Four Countries." *American Journal of Sociology* 108, no. 3: 533–79.
Banaszak, Lee Ann. 1996. *Why Movements Succeed or Fail: Opportunity, Culture, and the Struggle for Woman Suffrage.* Princeton: Princeton University Press.
Barker, Colin, Alan Johnson, and Michael Lavalette. 2001. *Leadership and Social Movements.* Manchester: Manchester University Press.
Bartra, Armando. 1977. "Seis años de lucha campesina." *Investigación Económica,* no. 3 (January): 157–209.
———. 1985. *Los herederos de Zapata: Movimientos campesinos posrevolucionarios en México, 1920–1980.* Mexico City: Ediciones Era.
Bartra, Roger. 1974. *Estructura agraria y clases sociales en México.* Serie Popular Era 28. Mexico City: Ediciones Era.
———. 2002. *Blood, Ink, and Culture: Miseries and Splendors of the Post-Mexican Condition.* Durham: Duke University Press.
Basáñez, Miguel. 1990. *El pulso de los sexenios: 20 años de crisis en México.* Mexico City: Siglo Veintiuno Editores.

Becker, Marc. 2008. "Pachakutik and Indigenous Political Party Politics in Ecuador." In Stahler-Sholk, Vanden, and Kuecker 2008, 165–80.
Beer, Caroline C. 2003. *Electoral Competition and Institutional Change in Mexico.* Notre Dame: University of Notre Dame Press.
Benford, Robert D., and David Snow. 2000. "Framing Processes and Social Movements: An Overview and Assessment." *Annual Review of Sociology* 26:611–39.
Bennett, Vivienne. 1992. "The Evolution of Urban Popular Movements in Mexico Between 1968 and 1988." In Escobar and Alvarez 1992, 240–59.
———. 1993. "Orígenes del movimiento urbano popular Mexicano: Pensamiento político y organizaciones políticas clandestinas, 1960–1980." *Revista Mexicana de Sociología* 55, no. 4 (July–September): 89–102.
Besserer, Federico, Victoria Novelo, and Juan Luis Sariego. 1983. *El sindicalismo minero en México, 1900–1952.* Mexico City: Ediciones Era.
Boudreau, Vincent. 1996. "Northern Theory, Southern Protest: Opportunity Structure Analysis in Cross-National Perspective." *Mobilization* 1, no. 2: 175–89.
———. 2005. "Precarious Regimes and Matchup Problems in the Explanation of Repressive Policy." In Davenport, Johnston, and Mueller 2005, 33–57.
Boudreaux, Richard. 2003. "360 Snipers Shot Students in '68, Mexican Inquiry Finds." *Los Angeles Times,* October 2.
Brachet-Marquez, Viviane. 1994. *The Dynamics of Domination: State, Class, and Social Reform in Mexico, 1910–1990.* Pittsburgh: University of Pittsburgh Press.
Brockett, Charles D. 1991. "The Structure of Political Opportunities and Peasant Mobilization in Central America." *Comparative Politics* 23, no. 3: 253–74.
———. 1995. "A Protest-Cycle Resolution of the Repression/Popular-Protest Paradox." In *Repertoires and Cycles of Collective Action,* edited by Mark Traugott, 117–44. Durham: Duke University Press.
Bruhn, Kathleen. 1997. *Taking on Goliath: The Emergence of a New Left Party and the Struggle for Democracy in Mexico.* University Park: Pennsylvania State University Press.
Bruhn, Kathleen, and Kenneth F. Greene. 2007. "Elite Polarization Meets Mass Moderation in Mexico's 2006 Elections." *Political Science and Politics* 40 (January): 33–38.
Brulle, Robert J. 1996. "Environmental Discourse and Social Movement Organizations: A Historical and Rhetorical Perspective on the Development of U.S. Environmental Organizations." *Sociological Inquiry* 66, no. 1: 58–83.
Buendía, Jorge. 2004. "The Changing Mexican Voter, 1991–2000." In Middlebrook 2004a, 108–29.
Burstein, Paul. 1999. "Social Movements and Public Policy." In *How Social Movements Matter,* edited by Marco G. Giugni, Doug McAdam, and Charles Tilly, 3–21. Minneapolis: University of Minnesota Press.
Calderón, Fernando. 1995. *Movimientos sociales y política: La década de los ochenta en Latinoamérica.* Mexico City: Siglo Veintiuno Editores.
Calhoun, Craig. 1991. "The Problem of Identity in Collective Action." In *Macro-Micro Linkages in Sociology,* edited by Joan Huber, 51–75. Newbury Park, Calif.: Sage.
Camp, Roderic Ai. 1989. *Entrepreneurs and Politics in Twentieth-Century Mexico.* New York: Oxford University Press.

———. 2004. "Citizen Attitudes Toward Democracy and Vicente Fox's Victory in 2000." In Domínguez and Lawson 2004, 25-46.
Canabal Cristiani, Beatriz. 1983. "El movimiento campesino en Sonora (1970-1976)." *Revista Mexicana de Ciencias Políticas y Sociales* 28, nos. 113-14 (July-December): 67-98.
———. 1984. *Hoy luchamos por la tierra*. Mexico City: Universidad Autónoma Metropolitana-Xochimilco.
Carbajal Ríos, Carola. 1988. "Una experiencia de participación de las campesinas en el movimiento popular." In *Las mujeres en el campo*, edited by Josefina Aranda Bezaury, 424-30. Oaxaca, Mexico: Instituto de Investigaciones Sociológicas de la Universidad Autónoma Benito Juárez de Oaxaca.
Carr, Barry. 1989. "The Left and Its Potential Role in Political Change." In *Mexico's Alternative Political Futures*, edited by Wayne A. Cornelius, Judith Gentleman, and Peter H. Smith, 367-87. San Diego: Center for U.S.-Mexican Studies, UCSD.
———. 1992. *Marxism and Communism in Twentieth-Century Mexico*. Lincoln: University of Nebraska Press.
Carton de Grammont, Hubert. 1989. "La Unión General de Obreros y Campesinos de México." In *Historia de la cuestión agraria mexicana*, vol. 8, *Política estatal y conflictos agrarios, 1950-1970*, edited by Julio Moguel, 222-60. Mexico City: Siglo Veintiuno Editores.
———. 1990. *Empresarios agrícolas y el estado: Sinaloa, 1893-1984*. Mexico City: Instituto de Investigaciones Sociales, UNAM.
Carton de Grammont, Hubert, and Horacio Mackinlay. 2009. "Campesino and Indigenous Social Organizations Facing Democratic Transition in Mexico, 1938-2006." *Latin American Perspectives* 36, no. 4: 21-37.
Carty, Victoria. 2006. "Transnational Labor Mobilizing in Two Mexican Maquiladoras." In Johnston and Almeida 2006, 215-29.
Castañeda, Jorge G. 2000. *Perpetuating Power: How Mexican Presidents Were Chosen*. New York: New Press.
Castells, Manuel, and Roberto Laserna. 1994. "The New Dependency: Technological Change and Socioeconomic Restructuring in Latin America." In *Comparative National Development*, edited by A. Douglas Kincaid and Alejandro Portes, 57-83. Chapel Hill: University of North Carolina Press.
Centro de Estudios Históricos del Agrarismo en México (CEHAM). 1988a. *La época de oro y el principio de la crisis de la agricultura mexicana, 1950-1970*. Edited by Julio Moguel. Vol. 7 of *Historia de la cuestión agraria mexicana*. Mexico City: Siglo Veintiuno Editores.
———. 1988b. *Modernización, lucha agraria, y poder político, 1920-1934*. Edited by Enrique Montalvo. Vol. 4 of *Historia de la cuestión agraria mexicana*. Mexico City: Siglo Veintiuno Editores.
———. 1989. *Política estatal y conflictos agrarios, 1950-1970*. Edited by Julio Moguel. Vol. 8 of *Historia de la cuestión agraria mexicana*. Mexico City: Siglo Veintiuno Editores.
———. 1990a. *El cardenismo: Un parteaguas histórico en el proceso agrario nacional, 1934-1940*. Part 1. Edited by Everardo Escárcega López and Saúl Escobar Toledo.

Vol. 5 of *Historia de la cuestión agraria mexicana*. Mexico City: Siglo Veintiuno Editores.

———. 1990b. *El cardenismo: Un parteaguas histórico en el proceso agrario nacional, 1934-1940*. Part 2. Edited by Saúl Escobar Toledo, Luis Hernández, Pilar López, and Rossana Cassigoli Salamón. Vol. 5 of *Historia de la cuestión agraria mexicana*. Mexico City: Siglo Veintiuno Editores.

———. 1990c. *Los tiempos de la crisis, 1970-1982*. Part 1. Edited by Julio Moguel. Vol. 9 of *Historia de la cuestión agraria mexicana*. Mexico City: Siglo Veintiuno Editores.

Chand, Vikram K. 2001. *Mexico's Political Awakening*. Notre Dame: University of Notre Dame Press.

Chang, Paul Y., and Byung-Soo Kim. 2007. "Differential Impact of Repression on Social Movements: Christian Organizations and Liberation Theology in South Korea (1972-1979)." *Sociological Inquiry* 77, no. 3: 326-55.

Chislett, William. 1985. "The Causes of Mexico's Financial Crisis and the Lessons to be Learned." In *Politics in Mexico*, edited by George Philip, 1-14. London: Croom Helm.

Clemens, Elisabeth S., and Debra C. Minkoff. 2004. "Beyond the Iron Law: Rethinking the Place of Organizations in Social Movement Research." In Snow, Soule, and Kriesi 2004, 155-70.

Coatsworth, John. H. 1999. "The United States and Democracy in Mexico." In *The United States and Latin America: The New Agenda*, edited by Victor Bulmer-Thomas and James Dunkerley, 141-58. London: Institute of Latin American Studies, University of London, with the David Rockefeller Center for Latin American Studies, Harvard University.

Collier, George. A. 1994. *Basta! Land and the Zapatista Rebellion in Chiapas*. With Elizabeth Lowery Quaratiello. Oakland: Food First Books.

Comisión Económica para América Latina (CEPAL). 1982. *Economía campesina y agricultura empresarial*. Mexico City: Siglo Veintiuno Editores.

Condés Lara, Enrique. 1990. *Los últimos años del Partido Comunista Mexicano (1969-1981)*. Mexico City: Grupo Editorial Eón.

Cornelius, Wayne A. 1992. "The Politics and Economics of Reforming the Ejido Sector in Mexico: An Overview and Research Agenda." *LASA Forum* 23, no. 3: 3-10.

———. 1996. *Mexican Politics in Transition: The Breakdown of a One-Party-Dominant Regime*. San Diego: Center for U.S.-Mexican Studies, UCSD.

———. 2004. "Mobilized Voting in the 2000 Elections: The Changing Efficacy of Vote Buying and Coercion in Mexican Electoral Politics." In Domínguez and Lawson 2004, 47-65.

Cornelius, Wayne A., Judith Gentleman, and Peter H. Smith. 1989. "Overview: The Dynamics of Political Change." In *Mexico's Alternative Political Futures*, edited by Wayne A. Cornelius, Judith Gentleman, and Peter H. Smith, 1-51. San Diego: Center for U.S.-Mexican Studies, UCSD.

Craig, Ann L. 1990. "Institutional Context and Popular Strategies." In Foweraker and Craig 1990, 271-84.

Crespo, José Antonio. 2004. "Party Competition in Mexico: Evolution and Prospects." In Middlebrook 2004a, 57-81.

Cress, Daniel M., and David A. Snow. 2000. "The Outcomes of Homeless Mobilization: The Influence of Organization, Disruption, Political Mediation, and Framing." *American Journal of Sociology* 105, no. 4: 1063–1104.

Dagnino, Evelina. 1998. "Culture, Citizenship, and Democracy: Changing Discourses and Practices of the Latin American Left." In Alvarez, Dagnino, and Escobar 1998, 33–63.

Dahl, Robert A. 1971. *Polyarchy: Participation and Opposition.* New Haven: Yale University Press.

Davenport, Christian. 2005. "Introduction: Repression and Mobilization: Insights from Political Science and Sociology." In Davenport, Johnston, and Mueller 2005, vii–xli.

Davenport, Christian, Hank Johnston, and Carol Mueller, eds. 2005. *Repression and Mobilization.* Minneapolis: University of Minnesota Press.

De la Cruz, Rafael. 1989. "Nuevos movimientos sociales en Venezuela." In *Los movimientos populares en América Latina,* edited by Daniel Camacho and Rafael Menjívar, 215–46. Mexico City: Siglo Veintiuno Editores.

de la Peña, Sergio, and Marcel Morales Ibarra. 1989. "En los umbrales de la Segunda Guerra Mundial." In *Historia de la cuestión agraria mexicana,* vol. 6, *El agrarismo y la industrialización de México, 1940–1950,* edited by Sergio de la Peña, 3–31. Mexico City: Siglo Veintiuno Editores.

della Porta, Donatella. 1988. "Recruitment Processes in Clandestine Political Organizations: Italian Left-Wing Terrorism." *International Social Movement Research* 1:155–72.

———. 1995. *Social Movements, Political Violence, and the State: A Comparative Analysis of Italy and Germany.* Cambridge: Cambridge University Press.

———. 1996. "Social Movements and the State: Thoughts on the Policing of Protest." In *Comparative Perspectives on Social Movements: Political Opportunities, Mobilizing Structure, and Cultural Framing,* edited by Doug McAdam, John D. McCarthy, and Mayer N. Zald, 62–92. Cambridge: Cambridge University Press.

Diaz-Cayeros, Alberto, and Beatriz Magaloni. 2001. "Party Dominance and the Logic of Electoral Design in Mexico's Transition to Democracy." *Journal of Theoretical Politics* 13, no. 3: 271–93.

Dixon, Kwame. 2008. "Transnational Black Social Movements in Latin America: Afro-Colombians and the Struggle for Human Rights." In Stahler-Sholk, Vanden, and Kuecker 2008, 181–95.

Domínguez, Jorge I. 2004. "Conclusion: Why and How Did Mexico's 2000 Presidential Election Campaign Matter?" In Domínguez and Lawson 2004, 321–44.

Domínguez, Jorge I., and Chappell H. Lawson. 2004. *Mexico's Pivotal Democratic Election: Candidates, Voters, and the Presidential Campaign of 2000.* Stanford: Stanford University Press.

Domínguez, Jorge I., and James A. McCann. 1995. "Shaping Mexico's Electoral Arena: The Construction of Partisan Cleavage in the 1988 and 1991 National Elections." *American Political Science Review* 89, no. 1 (March): 34–48.

———. 1996. *Democratizing Mexico: Public Opinion and Electoral Choices.* Baltimore: Johns Hopkins University Press.

Drake, Paul. W. 1996. *Labor Movements and Dictatorships: The Southern Cone in Comparative Perspective.* Baltimore: Johns Hopkins University Press.

Earl, Jennifer. 2004. "Controlling Protest: New Directions for Research on the Social Control of Protest." *Research in Social Movements, Conflicts and Change* 25:55–83.

Earl, Jennifer, Andrew Martin, John D. McCarthy, and Sarah A. Soule. 2004. "The Use of Newspaper Data in the Study of Collective Action." *Annual Review of Sociology* 30:65–80. Online advance publication January 7.

Earl, Jennifer, John D. McCarthy, and Sarah A. Soule. 2003. "Protest Under Fire? Explaining the Policing of Protest." *American Sociological Review* 68, no. 4: 581–606.

Eisenstadt, Todd. 2003. "Thinking Outside the (Ballot) Box: Informal Electoral Institutions and Mexico's Political Opening." *Latin American Politics and Society* 45, no. 1: 25–54.

———. 2004. *Courting Democracy in Mexico: Party Strategies and Electoral Institutions*. Cambridge: Cambridge University Press.

———. 2007. "The Origins and Rationality of the 'Legal Versus Legitimate' Dichotomy Invoked in Mexico's 2006 Post-Electoral Conflict." *Political Science and Politics* 40, no. 1: 39–43.

Enriquez, Sam. 2006. "Ex-Mexico Leader Under House Arrest: A Judge Says There Is Enough Evidence to Try Luis Echeverría in the 1968 Student Massacre." *Los Angeles Times*, July 1.

Escobar, Arturo, and Sonia Alvarez, eds. 1992. *The Making of Social Movements in Latin America: Identity, Strategy, and Democracy*. Boulder, Colo.: Westview Press.

Esteva, Gustavo. 1983. *The Struggle for Rural Mexico*. South Hadley, Mass.: Bergin and Garvey.

Evrensel, Ayse Y. 2002. "Effectiveness of IMF-Supported Stabilization Programs in Developing Countries." *Journal of International Money and Finance* 21, no. 5: 565–87.

Foley, Michael W. 1991. "Agenda for Mobilization: The Agrarian Question and Popular Mobilization in Contemporary Mexico." *Latin American Research Review* 26, no. 2: 39–74.

Foweraker, Joe. 1989. *Making Democracy in Spain: Grass-Roots Struggle in the South, 1955–1975*. Cambridge: Cambridge University Press.

———. 1990. "Popular Movements and Political Change in Mexico." In Foweraker and Craig 1990, 3–20.

———. 1993. *Popular Mobilization in Mexico: The Teachers' Movement, 1977–1987*. Cambridge: Cambridge University Press.

Foweraker, Joe, and Ann L. Craig, eds. 1990. *Popular Movements and Political Change in Mexico*. Boulder, Colo.: Lynne Rienner.

Foweraker, Joe, and Todd Landman. 1997. *Citizenship Rights and Social Movements: A Comparative and Statistical Analysis*. New York: Oxford University Press.

Fox, Jonathan, ed. 1990. *The Challenge of Rural Democratisation: Perspectives from Latin America and the Philippines*. London: Frank Cass.

———. 1994a. "The Difficult Transition from Clientelism to Citizenship: Lessons from Mexico." *World Politics* 46 (January): 151–84.

———. 1994b. "Political Change in Mexico's New Peasant Economy." In *The Politics of Economic Restructuring: State-Society Relations and Regime Change in Mexico*, edited by Maria Lorena Cook, Kevin Middlebrook, and Juan Molinar Horcasitas, 243–76. San Diego: Center for U.S.-Mexican Studies, UCSD.

Fox, Jonathan, and Gustavo Gordillo. 1989. "Between State and Market: The Campesinos' Quest for Autonomy." In *Mexico's Alternative Political Futures*, edited by Wayne A. Cornelius, Judith Gentleman, and Peter H. Smith, 131–59. San Diego: Center for U.S.-Mexico Studies, UCSD.

Fox, Jonathan, and Libby Haight. 2007. "Transparency Reforms in Mexico: Theory and Practice." In Fox, Haight, Hofbauer, and Sánchez Andrade 2007, 27–59.

Fox, Jonathan, Libby Haight, Helena Hofbauer, and Tania Sánchez Andrade, eds. 2007. *Mexico's Right-to-Know Reforms: Civil Society Perspectives*. Washington, D.C.: Woodrow Wilson International Center for Scholars.

Fox, Vicente Quesada. 1999. *A Los Pinos: Recuento autobiográfico y político*. Edited by Rogelio Carvajal Dávila. Mexico City: Editorial Océano de México.

Francisco, Ronald A. 2005. "The Dictator's Dilemma." In Davenport, Johnston, and Mueller 2005, 58–81.

Franco, Jean. 1998. "Defrocking the Vatican: Feminism's Secular Project." In Alvarez, Dagnino, and Escobar 1998, 278–89.

Gamson, William. 1990. *The Strategy of Social Protest*. 2nd ed. Belmont, Calif.: Wadsworth.

García Díez, Fátima. 2001. "The Emergence of Electoral Reforms in Contemporary Latin America." Working paper 191, Institut de Ciéncies Polítiques i Socials, Barcelona, Spain.

Garrido, Luis Javier. 1989. "The Crisis of Presidentialism." In *Mexico's Alternative Political Futures*, edited by Wayne A. Cornelius, Judith Gentleman, and Peter H. Smith, 417–34. San Diego: Center for U.S.-Mexican Studies, UCSD.

Garza, David T. 1964. "Factionalism in the Mexican Left: The Frustration of the MLN." *Western Political Quarterly* 17, no. 3 (September): 447–60.

Gates, Leslie C. 2009. "Theorizing Business Power in the Semiperiphery: Mexico, 1970–2000." *Theory and Society* 38, no. 1: 57–95.

Gilabert, Cesar. 1993. *El hábito de la utopía: Análisis del imaginario sociopolítico en el movimiento estudiantil de México, 1968*. Mexico: Instituto Mora, Miguel Angel Porrua.

Giugni, Marco. G., Doug McAdam, Charles Tilly. 1998. *From Contention to Democracy*. Lanham, Md.: Rowman and Littlefield.

———, eds. 1999. *How Social Movements Matter*. Minneapolis: University of Minnesota Press.

Goldfield, Michael. 1989. "Worker Insurgency, Radical Organization, and New Deal Labor Legislation." *American Political Science Review* 83, no. 4 (December): 1257–82.

Goldstein, Robert J. 1983. *Political Repression in Nineteenth-Century Europe*. London: Croom Helm.

Goldstone, Jack A. 1991. *Revolution and Rebellion in the Early Modern World*. Berkeley and Los Angeles: University of California Press.

———, ed. 2003. *States, Parties, and Social Movements*. Cambridge: Cambridge University Press.

Gómez Tagle, Silvia. 2004. "Public Institutions and Electoral Transparency in Mexico." In Middlebrook 2004a, 82–105.

Gramsci, Antonio. 1971. *Selections from the Prison Notebooks*. Edited by Quintin Hoare and Geoffrey Nowell Smith. New York: International Publishers.
Grindle, Merilee S. 1986. *State and Countryside: Development Policy and Agrarian Politics*. Baltimore: Johns Hopkins University Press.
———. 2007. *Going Local: Decentralization, Democratization, and the Promise of Good Governance*. Princeton: Princeton University Press.
Guevara Niebla, Gilberto. 1988. *La democracia en la calle: Crónica del movimiento estudiantil mexicano*. Mexico City: Siglo Veintiuno Editores.
———. 1993. "Volver al 68." *Nexos* 190 (October): 31–43.
Gutelman, Michel. 1971. *Capitalismo y reforma agraria en México*. Mexico City: Ediciones Era.
Gutmann, Matthew. C. 2002. *The Romance of Democracy: Compliant Defiance in Contemporary Mexico*. Berkeley and Los Angeles: University of California Press.
Haber, Paul Lawrence. 1996. "Identity and Political Process: Recent Trends in the Study of Latin American Social Movements." *Latin American Research Review* 31, no. 1: 171–88.
———. 2007. *Power from Experience: Urban Popular Movements in Late Twentieth-Century Mexico*. University Park: Pennsylvania State University Press.
Hansen, Roger D. 1971. *The Politics of Mexican Development*. Baltimore: Johns Hopkins University Press.
Harvey, David. 2003. *The New Imperialism*. New York: Oxford University Press.
Harvey, Neil. 1990. "Peasant Strategies and Corporatism in Chiapas." In Foweraker and Craig 1990, 183–98.
———. 1998. *The Chiapas Rebellion: The Struggle for Land and Democracy*. Durham: Duke University Press.
Heath, John. 1985. "Contradictions in Mexican Food Policy." In *Politics in Mexico*, edited by George Philip, 97–136. Sydney: Croom Helm.
Heitlinger A. 1996. "Framing Feminism in Post-Communist Czech Republic." *Communist and Post-Communist Studies* 29, no. 1: 77–93.
Hellman, Judith Adler. 1992. "The Study of New Social Movements in Latin America and the Question of Autonomy." In Escobar and Alvarez 1992, 52–61.
———. 1994. "Mexican Popular Movements, Clientelism, and the Process of Democratization." *Latin American Perspectives* 21, no. 2: 124–42.
Hernández Castillo, Rosalva Aída. 2006. "The Indigenous Movement in Mexico: Between Electoral Politics and Local Resistance." *Latin American Perspectives* 33, no. 2: 115–31.
Hernández Navarro, Luis, and Laura Carlsen. 2004. "Indigenous Rights: The Battle for Constitutional Reform in Mexico." In Middlebrook 2004a, 440–65.
Hernández Rodríguez, Rogelio. 1986. "La política y los empresarios después de la nacionalización bancaria." *Foro Internacional* 27, no. 2: 247–65.
———. 2003. "The Renovation of Old Institutions: State Governors and the Political Transition in Mexico." *Latin American Politics and Society* 45, no. 4: 97–127.
Hess, David, and Brian Martin. 2006. "Repression, Backfire, and the Theory of Transformative Events." *Mobilization* 11, no. 2: 249–67.
Hinojosa-Ojeda, Raúl, Curt Dowds, Robert McCleery, Sherman Robinson, David Runsten, Craig Wolff, and Goetz Wolff. 1996. *North American Integration Three*

*Years After NAFTA: A Framework for Tracking, Modeling, and Internet Accessing the National and Regional Labor Market Impacts.* Los Angeles: North American Integration and Development Center, UCLA.

Holzner, Claudio. 2006. "Clientelism and Democracy in Mexico: The Role of Strong and Weak Networks." In Johnston and Almeida 2006, 77–95.

Human Rights Watch. 1999. *Systemic Injustice: Torture, "Disappearance," and Extrajudicial Execution in Mexico.* New York: Human Rights Watch.

——. 2008. *Mexico's National Human Rights Commission: A Critical Assessment.* Vol. 20, no. 1(B), February. New York: Human Rights Watch.

Huntington, Samuel. 1991. *The Third Wave: Democratization in the Late Twentieth Century.* Norman: University of Oklahoma Press.

Imaz Bayona, Cecilia. 1975. "El apoyo popular al movimiento estudiantil de 1968." *Revista Mexicana de Sociología* 37, no. 2: 363–92.

Issa, Daniela. 2008. "Praxis of Empowerment: Mística and Mobilization in Brazil's Landless Rural Workers' Movement." In Stahler-Sholk, Vanden, and Kuecker 2008, 131–45.

Jenkins, J. Craig. 1995. "Social Movements, Political Representation, and the State: An Agenda and Comparative Framework." In *The Politics of Social Protest: Comparative Perspectives on States and Social Movements,* edited by J. Craig Jenkins and Bert Klandermans, 14–35. Minneapolis: University of Minnesota Press.

Johnston, Hank. 2005. "Talking the Walk: Speech Acts and Resistance in Authoritarian Regimes." In Davenport, Johnston, and Mueller 2005, 108–137.

Johnston, Hank, and Paul Almeida, eds. 2006. *Latin American Social Movements: Globalization, Democratization, and Transnational Networks.* Lanham, Md.: Rowman and Littlefield.

Katz, Friedrich. 1998. *The Life and Times of Pancho Villa.* Stanford: Stanford University Press.

Kaufman, Robert R., Carlos Bazdresch, and Blanca Heredia. 1994. "Mexico: Radical Reform in a Dominant Party System." In *Voting for Reform: Democracy, Political Liberalization, and Economic Adjustment,* edited by Stephan Haggard and Steven B. Webb, 360–410. New York: Oxford University Press.

Kitschelt, Herbert P. 1986. "Political Opportunity Structures and Political Protest: Anti-Nuclear Movements in Four Democracies." *British Journal of Political Science* 16, no. 1: 57–85.

Klesner, Joseph L. 2004. "The Structure of the Mexican Electorate: Social, Attitudinal, and Partisan Bases of Vicente Fox's Victory." In Domínguez and Lawson 2004, 91–122.

——. 2005. "Electoral Competition and the New Party System in Mexico." *Latin American Politics and Society* 47, no. 2: 103–41.

——. 2006. "Social and Regional Factors in the 2006 Presidential Election: Some County-Level Aggregate Data Findings." http://web.mit.edu/polisci/research/meixco06/KlesnerMemo.pdf (accessed August 9, 2006).

——. 2007. "The 2006 Mexican Election and Its Aftermath: Editor's Introduction." *Political Science and Politics* 40, no. 1: 11–14.

Knight, Alan. 1986. *The Mexican Revolution.* 2 vols. Cambridge: Cambridge University Press.

———. 1990. "Historical Continuities in Social Movements." In Foweraker and Craig 1990, 78–102.
Koopmans, Ruud, and Paul Statham. 1999. "Ethnic and Civic Conceptions of Nationhood and the Differential Success of the Extreme Right in Germany and Italy." In *How Social Movements Matter,* edited by Marco G. Giugni, Doug McAdam, and Charles Tilly, 225–51. Minneapolis: University of Minnesota Press.
Krain, Matthew. 1997. "State-Sponsored Mass Murder: The Onset and Severity of Genocides and Politicides." *Journal of Conflict Resolution* 41, no. 3: 331–60.
Kriesi, Hanspeter. 1995. "The Political Opportunity Structure of New Social Movements: Its Impact on Their Mobilization." In *The Politics of Social Protest: Comparative Perspectives on States and Social Movements,* edited by J. Craig Jenkins and Bert Klandermans, 167–98. Minneapolis: University of Minnesota Press.
———. 2004. "Political Context and Opportunity." In Snow, Soule, and Kriesi 2004, 67–90.
Kriesi, Hanspeter, Ruud Koopmans, Jan Willem Duyvendak, and Marco G. Giugni. 1995. *The Politics of New Social Movements in Western Europe: A Comparative Analysis.* Minneapolis: University of Minnesota Press.
Kuecker, Glen David. 2008. "Fighting for the Forests Revisited: Grassroots Resistance to Mining in Northern Ecuador." In Stahler-Sholk, Vanden, and Kuecker 2008, 97–112.
Kuecker, Glen David, Richard Stahler-Sholk, and Harry E. Vanden. 2008. "Challenges Ahead for Latin America's Social Movements." In Stahler-Sholk, Vanden, and Kuecker 2008, 337–42.
Kurzman, Charles. 1998. "Organizational Opportunity and Social Movement Mobilization: A Comparative Analysis of Four Religious Movements." *Mobilization* 3, no. 1: 23–49.
La Botz, Dan. 1995. *Democracy in Mexico.* Boston: South End Press.
Lawson, Chappell. 2002. *Building the Fourth Estate: Democratization and the Rise of a Free Press in Mexico.* Berkeley and Los Angeles: University of California Press.
———. 2004. "Building the Fourth Estate: Media Opening and Democratization in Mexico." In Middlebrook 2004a, 373–402.
———. 2007. "How Did We Get Here? Mexican Democracy After the 2006 Elections." *Political Science and Politics* 40, no. 1: 45–48.
Lawson, Chappell, and Joseph L. Klesner. 2004. "Political Reform, Electoral Participation, and the Campaign of 2000." In Domínguez and Lawson 2004, 67–87.
Levy, Daniel C. 1980. *University and Government in Mexico: Autonomy in an Authoritarian System.* New York: Praeger.
Levy, Daniel C., and Kathleen Bruhn. 2006. *Mexico: The Struggle for Democratic Development.* 2nd ed. Berkeley and Los Angeles: University of California Press.
Levy, Daniel C., and Gabriel Székely. 1987. *Mexico: Paradoxes of Stability and Change.* Boulder, Colo.: Westview Press.
Li, Quan, and Rafael Reuveny. 2003. "Economic Globalization and Democracy: An Empirical Analysis." *British Journal of Political Science* 33, no. 1: 29–54.
Lins Ribeiro, Gustavo. 1998. "Cybercultural Politics: Political Activism at a Distance in a Transnational World." In Alvarez, Dagnino, and Escobar 1998, 325–52.
Lipset, Seymour Martin. 1994. "The Social Requisites of Democracy Revisited: 1993 Presidential Address." *American Sociological Review* 59, no. 1 (February): 1–22.

Loaeza, Soledad. 1987. "El Partido Acción Nacional: De la oposición leal a la impaciencia electoral." In *La vida política mexicana en la crisis*, edited by Soledad Loaeza y Rafael Segovia, 77–105. Mexico City: El Colegio de México.

———. 1990. "Derecha y democracia en el cambio político mexicano: 1982–1988." *Foro Internacional* 30, no. 4 (June): 631–58.

———. 1993. "México, 1968: Los orígenes de la transición." In *La transición interrumpida: México, 1968–1988*, edited by Ilán Semo, 15–47. Mexico City: Nueva Imagen.

Lomelí Meillon, Luz. 2006. "Los órganos electorales, un espacio de participación ciudadana." *Espiral* 12, no. 36 (May–August): 41–60.

Loveman, Mara. 1998. "High-Risk Collective Action: Defending Human Rights in Chile, Uruguay, and Argentina." *American Journal of Sociology* 104, no. 2: 477–525.

Lúa, Graciela Flores, Luisa Paré, and Sergio Sarmiento. 1988. *Las voces del campo: Movimiento campesino y política agraria, 1976–1984*. Mexico City: Siglo Veintiuno Editores.

Luna, Matilde, Ricardo Tirado, and Fracisco Valdés. 1987. "Businessmen and Politics in Mexico, 1982–1986." In *Government and Private Sector in Contemporary Mexico*, edited by Silvia Maxfield and Ricardo Anzaldua, 13–43. San Diego: Center for U.S.-Mexican Studies, UCSD.

Luna, Matilde Ledesma. 1992. *Los empresarios y el cambio político: México, 1970–1987*. Mexico City: Ediciones Era.

Luna, Matilde Ledesma, and Ricardo Tirado. 1992. *El Consejo Coordinador Empresarial: Una radiografía*. Mexico City: Facultad de Ciencias Política y Sociales, Instituto de Investigaciones Sociales, UNAM.

Mabry, Donald J. 1982. *The Mexican University and the State: Student Conflicts, 1910–1971*. College Station: Texas A&M University Press.

Mackinlay, Horacio. 2004. "Rural Producers' Organizations and the State in Mexico: The Political Consequences of Economic Restructuring." In Middlebrook 2004a, 286–331.

Magaloni, Beatriz. 2006. *Voting for Autocracy: Hegemonic Party Survival and Its Demise in Mexico*. Cambridge: Cambridge University Press.

Magaloni, Beatriz, and Guillermo Zepeda. 2004. "Democratization, Judicial and Law Enforcement Institutions, and the Rule of Law in Mexico." In Middlebrook 2004a, 168–97.

Mahoney, James. 2000. "Path Dependence in Historical Sociology." *Theory and Society* 29, no. 4: 507–48.

Markoff, John. 1996. *Waves of Democracy: Social Movements and Political Change*. Thousand Oaks, Calif.: Pine Forge Press.

Martin, JoAnn. 2005. *Tepoztlán and the Transformation of the Mexican State: The Politics of Loose Connections*. Tucson: University of Arizona Press.

Martínez, Marielle P. L., Luis Foncerrada, and Esperanza Oteo Bautista. 1980. *Los caminos de mano de obra como factores de cambio socioeconómico: Análisis de una encuesta a 423 familias campesinas mexicanas*. Mexico City: Centro de Estudios Sociológicos, El Colegio de México.

Martínez-Torres, María Elena, and Peter M. Rosset. 2008. "La Vía Campesina: Transnationalizing Peasant Struggle and Hope." In Stahler-Sholk, Vanden, and Kuecker 2008, 307–22.

Maxfield, Sylvia. 1990. *Governing Capital: International Finance and Mexican Politics.* Ithaca: Cornell University Press.
McAdam, Doug. 1996. "Conceptual Origins, Current Problems, Future Directions." In *Comparative Perspectives on Social Movements: Political Opportunities, Mobilizing Structures, and Cultural Framing,* edited by Doug McAdam, John D. McCarthy, and Mayer N. Zald, 23–40. Cambridge: Cambridge University Press.
McAdam, Doug, Sidney Tarrow, and Charles Tilly. 2001. *Dynamics of Contention.* Cambridge: Cambridge University Press.
McMichael, Philip. 2006. "Peasant Prospects in the Neoliberal Age." *New Political Economy* 11, no. 3 (September): 407–19.
Meyer, David S. 2004. "Protest and Political Opportunities." *Annual Review of Sociology* 30:125–45.
Meyer, David S., and Suzanne Staggenborg. 1996. "Movements, Countermovements, and the Structure of Political Opportunity." *American Journal of Sociology* 101, no. 6: 1628–60.
Middlebrook, Kevin J. 1995. *The Paradox of Revolution: Labor, the State, and Authoritarianism in Mexico.* Baltimore: Johns Hopkins University Press.
———, ed. 2004a. *Dilemmas of Political Change in Mexico.* London: Institute of Latin American Studies, University of London.
———. 2004b. "Mexico's Democratic Transitions: Dynamics and Prospects." In Middlebrook 2004a, 1–53.
Migdal, Joel S. 1974. *Peasants, Politics, and Revolution: Pressures Toward Political and Social Change in the Third World.* Princeton: Princeton University Press.
Mills, C. Wright. 1956. *The Power Elite.* New York: Oxford University Press.
Mitchell, Kenneth Edward. 2001. *State-Society Relations in Mexico: Clientelism, Neoliberal State Reform, and the Case of Conasupo.* Aldershot, U.K.: Ashgate.
Molinar Horcasitas, Juan. 1991. *El tiempo de la legitimidad.* Mexico City: Cal y Arena.
Monsiváis, Carlos. 1987. *Entrada libre: Crónicas de una sociedad que se organiza.* Mexico City: Ediciones Era.
Montes de Oca Luján, Rosa Elena. 1977. "La cuestión agraria y el movimiento campesino: 1970–1976." *Cuadernos Políticos,* no. 14:58–71.
Mora, Mariana. 2008. "Zapatista Anti-Capitalist Politics and the 'Other Campaign': Learning from the Struggle for Indigenous Rights and Autonomy." In Stahler-Sholk, Vanden, and Kuecker 2008, 151–64.
Moreno, Alejandro. 2001. "Democracy and Mass Belief Systems in Latin America." In *Citizen Views of Democracy in Latin America,* edited by Roderic Ai Camp, 27–50. Pittsburgh: University of Pittsburgh Press.
———. 2003. *El votante mexicano: Democracia, actitudes políticas y conducta electoral.* Mexico City: Fondo de Cultura Económica.
———. 2007. "The 2006 Mexican Presidential Election: The Economy, Oil Revenues, and Ideology." *Political Science and Politics* 40, no. 1: 15–19.
Moreno, Alejandro, and Keith Yanner. 2000. "Predictors of Voter Preferences in Mexico's 1994 Presidential Election." Working Papers in Political Science, no. 2000-07, Departamento Académico de Ciencia Política, Instituto Tecnológico Autónomo de México.
Morris, Aldon D., and Suzanne Staggenborg. 2004. "Leadership in Social Movements." In Snow, Soule, and Kriesi 2004, 171–96.

Muller, Edward N., and Erich Weede. 1990. "Cross-National Variation in Political Violence: A Rational Action Approach." *Journal of Conflict Resolution* 34, no. 4: 624–51.

Munck, Gerardo. 1990. "Identity and Ambiguity in Democratic Struggles." In Foweraker and Craig 1990, 23–42.

Noonan, Rita K. 1995. "Women Against the State: Political Opportunities and Collective Action Frames in Chile's Transition to Democracy." *Sociological Forum* 10:81–111.

Nun, José. 1993. "Democracy and Modernization, Thirty Years Later." *Latin American Perspectives* 10, no. 4: 7–27.

O'Donnell, Guillermo, Philippe C. Schmitter, and Laurence Whitehead. 1986. *Transitions from Authoritarian Rule: Latin America*. Baltimore: Johns Hopkins University Press.

Olesen, Thomas. 2006. "The Zapatistas and Transnational Framing." In Johnston and Almeida 2006, 179–96.

Oliver, Pamela E., and Hank Johnston. 2000. "What a Good Idea! Ideologies and Frames in Social Movement Research." *Mobilization* 5, no. 1: 37–54.

Oliver, Pamela E., Gregory M. Maney. 2000. "Political Processes and Local Newspaper Coverage of Protest Events: From Selection Bias to Triadic Interactions." *American Journal of Sociology* 106, no. 2: 463–505.

Olvera, Alberto J. 2004. "Civil Society in Mexico at Century's End." In Middlebrook 2004a, 403–39.

Ondetti, Gabriel. 2008. *Land, Protest, and Politics: The Landless Movement and the Struggle for Agrarian Reform in Brazil*. University Park: Pennsylvania State University Press.

Oporto, Henry. 1991. *La revolución democrática: Una nueva manera de pensar Bolivia*. La Paz, Bolivia: Los Amigos del Libro.

Ortíz Mena, Raúl, Victor L. Urquidi, Albert Waterston, and Jonas H. Haralz. 1953. *El desarrollo económico de México y su capacidad para obsorber capital del exterior*. Mexico: Nacional Financiera.

Otero, Gerardo. 2000. "Neoliberal Reform in Rural Mexico: Social Structural and Political Dimensions." *Latin American Research Review* 35, no. 1: 187–207.

Paige, Jeffery M. 1997. *Coffee and Power: Revolution and the Rise of Democracy in Central America*. Cambridge: Harvard University Press.

Páramo, Teresa. 1983. "La polarización en el agro y el campesinado en México (1960–1970)." *Revista Mexicana de Ciencias Políticas y Sociales* 28, nos. 113–14 (July–December): 7–42.

Paré, Luisa. 1990. "Rural Democratisation in Mexico." In *The Challenge of Rural Democratisation: Perspectives from Latin America and the Philippines*, edited by Jonathan Fox, 79–96. London: Frank Cass.

Paré Ouellet, Luisa. 1992. "El estado y los campesinos." In *El nuevo estado mexicano*, vol. 3, *Estado, actores y movimientos sociales*, edited by J. Alonso, A. Aziz, and J. Tamayo, 125–43. Mexico City: Nueva Imagen.

Peláez, Gerardo. 1980. *Partido Comunista Mexicano: 60 años de historia*. Culiacán, Sinaloa, Mexico: Universidad Autónoma de Sinaloa.

Pérez Arce, Francisco. 1990. "The Enduring Union Struggle for Legality and Democracy." In Foweraker and Craig 1990, 105–20.

Pick, James B., Edgar W. Butler, and Elizabeth L. Lanzer. 1989. *Atlas of Mexico*. Boulder, Colo.: Westview Press.
Piven, Frances Fox, and Richard A. Cloward. 1977. *Poor People's Movements: Why They Succeed, How They Fail*. New York: Pantheon.
Poniatowska, Elena. 1977. *La noche de Tlatelolco*. Mexico: Ediciones Era.
Preston, Julia, and Samuel Dillon. 2004. *Opening Mexico*. New York: Farrar, Straus, and Giroux.
Prud'home, Jean-François. 1998. "The Instituto Federal Electoral (IFE): Building an Impartial Electoral Authority." In *Governing Mexico: Political Parties and Elections*, edited by Mónica Serrano, 139–55. London: Institute of Latin American Studies, University of London.
Putnam, Robert. 1993. *Making Democracy Work: Civic Traditions in Modern Italy*. Princeton: Princeton University Press.
Ramírez Mercado, Manuel. 2006. "La distribución del voto en las entidades federativas. Análisis sobre las elecciones presidenciales en México, 1988–2006." *El Cotidiano* 21, no. 141: 17–30.
Ramírez Sáiz, Juan Manuel. 1992. "Entre el corporativismo social y la lógica electoral. El estado y el movimiento urbano popular." In *El nuevo estado mexicano*, vol. 3, *Estado, actores y movimientos sociales*, edited by J. Alonso, A. Aziz, and J. Tamayo, 171–94. Mexico City: Nueva Imagen.
Reis, Fábio Wanderley. 1996. "The State, the Market, and Democratic Citizenship." In *Constructing Democracy: Human Rights, Citizenship, and Society in Latin America*, edited by Elizabeth Jelin and Eric Hershberg, 121–37. Boulder, Colo.: Westview Press.
Riding, Alan. 1976. "Paper in Mexico Ends Liberal Tone." *New York Times*, July 10.
———. 1986. *Distant Neighbors: A Portrait of the Mexicans*. New York: Vintage Books.
Robles, Rosario, and Julio Moguel. 1990. "Los nuevos movimientos rurales, por la tierra y por la apropriación del ciclo productivo." In *Historia de la cuestión agraria mexicana*, vol. 9, *Los tiempos de la crisis, 1970–1982*, part 2, edited by Pilar López Sierra, Francis Mestries, Julio Moguel, and Rosario Robles, 377–450. Mexico City: Siglo Veintiuno Editores.
Rodríguez, Victoria E. 1997. *Decentralization in Mexico: From Reforma Municipal to Solidaridad to Nuevo Federalismo*. Boulder, Colo.: Westview Press.
———. 1998. "Recasting Federalism in Mexico." *Journal of Federalism* 28, no. 1 (Winter): 235–54.
Romero, Laura. 1986. "El movimiento fascista en Guadalajara." In *Perspectivas de los movimientos sociales en la región Centro-Occidente*, edited by Jaime Tamayo, 31–102. Mexico City: Editorial Linea.
Rubin, Jeffrey W. 1997. *Decentering the Regime: Ethnicity, Radicalism, and Democracy in Juchitán, Mexico*. Durham: Duke University Press.
Rubio, Blanca V. 1987. *Resistencia campesina y explotación rural en México*. Mexico City: Ediciones Era.
———. 1988. "Estructura de la producción agropecuaria y cultívos básicos, 1960–1970." In *Historia de la cuestión agraria mexicana*, vol. 7, *La epoca de oro y el principio de la crisis de la agricultura mexicana, 1950–1970*, edited by Julio Moguel, 146–276. Mexico City: Siglo Veintiuno Editores.

———. 1990. "Agricultura, economía y crisis durante el periodo 1970–1982." In *Historia de la cuestión agraria mexicana*, vol. 9, *Los tiempos de la crisis, 1970–1982*, part 1, edited by Julio Moguel, 15–137. Mexico City: Siglo Veintiuno Editores.

Rummel, R. J. 1995. "Democracy, Power, Genocide, and Mass Murder." *Journal of Conflict Resolution* 39, no. 1: 3–26.

Sanderson, Steven E. 1979. "La lucha agraria en Sonora, 1970–1976: Manipulación, reforma y la derrota del populismo." *Revista Mexicana de Sociología* 41, no. 3: 1181–1232.

———. 1986. *The Transformation of Mexican Agriculture: International Structure and the Politics of Rural Change*. Princeton: Princeton University Press.

Sanderson, Susan R. Walsh. 1984. *Land Reform in Mexico: 1910–1980*. New York: Academic Press.

Schedler, Andreas. 2000. "Mexico's Victory: The Democratic Revelation." *Journal of Democracy* 11, no. 4: 5–19.

Schild, Verónica. 1998. "New Subjects of Rights? Women's Movements and the Construction of Citizenship in the 'New Democracies.'" In Alvarez, Dagnino, and Escobar 1998, 93–117.

Schmidt, Samuel. 1991. *The Deterioration of the Mexican Presidency: The Years of Luis Echeverría*. Tucson: University of Arizona Press.

Schmitt, Karl M. 1965. *Communism in Mexico: A Study in Political Frustration*. Austin: University of Texas Press.

Schmitter, Philippe. 1974. "Still the Century of Corporatism." *Review of Politics* 36, no. 1: 85–131.

Schneider, Cathy. 1992. "Radical Opposition Parties and Squatters Movements in Pinochet's Chile." In Escobar and Alvarez 1992, 260–75.

———. 1995. *Shantytown Protest in Pinochet's Chile*. Philadelphia: Temple University Press.

Schock, Kurt. 1999. "People Power and Political Opportunities: Social Movement Mobilization and Outcomes in the Philippines and Burma." *Social Problems* 46, no. 3: 355–75.

———. 2005. *Unarmed Insurrections: People Power Movements in Nondemocracies*. Minneapolis: University of Minnesota Press.

Schryer, Frans J. 1990. *Ethnicity and Class Conflict in Rural Mexico*. Princeton: Princeton University Press.

Sellers, Charles. 1965. "The Equilibrium Cycle in Two-Party Politics." *Public Opinion Quarterly* 29 (Spring): 16–38.

Serrano, Monica, and Victor Bulmer-Thomas. 1996. *Rebuilding the State: Mexico After Salinas*. London: Institute of Latin American Studies, University of London.

Sevilla Mascareñas, Mario. 1977. *Aquí, Sonora, S.O.S.* Mexico: Ciclo Ediciones Calpuleque.

Shadlen, Kenneth C. 2000. "Neoliberalism, Corporatism, and Small Business Political Activism in Contemporary Mexico." *Latin American Research Review* 35, no. 2: 73–106.

Shapira, Yoram. 1977. "The Impact of the 1968 Student Protest on Echeverría's Reformism." *Journal of Interamerican Studies and World Affairs* 19, no. 4: 557–80.

Sharp, Gene. 2005. *Waging Nonviolent Struggle: Twentieth-Century Practice and Twenty-First-Century Potential*. Boston: Extending Horizons Books.

Shefner, Jon. 2001. "Coalitions and Clientelism in Mexico." *Theory and Society* 30, no. 5: 593–628.
Shefner, Jon, George Pasdirtz, and Cory Blad. 2006. "Austerity Protests and Immiserating Growth in Mexico and Argentina." In Johnston and Almeida 2006, 19–41.
Shirk, David. 2005. *Mexico's New Politics: The PAN and Democratic Change*. Boulder, Colo.: Lynne Rienner.
Sikkink, Kathryn. 1993. "Human Rights, Principled Issue-Networks, and Sovereignty in Latin America." *International Organization* 47, no. 3: 411–41.
Sikkink, Kathryn, and Jackie Smith. 2002. "Infrastructures for Change: Transnational Organizations, 1952–1993." In *Restructuring World Politics: Transnational Social Movements, Networks, and Norms*, edited by Sanjeev Khagram, Kathryn Sikkink, and James Riker, 24–43. Minneapolis: University of Minnesota Press.
Skocpol, Theda. 1979. *States and Social Revolutions*. Cambridge: Cambridge University Press.
———. 1985. "Bringing the State Back In: Strategies of Analysis in Current Research." In *Bringing the State Back In*, edited by Peter B. Evans, Dietrich Rueschemeyer, and Theda Skocpol, 3–43. Cambridge: Cambridge University Press.
Slater, David. 2008. "Power and Social Movements in the Other Occident: Latin America in an International Context." In Stahler-Sholk, Vanden, and Kuecker 2008, 21–38.
Snow, David A., and Robert D. Benford. 1988. "Ideology, Frame Resonance, and Participant Mobilization." *International Social Movement Research* 1:197–218.
Snow, David A., Sarah A. Soule, and Hanspeter Kriesi, eds. 2004. *The Blackwell Companion to Social Movements*. Malden, Mass.: Blackwell.
Spalding, Rose J. 2008. "Neoliberal Regionalism and Resistance in Mesoamerica: Foro Mesoamericano Opposition to Plan Puebla-Panamá and CAFTA." In Stahler-Sholk, Vanden, and Kuecker 2008, 323–36.
Spronk, Susan, and Jeffery R. Webber. 2008. "Struggles Against Accumulation by Dispossession in Bolivia: The Political Economy of Natural Resource Contention." In Stahler-Sholk, Vanden, and Kuecker 2008, 77–91.
Stahler-Sholk, Richard. 2008. "Resisting Neoliberal Homogenization: The Zapatista Autonomy Movement." In Stahler-Sholk, Vanden, and Kuecker 2008, 113–29.
Stahler-Sholk, Richard, Harry E. Vanden, and Glen David Kuecker, eds. 2008. *Latin American Social Movements in the Twenty-First Century*. Lanham, Md.: Rowman and Littlefield.
Stepan-Norris, Judith, and Maurice Zeitlin. 1989. "'Who Gets the Bird?' or, How the Communists Won Power and Trust in America's Unions: The Relative Autonomy of Intraclass Political Struggles." *American Sociological Review* 54, no. 4: 503–23.
Stephan, Maria J., and Erica Chenoweth. 2008. "Why Civil Resistance Works: The Strategic Logic of Nonviolent Conflict." *International Security* 33, no. 1: 7–44.
Stephen, Lynn. 1992. "Women in Mexico's Popular Movements: Survival Strategies Against Ecological and Economic Impoverishment." *Latin American Perspectives* 19, no. 1: 73–96.
———. 1997. "Election Day in Chiapas: A Low-Intensity War." *NACLA Report on the Americas* 32, no. 2: 10.

Stevens, Evelyn P. 1974. *Protest and Response in Mexico.* Cambridge: MIT Press.
Stewart, Julie. 2006. "When Local Troubles Become Transnational: The Transformation of a Guatemalan Indigenous Rights Movement." In Johnston and Almeida 2006, 197–214.
Stokes, Donald E., and Gudmund R. Iversen. 1962. "On the Existence of Forces Restoring Party Competition." *Public Opinion Quarterly* 26 (Summer): 159–71.
Swidler, Ann. 1986. "Culture in Action: Symbols and Strategies." *American Sociological Review* 51, no. 2: 273–86.
Tamayo, Jaime. 1990. "Neoliberalism Encounters *Neocardenismo.*" In Foweraker and Craig 1990, 121–36.
Tamayo Flores-Alatorre, Sergio. 1999. *Los veinte octubres mexicanos: La transición a la modernización y la democracia, 1968–1988.* Mexico City: Universidad Autónoma Metropolitana–Azcapotzalco.
Tarrow, Sidney. 1994. *Power in Movement: Social Movements, Collective Action, and Politics.* Cambridge: Cambridge University Press.
———. 1995. "Mass Mobilization and Elite Exchange: Democratization Episodes in Italy and Spain." *Democratization* 2, no. 3: 221–45.
Taylor, Verta. 1989. "Social Movement Continuity: The Women's Movement in Abeyance." *American Sociological Review* 54, no. 5: 761–75.
Thacker, Strom. C. 1999. "NAFTA Coalitions and the Political Viability of Neoliberalism in Mexico." *Journal of Interamerican Studies and World Affairs* 41, no. 2 (Summer): 57–89.
———. 2000. *Big Business, the State, and Free Trade: Constructing Coalitions in Mexico.* Cambridge: Cambridge University Press.
Tilly, Charles. 1978. *From Mobilization to Revolution.* New York: McGraw-Hill.
———. 1999. "From Interactions to Outcomes in Social Movements." In *How Social Movements Matter,* edited by Marco Giugni, Doug McAdam, and Charles Tilly, 253–70. Minneapolis: University of Minnesota Press.
———. 2005. "Regimes and Contention." In *The Handbook of Political Sociology: States, Civil Societies, and Globalization,* edited by Thomas Janoski, Robert Alford, Alexander Hicks, and Mildred A. Schwartz, 423–40. Cambridge: Cambridge University Press.
Tirado, Ricardo. 1982. "Las organizaciones empresariales del sector agropecuario en México: La CNPP y la CNG." Unpublished paper prepared for the Instituto de Investigaciones Sociales, UNAM.
Touraine, Alain. 1997. *What is Democracy?* Boulder, Colo.: Westview Press.
Trevizo, Dolores. 2002. "Dispersed Communist Networks and Grassroots Leadership of Peasant Revolts in Mexico." *Sociological Perspectives* 45, no. 3 (Autumn): 285–315. http://caliber.ucpress.net/doi/abs/10.1525/sop.2002.45.3.285 (accessed June 25, 2010).
———. 2003. "Interclass Conflict and Political Divisions Among Capitalists: The Remaking of an Agrarian Capitalist Class in Mexico, 1970–75." *Social Science History* 27, no. 1 (Spring): 75–108.
———. 2006. "Between Zapata and Che: A Comparison of Social Movement Success and Failure in Mexico." *Social Science History* 30, no. 2 (Summer): 197–229.
Tutino, John. 1986. *From Insurrection to Revolution in Mexico: Social Bases of Agrarian Revolution, 1750–1940.* Princeton: Princeton University Press.

Ulloa Bornemann, Alberto. 2007. *Surviving Mexico's Dirty War: A Political Prisoner's Memoir*. Philadelphia: Temple University Press.
Valdés Ugalde, Francisco. 1997. *Autonomía y legitimidad: Los empresarios, la política y el estado en México*. Mexico City: Siglo Veintiuno Editores.
Vanden, Harry E. 2008. "Social Movements, Hegemony, and New Forms of Resistance." In Stahler-Sholk, Vanden, and Kuecker 2008, 39–55.
Velasco, José Luis. 2005. *Insurgency, Authoritarianism, and Drug Trafficking in Mexico's "Democratization."* New York: Routledge.
Villalón, Roberta. 2008. "Neoliberalism, Corruption, and Legacies of Contention: Argentina's Social Movements, 1993–2006." In Stahler-Sholk, Vanden, and Kuecker 2008, 253–69.
Villarreal, Andrés. 2002. "Political Competition and Violence in Mexico: Hierarchical Social Control in Local Patronage Structures." *American Sociological Review* 67, no. 4 (August): 477–98.
Wada, Takeshi. 2006. "Claim Network Analysis: How Are Social Protests Transformed into Political Protests in Mexico?" In Johnston and Almeida 2006, 95–111.
Warman, Arturo. 1980. *We Come to Object: The Peasants of Morelos and the National State*. Baltimore: Johns Hopkins University Press.
Warren, Kay B. 1998. *Indigenous Movements and Their Critics: Pan-Maya Activism in Guatemala*. Princeton: Princeton University Press.
Weldon, Jeffrey A. 2004. "Changing Patterns of Executive-Legislative Relations." In Middlebrook 2004a, 134–67.
Weyland, Kurt. 1996. *Democracy Without Equity: Failures of Reform in Brazil*. Pittsburgh: University of Pittsburgh Press.
Whitmeyer, Joseph M., and Rosemary L. Hopcroft. 1996. "Community, Capitalism, and Rebellion in Chiapas." *Sociological Perspectives* 39, no. 4: 517–38.
Whittier, Nancy. 2004. "The Consequences of Social Movements for Each Other." In Snow, Soule, and Kriesi 2004, 531–51.
Wilke, James W. 1967. *The Mexican Revolution: Federal Expenditure and Social Change Since 1910*. Berkeley and Los Angeles: University of California Press.
Williams, Heather L. 2001. *Social Movements and Economic Transition: Markets and Distributive Conflict in Mexico*. Cambridge: Cambridge University Press.
Wolf, Eric R. 1969. *Peasant Wars of the Twentieth Century*. New York: Harper Colophon Books.
Womack, John, Jr. 1986. "The Mexican Revolution, 1910–1920." In *The Cambridge History of Latin America*, vol. 5, *C. 1870 to 1930*, edited by Leslie Bethell, 79–153. Cambridge: Cambridge University Press.
———. 1999. *Rebellion in Chiapas: An Historical Reader*. New York: New Press.
Yashar, Deborah. 2005. *Contesting Citizenship in Latin America: The Rise of Indigenous Movements and the Postliberal Challenge*. Cambridge: Cambridge University Press.
Yúdice, George. 1998. "The Globalization of Culture and the New Civil Society." In Alvarez, Dagnino, and Escobar 1998, 353–79.
Zald, Mayer N. 1996. "Culture, Ideology, and Strategic Framing." In *Comparative Perspectives on Social Movements: Political Opportunities, Mobilizing Structures, and Cultural Framings*, edited by Doug McAdam, John D. McCarthy, and Mayer N. Zald, 261–74. Cambridge: Cambridge University Press.

Zeitlin, Maurice. 1984. *The Civil Wars in Chile*. Princeton: Princeton University Press.
Zeitlin, Maurice, and Richard Earl Ratcliff. 1988. *Landlords and Capitalists: The Dominant Class of Chile*. Princeton: Princeton University Press.
Zermeño, Sergio. 1978. *México, una democracia utópica: El movimiento estudiantil del 68*. Mexico City: Siglo Veintiuno Editores.
———. 1989. "El regreso del líder: Crisis, neoliberalismo y desorden." *Revista Mexicana de Sociología* 101 (October–December): 115–50.
Zwerman, Gilda, and Patricia Steinhoff. 2005. "When Activists Ask for Trouble: State-Dissident Interactions and the New Left Cycle of Resistance in the United States and Japan." In Davenport, Johnston, and Mueller 2005, 85–107.

# Index

Page numbers in *italics* indicate illustrations.

Abruch Linder, Miguel, 132
agriculture, 100–101
   labor force in, 213–14
   *See also* land ownership; peasants
Aguilar Zínser, Adolfo, 87
Alianza Cívica, 81, 189
Almeida, Paul, 34
Álvarez Garín, Raúl, 64
Amenta, Edwin, 39 n. 18, 40
amnesty, 76, 82, 171 n. 15
Amnesty International, 171
Andrews, Kenneth T., 53
austerity, 35, 141, 173
   protests against, 33, 36
   *See also* neoliberalism
authoritarianism, 6, 137, 146, 175
   "soft" nature of, 2, 11
   struggle against, 168, 194
   Tlatelolco as symbol of, 70, 82, 88, 188
Avritzer, Leonardo, 44, 189

Baja California Sur, 178, 182 n. 26
bank nationalization, 138, 147
   capitalists' response to, 139–40, 145, 151, 190
Barrio Terrazas, Pancho, 148 n. 23
Bartra, Armando, 110 n. 34, 202
Bartra, Roger, 9 n. 22, 97 n. 11
Basogoiti, José María, 139, 140, 147–48, 151–52
Benford, Robert D., 50
Bolivia, 29 n. 4, 34, 55
Bonfil, Guillermo, 184
Brazil, 29 n. 4, 34, 55
Bruhn, Kathleen, 11 n. 30, 23 n 47, 35, 142
   on PRD support, 154, 157, 158, 175
Buendía, Jorge, 176
businessmen. *See* capitalists

Cabañas, Lucio, 70 n. 4, 103 n. 22, 116 n. 41
Calderón, Felipe, 15, 141, 149
Calhoun, Craig, 45, 93
Cámara Nacional de la Industria de la Transformación (CANACINTRA), 23 n. 47, 127 n. 1

Camp, Roderic Ai, 18 n. 41
Campeche, 178
Canales Clariond, Fernando, 148 n. 23
capitalists
   agrarian, 3, 23, 96–99, 133 n. 8, 151–52
   alliances with middle-class groups, 18, 23, 141, 152, 191, 197
   assault on presidentialism by, 139, 140, 146, 151
   and corporatism, 9, 126, 134, 136, 137, 151
   countermovement by, 1, 3, 54, 152–53
   defined, 97 n. 8
   and democratization, 51, 146, 150, 151, 152, 153, 191, 197
   efforts to strengthen civil society by, 127, 141
   framing by, 51, 151, 152, 191, 197
   ideological work of, 133
   and interclass struggle, 17, 18–19, 126, 134, 137, 147, 152–53
   and land struggle, 97–98, 126, 132
   and Mexican government, 9, 128–29, 131–32, 136, 142–43
   neoliberal agenda of, 23, 38, 54, 126–27, 138, 141–46, 151
   organizational structure and political orientation, 135
   peak associations of, 23, 126, 127, 137, 139, 142, 150, 151, 198
   and political activity, 11, 24, 127, 190
   PRI exclusion of, 9, 128
   protest tactics of, 133, 135 n. 10, 139, 140–41
   radicalization of, 145, 152–53, 190
   response to bank nationalizations, 139–40, 145, 151, 190
   revitalization of PAN by, 18, 23, 54, 127, 132, 140, 147, 150, 191
   and social pact, 131, 132, 145, 147–48
   support of repression by, 82
   trade associations of, 9, 131
Cárdenas, Cuauhtémoc, 59
   in 1988 elections, 15 n. 36, 148, 158, 174–75, 179
Cárdenas, Lázaro, 105, 106, 128, 132, 146

Carruthers, Bruce G., 39 n. 18
Carton de Grammont, Hubert, 161 n. 7
Castañeda, Jorge G., 87
Castillo, Heberto, 74
Catholic Church, 11, 193
cattle ranching, 94–95 n. 3, 97 n. 8
Central Campesina Independiente (CCI), 106–7
Central Independiente de Obreros Agrícolas y Campesinos (CIOAC), 162, 170, 171, 173, 177, 179
  ties to PCM, 26 n. 51, 107
Central Intelligence Agency (CIA), 65
Cervantes Cabeza de Vaca, Luís Tomás, 69
Chiapas, 26 n. 51, 124, 163–64, 171
  elections in, 178–79, 182 n. 26
  Zapatista rebellion in, 22 n. 46, 27, 34 n. 9, 171 n. 16
Chislett, William, 71 n. 5
citizenship rights, 5–6, 29, 35–36
civil society
  as battlefield, 30
  capitalists' efforts to strengthen, 127, 141
  and corporatism, 10, 75, 190
  and democratization, 18, 19, 44, 56
  role of leadership in, 22
  and social movements, 37, 38, 55
  strengthening of, 36, 75, 193–94
  weakness of, 10, 11, 12
clientelism, 14 n. 34, 185–86
Clouthier, Manuel de Jesús, 137, 139, 140, 143, 150
  background of, 134
  and PAN, 18, 147–48
  political leadership by, 134, 151–52, 196
Cloward, Richard A., 39
Coalición de Ejidos Colectivos de los Valles del Yaqui y Mayo (CECVYM), 161–62
Coalición de Obreros, Campesinos y Estudiantes del Istmo (COCEI), 162, 172
Coindreau, José Luis, 126, 137, 148 n. 23
Collier, George, 113
Colosio, Luis Donaldo, 201
Comandos Armados del Pueblo (CAP), 73
Comisión Federal Electoral, 80, 81, 193
Comisión Nacional de Derechos Humanos (CNDH), 58, 83, 86, 89, 194
  assessment of, 86–87
Comité Político de Familiares, 83
communism
  as capitalists' bogeyman, 133–34, 139, 152
  as Cold War bogeyman, 65–66

Communist parties, 46–47
Communist Party, Mexican. *See* Partido Comunista Mexicano (PCM)
Compañía Nacional de Subsistencias Populares (CONASUPO), 101 n. 19
Concello, José Angel, 147
Confederación de Asociaciones Agrícolas del Estado de Sinaloa (CAADES), 133
Confederación de Cámaras Industriales (CONCAMIN), 82, 140
Confederación de Cámaras Nacionales de Comercio (CONCANACO), 82, 137
Confederación de Trabajadores Mexicanos (CTM), 8
Confederación Nacional Campesina (CNC), 3 n. 3, 26 n. 51, 91, 124
  as corporatist organization, 8–9, 161, 186, 206
Confederación Nacional de la Pequeña Propiedad (CNPP), 8 n. 18
Confederación Nacional de Organizaciones Populares (CNOP), 8
Confederación Patronal de la República Mexicana (COPARMEX), 127, 131 n. 7, 134, 137, 140
  on bank nationalization, 139
  history of, 133
  political involvement of, 148
conflict networks, 47, 114, 124, 199
  informal, 48–50
Consejo Coordinador Empresarial (CCE), 127, 135 n. 10, 145
  on bank nationalization, 139
  establishment of, 134, 136
  and México en Libertad, 140
  political changes achieved by, 142, 143, 153
Consejo Nacional Agropecuario (CNA), 134
Consejo Nacional de Huelga (CNH), 60–61, 64, 67
Constitution of 1917, 1, 6, 60
  on Catholic Church, 11
  concessions to peasants in, 5, 94, 131
  contradictory principles in, 4–5, 128, 129
  and Native American recognition, 26–27
  1992 amendment of, 95 n. 5, 141, 143, 144, 153
co-optation, 35, 39, 43, 44, 109, 190
  as part of *pan y palo* tactics, 12, 55, 103–4
Coordinadora Nacional Plan de Ayala (CNPA), 107, 162, 164–65, 173, 209
  demands and slogans, 167–68
  protests by, 169–70, 171, 177

Corenelius, Wayne, 8
Corona del Rosal, Alfonso, 59
corporatism, 57, 167
   capitalists' challenge to, 126, 134, 136, 137, 151
   as central pillar of Mexican system, 8–10, 137
   and civil society, 10, 75, 190
   defined, 8 n. 17
   organizational structure of, 7
   of PRI, 2, 3
   and social control, 9–10
Corriente Socialista, 112
corruption, 9, 86 n. 17, 139, 205
Cortés González, Claudia, 65
countermovements
   of capitalists, 1, 3, 54, 152–53
   as concept, 53–54
   mobilizations by, 198
courts, 6, 17, 80 n. 12, 83, 88
Craig, Ann, 166–67
Crespo, José Antonio, 15 n. 35, 81 n. 14
Cuban Revolution, 65–66, 84
cultural autonomy, 33, 36

Danzós Palomino, Ramón, 106, 111, 114, 196
   jailing of, 107, 109–10
debt crisis (1982), 34–35, 36, 138
de la Madrid, Miguel, 140, 141, 170–71, 172
democracy and democratization, 1, 137, 156–57, 172, 188, 191
   and arbitrary government, 89
   capitalists and, 24, 51, 146, 150, 151, 152, 153, 191, 197
   civil society and, 18, 19, 44, 56
   critical publics and, 24
   definitions of, 15–16, 33 n. 8
   as demand of peasant movement, 24, 172
   globalization and, 32, 33, 36, 195
   in Latin America, 29
   Lipset on, 15–16, 192
   neoliberalism and, 16–17, 32–33, 195
   prerequisites of, 192
   and social justice, 24, 192–93
   social movements and, 29–32, 30, 31, 39, 55–56, 190, 195, 198
   uneven nature of, 14
Díaz Ordaz, Gustavo, 71, 107
   and dirty war, 57, 70 n. 4, 87–88
   and 1968 student movement, 60, 65, 67, 68, 70

dirty war, 12–13, 23, 82, 177, 188
   Communists as target of, 27, 66, 109, 165
   Díaz Ordaz and, 57, 70 n. 4, 87–88
   under Echeverría, 57, 72, 87–88, 91, 103, 104, 109
   extrajudicial killings, 12, 27, 57, 70, 103 n. 22
   in Guerrero, 70 n. 4, 72, 91, 103, 123, 182
   human rights organizations on, 194
   in Latin America, 36
   under López Portillo, 57, 87–88, 167–68
   start of, 70 n. 4
   *See also* repression
Distrito Federal, 178
Domínguez, Jorge I., 192
Drake, Paul, 41, 46
drug trade, 15, 192

Earl, Jennifer, 202–3
Echeverría, Luis, 70, 71–72, 100, 101, 130, 132
   and dirty war, 57, 72, 87–88, 91, 103, 104, 109
   and land invasions, 91, 118, 123
   rural development policies of, 5 n. 9, 91, 104 n. 26, 132
economy
   agricultural production, 100
   capitalist nature of, 38, 95–96, 128, 129, 132
   debt crisis of 1982, 34–35, 36, 138
   foreign investment, 35, 129–30, 141
   and inequality, 192–93
   neoliberal measures, 35, 141–42, 173
   social safety net, 157–58
   state's involvement in, 130, 131, 137, 138, 147, 157
   trade with U.S., 142–43
Ecuador, 34
Eisenstadt, Todd, 76, 80, 148, 182 n. 25, 187
Ejército Zapatista de Liberación Nacional (EZLN), 22 n. 46, 27, 171 n. 16
   electoral abstentionism of, 184
   and indigenous movement, 193–94
*ejido* system
   collectivization plan for, 100, 101
   as communal village structure, 5 n. 8, 118
   in Constitution, 5, 94–96
   constitutional amendment authorizing privatization of, 95 n. 5, 141, 143, 144, 153
El Barzón movement, 22 n. 46, 193
elections
   Alianza Cívica and, 81, 189
   antiparliamentarist view of, 74, 166

elections (*continued*)
 Federal Electoral Tribunal (TRIFE) and, 15 n. 37
 fraud in, 1, 9, 15, 152, 172, 175
 growing competitiveness, 14, 16–17, 24, 36, 89, 150, 189, 191–92
 ideological nature of in Mexico, 24, 155
 Native Americans and, 172, 183–84
 under old political system, 10, 11
 presidential (1970), 71
 presidential (1976), 11
 presidential (1988), 15 n. 36, 148, 154, 158, 172–73, 174–75, 179
 presidential (2000), 18 n. 42, 149, 151, 155 n. 1, 158, 189
 presidential (2006), 13, 15, 24, 38 n. 17, 150–51, 155, 176–77, 178, 191
 regional nature of, 13 n. 32, 155–56, 178
 voting age, 181
 voting procedures, 185–86, 191 n. 1
electoral law, 10, 38
 list of reforms to, 78–79
 1977 reform of (LFOPPE), 17, 75–77, 80, 81, 89, 172, 174, 189
 1990 reform of, 81
 of 1946, 74
Elizondo, Rodolfo, 148 n. 23
ethnic organizations, 161–62
¡Eureka!, 83
*Excelsior*, 111, 115–16, 207
 government purge of, 72, 206
 political independence of, 90 n. 1, 202, 205–6

fascist movements, 158
Federación de Partidos del Pueblo Mexicano (FPPM), 10 n. 27
Figueroa Figueroa, Rubén, 103 n. 22
foreign investment, 35, 129–30, 141
Foweraker, Joe, 2 n. 2, 12, 49, 171 n. 16
 on civil society, 18, 30
 on communist organizations, 46–47, 115
 on democratization, 18, 56, 191
 on politicization of demands, 24, 172
 on popular movements after 1968, 75, 91
Fox, Jonathan, 14 n. 34, 90, 102
Fox Quesada, Vicente, 87, 141, 148 n. 23
 and capitalists, 150
 presidential victory of, 149, 189
framing, 80, 199
 by capitalists, 51, 151, 152, 191, 197
 by PCM, 92, 113, 124

 by peasant movement, 50–51, 197
 and political ideology, 51–52
 role of leadership in, 52, 53
 by social movements, 50–53, 196, 197
 by student movement in 1968, 51, 65, 67, 69–70, 88, 197
Francisco, Ronald A., 40, 43 n. 25
Frente Democrático Nacional (FDN), 174–75
Frente Revolucionario Armado del Pueblo (FRAP), 73, 74
Frente Urbano Zapatista (FUZ), 73

Galván, Ignacio, 68
Gamson, William, 30 n. 5, 39, 69–70
Garza, David T., 105
Garza Sado, Eugenio, 134
Garzón, Alfonso, 106
Gates, Leslie, 17, 145
General Agreement on Tariffs and Trade (GATT), 141
Gentleman, Judith, 8
globalization, 16, 22, 34
 and democratization, 32, 33, 36, 195
Goichochea, Emilio, 148 n. 23
Goldstone, Jack A., 21, 55, 100
Gómez Tagle, Silvia, 81 n. 14
Gómez Villanueva, Augusto, 83, 101–2
González de Alba, 61, 64
González Morfín, José, 147
Gordillo, Gustavo, 90, 102
Gramsci, Antonio, 52, 124
Granados Cortes, Fernando, 109 n. 33
"great men" theory, 52, 152
Guatemala, 33, 34 n. 9
Guerrero, 182 n. 26
 dirty war in, 70 n. 4, 72, 91, 103, 123, 182
guerrilla movements, 12, 27, 123
 growth of, 72 n. 7, 73–74
 kidnappings by, 73 n. 9, 74, 134
Guevara, Che, 64, 65, 66
Guevara Niebla, Gilberto, 60, 68

*Hacia una política popular* (Orive), 113
Halcones, 72, 73 n. 8
Harvey, Neil, 3 n. 3, 124, 171, 178–79
Hellman, Judith Adler, 20 n. 43, 49
*Heraldo, El*, 66
Hernández, Octavio, 66
Hernández Castillo, Rosalva Aída, 184
Hernández Rodríguez, Rogelio, 14
Hidalgo, 177, 178

Holzner, Claudio, 14 n. 34
Horcasitas, Molinar, 80
human rights organizations, 88, 194
  CNDH and, 58, 83, 86–87, 89, 194
  and democracy, 89, 194
  list of, *84–85*
  rise of, 23, 58, 82–83, 88, 194
Human Rights Watch, 86, 87

Ibarra de Piedra, Rosario, 83 n. 15
illiteracy rate, 99, 100 n. 14
import substitution industrialization (ISI), 129–30, 131, 132, 145
indigenous peoples. *See* Native Americans
Información Sistemática, 159
Instituto Federal Electoral (IFE), 81, 189
Instituto Politécnico Nacional (IPN), 59
International Monetary Fund (IMF), 17, 34–35, 151

Jacobo García, Rafael, 109 n. 33, 114
Jaramillo, Rubén, 116 n. 40
Johnston, Hank, 34, 45–46
Juventud Comunista Mexicana (JCM), 61, 64, 108, 124

Klesner, Joseph, 156, 157, 181
Knights of Columbus, 82
Kriesi, Hanspeter, 39 n. 19

La Botz, Dan, 113
Lacandones, 73
land invasions
  agrarian capitalists and, 97, 126
  Echeverría and, 91, 118, 123
  and government redistribution, 102, 121
  legal incentive for, 129
  made illegal, 168
  PCM involvement in, 109–10, 111–12, 114–15, 122
  reasons for, 111–12
  repression of, 91, *102*, 123
Landman, Todd, 2 n. 2, 12, 171 n. 16
land ownership
  by agrarian capitalists, 96–97
  *ejido* system, 5, 94–96, 141, 143, 144, 153
  government caps on, 5, 129
  and government redistribution, 5, 71, 94, 97–98, 121, 132, 152
  *minifundismo*, 98, 119, 120–21
  *neolatifundia*, 97

Latin America, 11 n. 29, 12, 36
  democratic transitions in, 29, 38, 41
  and neoliberalism, 17, 33
  social movements in, 34
Lawson, Chappell, 10 n. 26, 17
legitimacy
  Mexican system's crisis of, 35, 57, 71, 75, 82, 188
  PRI loss of, 35, 148, 172
Levy, Daniel C., 11 n. 30, 23 n. 47, 35, 142
Ley Federal de Organizaciones Políticas y Procesos Electorales (LFOPPE), 80, 81
  provisions and significance, 75–77, 89, 172, 174, 189
Liga Comunista 23 de Septiembre, 73 n. 9, 134
Liga Comunista Espartaco (LCE), 73, 74
Línea Proletaria, 26 n. 51, 93, 113, 115, 161
Lipset, Seymour Martin, 14–15, 16, 192
Lombardo Toledano, Vicente, 105
López, J. Dolores, 108
López Obrador, Andrés Manuel, 15, 156, 158
López Portillo, José, 11, 168
  amnesty under, 76, 171 n. 15
  electoral reform of, 75, 81, 189
  repression under, 57, 87–88, 167–68
  state economic role under, 138, 157
Lúa, Graciela Flores, 106 n. 31, 162, 166
Lugo Chávez, Héctor, 142, 143
Luna, Matilde Ledesma, 136, 148 n. 23

Mabry, Donald J., 59
Mackinlay, Horacio, 161 n. 7
Mahoney, James, 21
Maldonado, Braulio, 106
Maoists, 26 n. 51, 61, 73–74
  and peasant movement, 92, 93, 113, 166
*maquiladoras*, 129 n. 5
Marcos, Subcomandante, 184 n. 28
Markoff, John, 32
Martin, JoAnn, 27 n. 52, 158
Martínez Nateras, Arturo, 108
Martínez Verdugo, Arnoldo, 116 n. 41, 122
Marx, Karl, and Marxism, 54, 128
Massieu, José Ruiz, 201
McAdam, Doug, 15, 89
media, mass, 10, 77, 193, 205–6. See also *Excelsior*
Mexican Academy for Human Rights, 83
Mexico City earthquake (1985), 100 n. 16
*Mexico en Libertad*, 139–40, 146
Meyer, David S., 51, 53–54

Michoacán, 110, 114, 116, 122, 182 n. 26
Middlebrook, Kevin, 193
migration, urban, 99–100
Mills, C. Wright, 24
minimum wage, 138
Ministry of Agrarian Reform, 9 n. 23, 111–12, 124, 131, 171
moral economy theory, 117
Morales, Evo, 29 n. 4
Moreno, Alejandro, 16 n. 39, 156
Morris, Aldon D., 53
Movimento dos Trabalhadores Rurais Sem Terra (MST), 29 n. 4
Movimiento de Acción Popular (MAP), 161
Movimiento de Acción Revolucionaria (MAR), 73
Movimiento de Liberación Nacional (MLN), 105–6

nationalism, 51, 67
  and economic policy, 127, 129, 141, 145, 153, 157
  as public ideology, 6, 94, 129, 131, 157–58, 187
Native Americans, 6, 25–27, 163–64
  and peasant struggle, 163, 165
  population of, 26 n. 49, 164
  protests by, 26, 27 n. 52, 34
  voting by, 172, 183–84, 186–87
  Zapatista rebellion and, 193–94
Nayarit, 178
neoliberalism, 24, 144–45, 195
  as agenda of capitalists, 23, 38, 54, 126–27, 138, 141–46, 151
  businessmen opposing, 23 n. 47, 127 n. 1
  and democratization, 16–17, 32–33, 195
  economic measures of, 35, 141–42, 173
  international pressure for, 17, 34–35
  Mexico as one of first countries to adopt, 17, 146, 151
  protests against, 33–34, 36
Noonan, Rita K., 50
North American Free Trade Agreement (NAFTA), 35, 141, 142, 153
Núñez Esteva, Alberto, 139, 142, 143–44, 145

Oaxaca, 66, 182 n. 26
  peasant movement in, 114, 116, 163–64
  teachers movement in, 86, 193
Oliver, Pamela E., 45, 194
*Oposición*, 94, 108, 109 n. 33, 110, 114

Organización Campesina Emiliano Zapata (OCEZ), 26 n. 51, 171
Orive Berlinguer, Adolfo, 113
Orona, Arturo, 106
Otero, Gerardo, 8 n. 20

Panama, 34 n. 9
Paré, Luisa, 12, 35, 113–14
  on left involvement in peasant movement, 106 n. 31, 162, 166
Partido Acción Nacional (PAN), 80, 146–50
  and 1988 elections, 175 n. 1
  becomes catch-all opposition party, 148
  building middle-class base of, 18, 23, 152, 191
  capitalists' revitalization of, 18, 23, 54, 127, 132, 140, 147, 150, 191
  early history of, 10–11, 146–47
  ideology of, 146–47
  list of candidates elected, 149
  regional and demographic support for, 156, 187
  social movement origins of, 3, 191
  unseats PRI, 13, 31, 87, 149–50, 151, 189
Partido Auténtico de la Revolución Mexicana (PARM), 174–75
Partido Comunista Mexicano (PCM)
  cadres of, 46, 123, 124
  dissolution of, 174
  electoral banning of, 10 n. 27
  electoral registration of, 77, 173
  framing by, 92, 113, 124
  and guerrilla movements, 41, 116 n. 40
  ideological tempering by, 173
  ideology of, 46, 47–48, 112, 113, 123, 124
  leadership role in peasant movement, 105–7, 109–10, 114–15, 121–22, 125, 166
  long involvement in peasant struggles, 47, 91, 92–93, 105–6, 111–13, 114–15, 187, 188
  during 1982 debt crisis, 138
  political and organizational crisis, 107–8, 112 n. 36
  radicalization of, 109, 124, 199
  radicalizing youth breaking from, 73, 199
  relations with peasantry, 166
  repression against, 66, 92, 107, 110, 124
  rural base of support, 104–5, 116–17, 159, 201
  rural membership, 105, 108, 121–22
  semiformal and informal networks, 110, 111, 114–15
  in student movement of 1968, 61, 64

"third period" policy, 104–5
work in coalitions by, 47, 113–14
Partido de la Revolución Democrática (PRD)
blocked road to two-party system, 23–24, 154, 186
expansion of support base, 31, 148, 185
EZLN distancing from, 184 n. 28
factionalism in, 176
formation of, 173–74
governorships won by, 182
ideology of, 24, 154–55
indigenous support for, 186–87
as left unity party, 174
in 2000 presidential election, 149, 158
in 2006 presidential election, 13, 15, 24, 38 n. 17, 150–51, 155, 176–77, 178, 191
and peasant movement, 54
and prior left rural organizing, 19, 179, 180–81, 185, 187, 191
regional support for, 156, 178–79
repression against, 154, 176
rural support for, 23, 154, 157, 176–86, 191
and social movements, 3, 175, 176, 191
Partido de Los Pobres, 71 n. 7, 72 n. 7, 116 n. 41
Partido Mexicano de los Trabajadores (PMT), 74
Partido Mexicano Socialista (PMS), 174
Partido Revolucionario de los Trabajadores (PRT), 74, 83 n. 15, 162, 164
Partido Revolucionario Institucional (PRI), 10, 71, 77, 80, 182
adopts neoliberalism, 158, 173, 174
capitalists excluded from, 9, 128
ideological flexibility of, 2
loses majority in Congress, 148, 189
loss of legitimacy by, 35, 148, 172
monopoly of political power by, 1–2, 3, 10, 31, 157
nationalist discourse of, 157–58, 187
patronage of, 2, 8–9, 157–58
peasant support for, 3, 9, 157–58
technocrats' rise to dominance in, 142 n. 18, 174
Partido Socialista de los Trabajadores (PST), 74, 161
Partido Socialista Unificado de México (PSUM), 162, 174
patronage, 39 n. 18
by PRI, 2, 8–9, 157–58

peak associations, businessmen's, 23, 126, 139, 150, 151, 198
functioned like social movements, 127, 137
influence on government policy, 142
See also Confederación Patronal de la República Mexicana (COPARMEX); Consejo Coordinador Empresarial (CCE)
peasant movement, 1, 22, 101–2, 152
economic and political demands of, 24, 167–68, 169, 172
framing by, 50–51, 197
ideological orientation of, 160–61
labeled "anarchists," 83, 101–2
land invasions by, 90–91, 97, 102, 111–12, 114–15, 121, 122, 129, 190
PCM leadership role in, 105–7, 109–10, 114–15, 121–22, 125, 166
PCM long involvement in, 47, 91, 92–93, 105–6, 111–13, 114–15, 187, 188
and PRD, 54
protest targets, 210
radicalization of, 167, 172, 190
repression against, 91, 102, 103–4, 123, 170–71, 190
tactics of, 168–69, 170, 171, 211
peasants
and agricultural workers, 213–14
Constitution's concessions to, 5, 94, 131
and ejido system, 5, 94–96
and land ownership, 95, 96, 98, 119, 120–21
peasant-workers, 213
political predispositions of, 156–59
and PRI, 3, 9, 157–58
social characteristics of, 99
Pérez Arce, Francisco, 188
Petróleos Mexicanos (PEMEX), 130, 161
Piven, Frances Fox, 39
pluralism, 13–14, 16, 89, 190
police, 86 n. 17, 194
political opportunity theory, 39, 42
political parties
Mexican authoritarianism and, 10–11, 74
under 1977 electoral reform, 77, 80, 189
and social movements, 20–21, 49, 166–67
Poniatowska, Elena, 72 n. 8
Popular Party, 105
poverty, 35, 164, 192–93
presidentialism, 167
capitalists' challenge to, 139, 140, 146, 151
and Mexico's political system, 1–2, 6, 8

private property, 4–5, 136, 137
    and social property, 5, 94–96, 141
privatization, 35, 141
    of ejido system, 95 n. 5, 143, 153
Programa de Apoyos Directos al Campo (PROCAMPO), 8 n. 20
Programa de Inversiones para el Desarrollo Rural Integrado (PIDER), 100
Programa Nacional de Solidaridad (PRONASOL), 8 n. 20
*Propuestas de modernización al sector agropecuario*, 143
protected consultation, 15
protectionism, economic, 127, 141, 145
    capitalists' rejection of, 145
    ISI development model, 129–30, 131, 132, 145
Puebla, 66, 148, 163–64
    PCM in, 108, 111, 114, 116, 121–22

radicalization
    of capitalists, 145, 152–53, 190
    of PCM, 109, 124, 199
    of peasant movement, 167, 172, 190
    and repression, 40–41, 93, 167, 188, 199
    of social movements, 12, 88
    of youth after 1968, 73, 74, 88, 123
Ramírez Mercado, Manuel, 176
repression, 35, 65, 164 n. 11, 167, 177, 188
    defined, 40
    and dissent, 41
    functioning clandestinely to avoid, 22, 40, 58, 74–75, 159, 161, 166
    June 10, 1971, massacre, 72
    against Native Americans, 163–64
    as part of *pan y palo* tactics, 12, 55, 103–4
    against PCM, 66, 92, 107, 110, 124
    against peasant movement, 91, *102*, 103–4, 123, 170–71, 190
    against PRD, 154, 176
    protests against, 168, 177, *179*, *181*
    and radicalization, 40–41, 93, 167, 188, 199
    social movements and, 39, 94, 198–99
    torture used, 12, 57, 69, 72, 86, 103 n. 22
    *See also* dirty war; Tlatelolco massacre
resource mobilization theory, 93
Revolution of 1910, 1, 4
Reyes Heroles, Jesús, 76
Riding, Alan, 206
Rosas, Adalberto, 133–34

Rubio, Blanca, 26, 159, 177–78, 203, 209
    on peasant demands, 168, 171, 172
Ruffo Appel, Ernesto, 148 n. 23

Salinas de Gortari, Carlos, 95 n. 5
    amnesty under, 171 n. 15
    declared victor in 1988 elections, 15 n. 36, 158, 175
    neoliberal measures of, 141, 143, 144
    repression under, 170–71
Sánchez, Samuel, 110, 112, 122
Sánchez Navarro, Juan, 134 n. 10
Sarmiento, Sergio, 106 n. 31, 162, 166
Scherer García, Julio, 205–6
Schock, Kurt, 41–42
Shapira, Yoram, 66, 71, 74
Shirk, David, 150
Sinaloa, 148, 177 n. 23
    land expropriations in, 132, 133
    peasant movement in, 105, 114, 115, 116, 122, 134
Sistema Alimentario Mexicano (SAM), 138
Skocpol, Theda, 55
Smith, Peter, 8
Snow, David, 50
social movements
    businessmen's peak associations as, 127, 137
    and citizenship rights, 29
    and civil society, 37, 38, 55
    co-optation efforts toward, 39, 43, 190
    defined, 19–20
    and democratization, 29–32, 31, 55–56, 190, 195, 198
    framing by, 50–53, 196, 197, 198
    leadership in, 42–44, 45, 52, 53, 152, 196–97
    organization of, 42, 44–45
    political disruption by, 50 n. 32, 51, 89, 198
    and political ideology, 45, 47, 93, 124
    and political parties, 20–21, 49, 166–67
    and popular movements, 20 n. 43, 157 n. 3
    and PRD, 175, 176, 191
    and protest cycle following 1968, 22, 31, 37, 57, 74–75, 195
    radicalization of, 12, 88
    and repression, 22, 39, 94, 198–99
    by social group, 3
    success by, 22, 39, 73
    tactics and strategy of, 20 n. 43, 34, 42
    theory and scholarship on, 30–31, 39, 152
    *See also* peasant movement

Sonora, 104, 132, 133
  peasant movement in, 105, 107, 114, 115, 116
Staggenborg, Suzanne, 51, 53–54
student movement of 1968, 59–71
  chronology of events, 62–63
  conciliatory gestures to, 60
  demands and grievances of, 59–60, 64
  framing by, 51, 65, 67, 69–70, 88, 197
  as historical catalyst, 22, 57–58, 71
  initiated protest cycle, 22, 31, 37, 57, 74–75, 195
  and international youth movement, 36, 65, 69
  leadership of, 60–61
  repression of, 65, 67
  rioting in, 64
  *See also* Tlatelolco massacre
student radicals, former
  antiparliamentarian stance of, 74
  clandestine networks of, 74–75, 92
  and human rights movement, 23
  ideological commitment of, 23, 45, 46, 93, 123
  involvement with peasant movement, 24–25, 91, 92, 125, 188
  role in protest cycle, 22, 31, 57, 74–75

Tabasco, 182 n. 26
Tamayo, Jaime, 154
Tarrow, Sidney, 15, 89
Taylor, Verta, 45, 93
Teniza, Natalia, 111–12
Tepoztlán, 158
Thacker, Strom, 142, 144–45
Tilly, Charles, 15, 50 n. 32, 89
Tirado, Ricardo, 136, 148 n. 23
Tlatelolco massacre (1968)
  account of, 68
  anticommunist hysteria preceding, 66
  legitimacy crisis created by, 57, 71, 188
  and rise of human rights movement, 58, 86
  as symbol, 82, 83, 88
  *See also* student movement of 1968
Tlaxcala, 103 n. 23
  elections in, 178, 182 n. 26
  PCM in, 108, 111, 114, 116, 121–22, 163 n. 9
Torres, Biebrich, 104 n. 26
torture, 12, 57, 69, 72, 86, 103 n. 22
transparency laws, 194–95
Trotskyists, 61, 64, 74, 173
  and peasant movement, 92, 112–13, 164
  *See also* Partido Revolucionario de los Trabajadores (PRT)

Ulloa Bornemann, Alberto, 73
UNAM (Universidad Nacional Autónoma de México), 58–59, 67
unemployment, 98–99, 118–19, 120–21, 163, 165
Unión Agrícola Nacional (UNAN), 134, 152
Unión General de Obreros y Campesinos de México (UGOCM), 105, 109, 173
Unión Regional de Ejidos y Comunidades de la Huasteca Hidalguense (URECHH), 161–62
unions
  *charro*, 64
  and government corporatism, 8 n. 16, 9
United States, 130
  economic pressure from, 17, 34–35, 151
  *See also* North American Free Trade Agreement (NAFTA)

Valdés, Francisco, 148 n. 23
Vallejo, Demetrio, 74
Vanden, Harry E., 54
Vargas Llosa, Mario, 11
Vázquez, Genaro, 70 n. 4
Veracruz, 182 n. 26
  peasant movement in, 105 n. 28, 116, 163–64, 179
Villa, Francisco "Pancho," 65, 94
Villalón, Roberta, 33
*Voz de México, La,* 94

Warman, Arturo, 147
Williams, Heather L., 6 n. 12, 43, 47, 48, 51
women, 25, 75, 177
World Bank, 138

Young, M. P., 40

Zacatecas, 108, 113, 114, 116
  elections in, 178, 182 n. 26
Zald, Mayer, 51, 93, 124
Zapata, Emiliano, 65, 94
Zapatistas. *See* Ejército Zapatista de Liberación Nacional (EZLN)
Zarazua Sandoval, Carlos, 142
Zedillo, Ernesto, 141
Zermeño, Sergio, 60
Zuno, José Guadalupe, 74
Zylan, Yvonne, 39 n. 18

www.ingramcontent.com/pod-product-compliance
Lightning Source LLC
Chambersburg PA
CBHW032128010526
44111CB00033B/219